Opération Crevette

Opération Crevette

Benin, Mercenaries, and the Survival of a New State

Les Sosnowski and Monique Sosnowski

LEXINGTON BOOKS
Lanham • Boulder • New York • London

Published by Lexington Books
An imprint of The Rowman & Littlefield Publishing Group, Inc.
4501 Forbes Boulevard, Suite 200, Lanham, Maryland 20706
www.rowman.com

86-90 Paul Street, London EC2A 4NE

British Library Cataloguing in Publication Information Available

Library of Congress Cataloging-in-Publication Data

Names: Sosnowski, Les, author. | Sosnowski, Monique, author.
Title: Operation Crevette : Benin, mercenaries, and the survival of a new
    state / Les Sosnowski and Monique Sosnowski.
Other titles: Benin, mercenaries, and the survival of a new state
Description: Lanham : Lexington Books, [2024] | Includes bibliographical
    references and index.
Identifiers: LCCN 2023050132 (print) | LCCN 2023050133 (ebook) | ISBN
    9781666911237 (cloth) | ISBN 9781666911244 (ebook)
Subjects: LCSH: Denard, Bob, 1929-2007--Military leadership. | Mercenary
    troops--Benin. | Coups d'état--Benin. | Benin--History--Coup d'état,
    1977. | Benin--Politics and government--1960-1990.
Classification: LCC DT541.845 .S67 2024 (print) | LCC DT541.845 (ebook) |
    DDC 966.83051--dc23/eng/20231025
LC record available at https://lccn.loc.gov/2023050132
LC ebook record available at https://lccn.loc.gov/2023050133

Contents

Preface vii

Chapter 1: From French Colony to Military Rule 1

Chapter 2: "Sick Child of Africa" 9

Chapter 3: Enough Is Enough 21

Chapter 4: Revolutionary Changes 33

Chapter 5: The French Connection 43

Chapter 6: The Doctor's Orders 55

Chapter 7: Getting Armed and Ready 65

Chapter 8: *Bienvenue au Maroc*! (Welcome to Morocco!) 73

Chapter 9: Dr. Zinsou Sends the Dirty Ninety 85

Chapter 10: The Omegas Are Coming 95

Chapter 11: Facing Reality 101

Chapter 12: A Three-Hour Disaster 109

Chapter 13: The Aftermath 125

Chapter 14: Whose Victory? 135

Chapter 15: Pandora's Boxes 145

Chapter 16: No End to Troubles 153

Chapter 17: Justice Delayed 169

Chapter 18: The End of an Epoch 183

Appendix A: Presidents and Heads of State of Benin from 1960 to
    2006   195

Appendix B: European Mercenaries Listed by Benin's Authorities
    as Involved in Opération Crevette   197

Appendix C: African Mercenaries Listed by Benin's Authorities
    as Involved in Opération Crevette   199

Appendix D: Resolution 404 (1977) of 8 February 1977   201

Appendix E: Resolution 405 (1977) of 14 April 1977   203

Appendix F: UN Security Council Letter Dates 13 June 1979   205

Bibliography   213

Index   225

About the Authors   227

Preface

INTRODUCTORY NOTE

The authors relay in this book the various memoires and personal accounts of the participants involved in Opération Crevette. As is the case with most memoires, especially those written with help of the literary assistants, the reader needs to use caution in the uncritical acceptance of the testimonies, interpretations, or, sometimes, even facts presented in such works. Such a cautious approach is required especially in cases where covert intelligence and subversive operations obscure true details in the interests of their state and non-state actors; thus, the truth is not always revealed to the public by their participants or is even purposely hidden from the public eye.

The authors of this book undertook extensive research of available public records and publications in order to present the most reliable description of Opération Crevette to date.

BOB DENARD AND COMPANY

Bob Denard is unquestionably one the most widely known, celebrated, and colorful figures among soldiers of fortune. He, like other soldiers of fortune, gained his sometimes-questionable fame during colonial wars, postcolonial armed conflicts, internal wars, coup d'états, and regime changes that took place in 1950 and 1960s, mostly across the Africa continent.[1] Unlike other mercenaries of that time, Denard stood out by extensively and successfully using the print media, television, and radio to share and discuss his adventures. He even published an autobiography and has been the subject of several books dedicated to his infamous mercenary activities. Interestingly, however, his true identity has remained, at least in the media reporting, the subject of doubt. During his countless operations, he used various aliases alongside false passports and identification documents. To this day there is debate about whether his birth name was Robert (a.k.a. "Bob") Denard or Gilbert Bourgeaud.

Obituaries published after his death in 2007 by *Agence France-Press* initially referred to him as "Bob Denard (whose real name is Gilbert Bourgeaud),"[2] only to issue a correction the next day that his real name was Robert Denard, "pseudonym Gilbert Bourgeaud."[3] A month after his death, a leading French newspaper, *Le Monde*, then again claimed his actual name as Gilbert Bourgeaud.[4] Sources closest to him, such as his former associates and participants of his mercenary operations organized in the Orbs Patria Nostra (Latin for "The World is Our Homeland") organization, possibly the only sources with the answer, have skirted solving this mystery. The latest edition of his biography, *Le Colonel*, published on the *Orbs Patria Nostra* website, refers to his birth name as "Robert Denard, born on 7 April 1929, of Léonard Denard," omitting any reference to Gilbert Bourgeaud in relation to his family (birth) name.[5]

However, most evidence points to his true name being Robert ("Bob") Denard. A short biography with an introduction written by Denard's defense attorney—Elie Hatem—is titled *Bob Denard. L'histoire d'un home*;[6] and in his work on the decolonization of Africa and mercenaries, author Hugues Henri claims that Denard's father's name was, in fact, Léonce Denard.[7] In his book *Le Roi de Fortune* (French for "The King of Fortune"), Pierre Lunel, historian and essayist, chronicles Denard's mercenary adventures. It is his understanding, he states, that "in July 1968, Robert Denard leaves the stage and disappears for the benefit of Gilbert Bourgeaud, born in Caen [France] on January 30, 1929."[8] In some of the only insights into the derivation of the name, nay alias, Gilbert Bourgeaud, Denard is quoted, saying: "I took the name of one of my former companions from childhood from Grayan [friend from Gironde, France]. After Congo and Bukavu it was no longer possible to continue under the name of Denard to travel to Africa under that label. It was necessary to remake my virginity."[9] However, shuffling through photos of his forged passports, some of them produced with the help of the French special services, it becomes clear—as we will call him—more often than not, did not want to be known. His passports shed light on some of his assumed names taken on throughout his life for his mercenary operation. These include, but are not limited to: Jean-Paul Berthier, Bako, Albert Demol, Rémy Destrieux, Roger Dupuis, Mustapha M'Hadjou, Bernard Martin, Maurin, or Antoine Thomas.[10] Addressing the doubts about Denard's birth name and nationality, Alan Leluc concluded: "Bob Denard, alias Gilbert Bourgeaud, alias Jean Maurin, is definitely Robert Denard and is definitely of French nationality. Although, because of his penetrating blue eyes and his early career amidst mercenaries of Belgian nationality, there was some doubt about this at one time, his accent, profile and birth certificate proclaim that he is a Frenchman from the Gironde."[11]

Denard was born in 1929 in France (sometimes he is mistakenly identified as Belgian) and grew up witnessing the vast modern French colonial empire vanish post–World War II. In Africa, this empire consisted of the confederations of French West Africa and French Equatorial Africa, the western Maghreb, Djibouti in the Horn of Africa, and the Indian Ocean islands of Madagascar, Réunion, and Comoros. While the territories in sub-Saharan Africa were treated by Paris primarily as colonies for exploitation, the Maghreb region (comprised of present-day Algeria, Morocco, and Tunisia) was considered a settler-friendly colonial possession. All of them were exploited by the Hexagon[12] (an epithet of Metropolitan France, owing to the shape of its European mainland) for all kinds of natural resources required by the French economy. They were considered places where the French who wanted a career in the colonial administration or military could thrive and were a place where they could buy a piece of land which they could not afford to have in the continental homeland. The colonies also served France as a source of recruits for French participation not only in both World Wars but also in the colonial wars conducted by France in her other colonial dependencies.

At its height in the 1920s and 1930s, the French colonial empire extended over 5,200,000 square miles (13,500,000 square kilometers). On the eve of World War II, France and her colonial possessions totaled about 150 million inhabitants; in 1945, France had only forty million within its European borders. Most of the French did not want to lose their "golden geese" to the process of decolonization.[13] This led France, like some other colonial powers, to engage in several bloody colonial wars and interventions in Asia and Africa in early 1950s and 1960s. These typically involved regular French military forces, the Foreign Legion, and, last but not least, French and foreign mercenaries.

As a young man, Bob Denard personally observed the fall of French Indochina and witnessed failed efforts to maintain the colonial status of Madagascar and some territories in northern Africa, such as Algeria. Many French could not accept the breakup of what for almost a hundred years, in various changing forms of dependency, was considered by the French as the France's own backyard. Many, therefore, if not already fighting in the French military against anti-colonial independence movements, joined various paramilitary groups or enrolled themselves as mercenaries who were usually covertly supported by the French special services. As one of those dismayed by France's inability to keep the status of a colonial power, Denard became involved in the efforts to protect what was still left from the already disintegrating French colonial empire.

At the end of World War II (c. 1945), Denard joined the French guerilla resistance forces, *les maquis* (named after the "underbrush" that served as their cover), where he likely had his first exposure to firearms. Denard witnessed the disappearance of the modern French colonial empire beginning with the Asian and, later, African colonies. In the early 1950s, decolonization of countries on both continents was often a bloody process of wars fought by colonial powers—such as France, Great Britain, Portugal, or the Netherlands—against the national liberation movements nascent in their colonial possessions.

The son of a regimental sergeant major in a colonial French army, Denard enrolled (at the age of seventeen) at a naval mechanical academy, the Saint-Mandrier in Toulon, from which he graduated a marine mechanic with the rank equivalent of an army sergeant. After eighteen months, he quit school and enrolled at the Marine Nationale[14] in Cherbourg on the North Sea, where in 1947 he served as a mechanic on a minesweeper (a small warship designed to remove or detonate naval mines). A year later, he served in the French northwest regions of Saint-Malo and Saint-Servan on a naval escort vessel aboard which young recruits were being trained.

At the end of 1948, Denard joined French naval forces operating in Indochina (Flotte Amphibie Indochine Sud, FAIS). According to some sources, he served in FAIS as a quartermaster;[15] other sources claim he worked as a naval gunner,[16] and yet others claim as a marine rifle man.[17] In the beginning of 1950, he returned briefly to France again work on a minesweeper, and in 1951, was sent for a short apprenticeship at the military school in Lafayette (Louisiana) in the United States. In April of 1952, he returned to France and quit his service, which according to some was the consequence of fight at a bar, as a French marine to undergo police training. He then moved to Morocco to work as a construction worker and, later, became a policeman and member of an anti-terrorist unit, LUCOTER, in Casablanca, fighting members of the anti-colonial groups and movements looking for refuge in the country. While in Morocco, Denard had been accused of participation in a 1956 tentative conspiracy to murder of French socialist politician Pierre Mendèz France. After fourteen months in Moroccan jail, he was cleared of the charges and, under military escort, repatriated to France. This would not be the last accusation of murder to face throughout his long career as a mercenary; it also would not be his only acquittal for murder in a criminal trial. Denard then flew back from France to North Africa, where, in Algeria, he acquired work as a colonial policeman only to see his employment in police terminated after few months in 1958.[18] Jobless, he returned to France and for next three years accepted various jobs unrelated to his soldering ambitions.

Between 1961 and 1977, Bob Denard would participate in armed conflicts mainly taking place across Africa, namely in newly independent Congo; as part of a colonial war in Angola; on the side of royalist forces in Yemen, where he purportedly worked alongside British intelligence; in Nigeria during the Biafra war; as well as in Gabon, and the Comoros Islands, the last of which he worked under the direction of the SDECE[19] to stage a coup.

In 1961, Denard enlisted as a mercenary in the Congo (present day Democratic Republic of Congo) where his mercenary career really began. During the internal conflict in Congo, he switched up his allegiances and his employers, as mercenaries often do.[20] It was then, in 1967, that General Mobutu (later the president of the Democratic Republic of the Congo) nominated him a commander of a Francophone (French-speaking) battalion of about 1,200 foreign mercenaries with a grade of a colonel. This was how Denard, a French marine sergeant, became Colonel Denard. However, the French paper media (except for those on the political right) and his former associates and *affecionados* refer to Denard as "Colonel," using quotations marks to denote his questionable military officer status. Interestingly, English language literature and media apparently acknowledging the rank awarded by General Mobutu, referring to him as Colonel Denard without the use of quotation marks. His associates and subordinates called Denard simply *colonel*, or *patron* (meaning "boss") or *vieux* (meaning "old one"). However, to others, he was one of *les affreux*—the French term meaning the frightful, terrible, or horrible. In this case, *les affreux* referred to men belonging to a group of particularly brutal mercenaries[21] who served in Africa, especially in Congo, during the 1960s. They were accused of not following any generally recognized international rules of military conduct, as well as breaking rules of international humanitarian laws, committing atrocities against both armed personnel of the other parties to a conflict but also against civilian population not participating directly in the hostilities. Although some of them were former soldiers, mainly from noncommissioned ranks, of various Western-armed or special forces, they often showed lack of discipline when serving as mercenaries, which affected their performance in action. Many showed their contempt, if not openly racist attitude, toward the local populations of countries in which they were operating. Even some of their field commanders, like Colonel Mike Hoare, were sometimes very critical of their mercenary subordinates. It was Colonel Hoare who expressed in his memories from then Congo (now Democratic Republic of Congo) the following opinion about his mercenary subordinates: "The general standard was alarmingly low. There was too high a proportion of alcoholics, drunks, booze artists, bums, and layabouts, who were finding it difficult to find a job anywhere else and thought this a heaven-sent opportunity to make some easy money. In addition, I discovered . . . that there were a fair sprinkling of dagga" (*dagga* is South African slang for marijuana).[22] Similar opinions about mercenaries in the Congo were expressed by other authors: "There were troublemakers

Figure 0.1.   Close-Up Bob Denard A. Pretoria, 1991. Credit: Pool Girard / Sidler / Contributor / Gamma-Rapho / Getty Images.

too. These men of doubtful background, all thrown together in a situation where it appeared that they alone held the key to a nation's future, soon made their presence felt."[23] *Time* magazine described the Congo mercenaries who earned the nickname *les affreux* (the "terrible ones"): "mercenaries include Sahara-scorched French veterans of the *Organisation Armée Secrète* (OAS, English for Secret Armed Organization) uprising in Algeria, tough British colonial troops from the old Indian army, and unashamedly racist Rhodesians who joke about 'sending a Kaffir a day to heaven.'"[24]

An indicative example of conduct that earned mercenary troops in Congo nickname *les affreux* was presented by one of the senior mercenaries in a series of photograph showing how the mercenaries "not only shot and hanged their prisoners after torturing them but used them for target practice and gambled over number of shots needed to kill one."[25] The conduct of *les affreux* in Congo illustrates the statement of one of the mercenaries quoted in *The Reporter* magazine: "When we attack a village, we have no time to ask who a rebel is and who is not. . . . We come in with our guns up and we blast everything."[26] Rape, looting, or theft, burning of villages, and taking hostages also were often behavior of many mercenary troops in Congo. Despite occasional daring operations during their activities in Congo, like protecting endangered, by local rebels, white population of cities like Stanleyville (city in Congo, present day Democratic Republic of the Congo), it was their often-atrocious conduct against African populous that resulted in designating them not only by French term as *les affreux* but also "dogs of war" or even "whores of war" in English. Sometimes, to avoid being identified as mercenaries they liked to call themselves volunteers or experts. However, observes one author, the mercenary remains a poorly defined figure: "We can simply assume that, in a hierarchy of motivations, politics prevails in the volunteer, contrary to the mercenary."[27]

There is also a rather anecdotal way to explain the use of French term *les affreux* as a common description of the mercenaries. Huges Henri says that during the conflict in then-Congo, three military advisers to Moise Tshombe (former prime minister of the Democratic Republic of the Congo) noticed the mercenaries returning from the "front" through the streets of Elisabethville in neglected uniforms. One of the advisers looking at them heaved a sigh of discouragement and allegedly said to his companions: "My God, how dreadful they are."[28]

Although many such names are given to the mercenaries fighting in organized military units during armed conflicts, they still remain in use for mercenaries taking part in small scale operations, like coups d'état.

Today, the bigger scale mercenary military operations are organized by specialized private companies retained by governments, organizations, special services, or opposition groups, openly employing armed individuals as contract employee and thus called contractors. It gives them legal protection coming from international conventions, which old-time *affreux* had not had and, as a result, were sometimes subject to criminal proceedings under individual state jurisdiction, although they often commit similar atrocious crimes as those who acted in the so-called Third World countries in the 1960s and 1970s of the past century.

Apart from his adventures as a mercenary, Bob Denard also lived a colorful, intensive, celebrity-like private life. Born into Catholic parents, he would convert from Roman Catholicism to Judaism to Islam and back to Catholicism, be married six times, and father eight children. His personal records were further decorated by several criminal trials against him in France and abroad relating to his African mercenary activities.

During his service in Congo (present-day Democratic Republic of the Congo), he met many former professional soldiers from various countries who subsequently became famous professional mercenaries. Among them were Jean "Black Jack" Schramme, Jeremiah C. Puren, "Mad" Mike Hoare, Robert (Rene) Faulques, and Roger Trinquier. As former army officers, many of them had experience in commanding military units, which Denard, until then, lacked. A mercenary in the Congo, Denard joined forces that were already organized either by private individuals, foreign secret and intelligence services, the Congolese state, or Congolese local, provincial leaders. These were usually relatively small bands of foreigners who fought for pay for any party that hired them for a particular assignment. Only in 1967, when he was given by General Mobutu command more than 1,200 soldiers, did he gain experience in commanding a large group of fighting men in the context of military operation. Such experience, however, had limited use in organizing his future covert operations conducted with a small number of secretly recruited mercenaries.

As to the motives for mercenary service of Denard and many of his likes, one can quote the opinion that "[l]ike his native France, which clings determinedly to the remnants of empire, Denard seems driven as much by romantic self-gratification as by money or power."[29] Often, the mercenaries, including Bob Denard, also liked to add the very trendy Cold War era motivation slogan: fight against Communism in the so-called Third World countries. A convincing explanation for this attitude seems to be the fact that "[m]any French military commanders in Algeria, who had lived through the army's humiliations in 1940 and at Dien Bien Phu in 1954, believed their fight in Algeria was in defense not just of *Algerie française* and French glory but also against communist inspired subversion which threatened France's southern flank."[30] They often "held the view that nationalism in North Africa would and did equate with Soviet Communism, posing a direct strategic threat to France herself."[31] As a result, "such Cold War paranoia led to confusion between local nationalism and socialism and communism, between decolonisation and a threat to the free world."[32] It was an effect touching not only commanders by also many rank-file French, among them Bob Denard, fighting those loosing wars in Hexagon's or other countries colonies. It was *Le Monde* that published a death notice in which the author questioned Denard's efforts to separate himself from the bad image of the brutality of French soldiers fighting in the 1950s and 1960s during Algerian War of independence or the equally bad image of *les affreaux* participating in the Congolese internal conflicts. "Bob Denard—wrote Nicolas Boucier—symbol of French neocolonialism, cultivated this image of the 'special case,' which he defined for himself."[33]

To improve their public image and in attempt to avoid of being seen as "mercenaries,"[34] many of them often presented themselves as "volunteers." However, the meaning of the word "volunteer" is at least misleading. In this case, although mercenaries serve voluntarily as opposed to being conscripted, they serve for any state or non-state actor who hires them for pay. In all known cases, mercenaries sign a contract specifying the pay for their time and participation in a particular operation.[35] Denard was no exception to this rule and did not meet the common understanding of term "volunteer." "International volunteer combatants—submits Jean-Philippe Siebert—are individuals who leave their country of origin or residence to take part in an armed conflict abroad of their own free will, without being sent by their government and without having as their main motivation the hope of material gain. Unlike mercenaries and contractors, the lucrative aspect does not motivate their engagement. . . . If they are not integrated into a regular army, armed volunteers are no more entitled to the status of combatants or prisoners of war than mercenaries."[36]

In the 1960s and 1970s some mercenaries were subjects to criminal prosecution in the countries they were apprehended when acting as mercenaries.[37] France, although reluctantly, also later took legal action against Bob Denard.[38]

Opération Crevette was only the second coup d'état organized by Denard himself, from personally arranging contracts, recruiting participants, preparing the detailed plan of action, and taking exclusive command during all stages of its execution. Here is history of Opération Crevette.

NOTES

1. Walter Bruyére-Ostells tilted his monographie dedicated to presenting activities of French mercenaries between 1960 and 1989 *Dans l'ombre de Bob Denard. Les*

mercenaires français de 1960 à 1989 (Paris : Nouveau Monde Éditions, 2014), 480, placing all of them "In the shadow of Bob Denard."

2. *Agence France Presse*, "Décès de l'ancien mercenaire Bob Denard," *leparisien.fr*, October 13, 2007, https://www.leparisien.fr/politique/deces-de-l-ancien-mercenaire-bob-denard-14-10-2007-3291315907.php. Original quote: "Bob Denard (dont le véritable nom est Gilbert Bourgeaud)."

3. "Nom: Robert Denard, pseudonyme: Gilbert Bourgeaud," *Agence France Presse*, October 15, 2007.

4. Nicolas Bourcier, "Disparitions: Bob Denard, mercenaire," *Le Monde*, October 17, 2007. https://www.lemonde.fr/disparitions/article/2007/10/17/bob-denard-mercenaire_967897_3382.html.

5. "Le Colonel," *Orbs Patria Nostra* webpage: https://www.orbspatrianostra.com/documents/documents-colonel.html.

6. Philippe Hugounenc, *Bob Denard, l'Histoire d'un Homme* (Paris: Philippe Hugounenc Editeur, 2020).

7. Hugues Henri, "La décolonisation de l'Afrique et les mercenaires," n.d., 13.

8. Pierre Lunel, *Bob Denard : Le Roi de Fortune* (Edition⁰ 1, 1991), 406. Original quote: "En juillet 1968, Robert Denard quitte la scène et disparaît au profit de Gilbert Bourgeaud, né à Caen, le 30 janvier 1929. . . . J'ai pris le nom d'un de mes anciens copains d'enfance de Grayan. Après le Congo et Bukavu, ce n'était plus possible de continuer sous le nom de Denard, de voyager en Afrique sous cette étiquette-là. . . . Il m'a bien fallu me refaire une virginité."

9. Ibid.

10. Documents—"Le Colonel," *Orbs Patria Nostra*.

11. Alain Leluc, "Vingt ans de mercenariat," *Historia*, no. 406 (1980): 2.

12. The Hexagon (*l'Hexagone*) is an epithet for Metropolitan France, owing to the shape of its European mainland.

13. Benard Droz, *Histoire de la décolonisation: Au xxe siecle* (Paris: Contemporary French Fiction; Points histoire edition, 2009), 80–93, 153–218, and 245–62.

14. The French Navy, also known as *La Royale* or the maritime branch of the French Armed Forces.

15. Bourcier, "Disparitions: Bob Denard, mercenaire."

16. Denard's service in FAIS as a naval gunner is listed in section "Le Colonel" listed at the *Orbs Patria Nostra* website.

17. "Une Vie de Mercenaire," *La Liberte*, October 21, 2006, 2.

18. Ibid.

19. Service de Documentation Extérieure et de Contre-Espionnage (SDECE), in English the "External Documentation and Counter-Espionage Service."

20. Interesting details of mercenary recruitment in case of Congo could be found in George H. Dodenhoff, "The Congo: A Case Study of Mercenary Employment," *Naval War College Review* 21, no. 8 (1969): 44–70.

21. For an interesting article on that subject see Walter Bruyere-Ostells, "The 'Affreux': French Mercenaries, Types of Violence and Systems of Domination by Extra-African Forces (1960–1989)" (2014), https://hal.archives-ouvertes.fr/hal-01353545.

22. Mike Hoare, *Congo Mercenary* (London: Robert Hall, 1967), 66.

23. Stephen John Gordon Clarke, *The Congo Mercenary: A History and Analysis* (Johannesburg: South African Institute of International Affairs, 1968), 43.

24. "Mercenaries: The Terrible Ones," *Time*, Friday, August 11, 1967 (online: http://content.time.com/time/subscriber/article/0,33009,899700-1,00.html). According to *Merriam-Webster* dictionary in South Africa, the use of the term "Kaffir" to refer to a black African is a profoundly offensive and inflammatory expression of contemptuous racism.

25. Guy Arnold, *Mercenaries: Scourge of the Developing World* (London: Palgrave Macmillan, 1999), 12.

26. Peter Schmid, "Tshombe's Four Hundred," *The Reporter*, December 17, 1964, 26.

27. Walter Bruyère-Ostells, "Mercenaires et/ou volontaires Engagements de combattants français de la Rhodésie à la Yougoslavie (1976–1995)," Études Géostratégiques, April 13 and 14, 2012, https://etudesgeostrategiques.com/files/ougoslavie-1976-1995_ghw7jonwovxwnh5biad7fb/#_ftn2.

28. Hugues Henri, "La décolonisation de l'Afrique et les mercenaires," n.d., 2, https://www.academia.edu/37523937/La_décolonisation_de_lAfrique_et_les_mercenaires.

29. Howard French, "The Mercenary Position," *Transition* (Kampala, Uganda), no. 73 (1997): 112.

30. Mel William Edward McNulty, "Military Intervention in Theory and Practice: French Policy in Sub-Saharan Africa Since 1960" (PhD diss., University of Portsmouth, 1999), 69, and also French authors quoted by him: https://pure.port.ac.uk/ws/portalfiles/portal/12992283/McNulty_M.W.E._PhD.

31. Ibid., 70.

32. Ibid.

33. Bourcier, "Disparitions: Bob Denard, mercenaire."

34. Non legal, pejorative term used often in media instead of "mercenary" is *affreaux*, "dog of war," "whore of war," and, on the other hand, are complimentary terms like "soldier of fortune," "wild geese," or "technical" advisors.

35. George H. Dodenhoff, "The Congo: A Case Study of Mercenary Employment Source," *Naval War College Review* 21, no. 8 (April 1969), 50. The author describes monetary pay provided by contract for foreing mercenaries recruited for Congo crisis of 1960s.

36. Jean-Philippe Siebert, "Militaires, mercenaires, contractors, volontaires . . . à ne pas confondre," *Les Surligneur*, March 21, 2023, https://www.lessurligneurs.eu/militaires-mercenaires-contractors-volontaires-a-ne-pas-confondre/.

37. Rolf Steiner in 1971 in Khartoum, Sudan, and a 1976 trial of group of mercenaries in Luanda, Angola.

38. See chapter 17 of this book.

Chapter 1

From French Colony
to Military Rule

Shaped by Togo, Burkina Faso, Niger, and Nigeria, Benin is comprised of a narrow, five-hundred-mile-long strip of land. It stretches from the Niger River in the north to the Gulf of Guinea in the south. As one of the smaller countries in West Africa, Benin has eight times less land mass than its eastern neighbor, Nigeria, but is twice as large as Togo, its neighbor to the west.

Located in what is now southern Benin, the Kingdom of Dahomey (1600 –1904) was a powerful regional kingdom in precolonial West Africa. Founded on the Abomey Plateau, the kingdom was first known as Abomey, later becoming known as Dahomey. Prior to centralization, this expanse of the Abomey Plateau was home to various small tribes that were considered resource poor, particularly in comparison to the Oyo empire (in present-day Nigeria), that was at the peak of its power. Around 1600, the stretch of land was formalized into the Kingdom of Dahomey by the Fon people, who were dominant at the time. The foundational king of Dahomey is often considered to be Houegadja (c. 1645–1685); he built the royal palaces in the kingdom and began raiding and conquering towns beyond the Abomey Plateau. It was at this time that the (Atlantic) slave trade was also growing, and Dahomey capitalized, becoming a major source of slaves as it captured prisoners caught in the midst of its expansion. The Kingdom of Dahomey grew in prosperity from its resource-poor origins as it sold slaves into the Atlantic slave trade in exchange for European goods, such as rifles, tobacco, fabrics, and alcohol.

Prosperity, however, did not last very long. The kingdom began to struggle around the 1840s and 1850s. The British, who were major supporters of the Dahomean economy as purchasers of slaves, shifted gears and took an active stance on abolishing the slave trade.

During the eighteenth and nineteenth centuries, the Kingdom of Dahomey was one of the most powerful kingdoms in Africa. At the time, the Dahomey had one of the largest armies in Africa that had 150,000 males and five

1

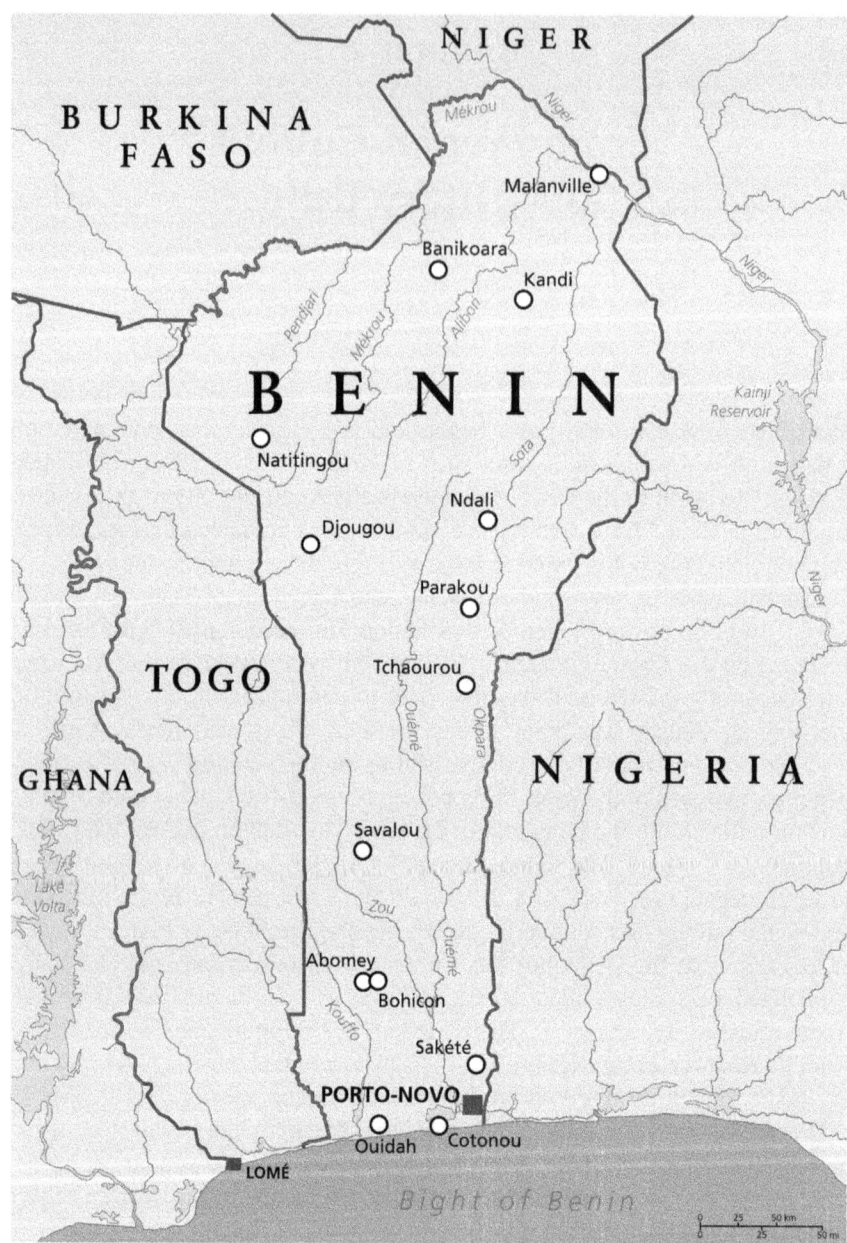

Figure 1.1. Map of the West African State of Benin. Credit: Panther Media GmbH / Alamy Stock Vector.

thousand females; although this army hardly matched the well-armed and equipped French army. The French takeover and colonization of the Kingdom of Dahomey began in 1872, resulting in two Franco–Dahomean wars. The First Franco–Dahomean War took place in 1890; France emerged the victor after winning the Battle of Abomey. Then in 1892, through negotiated agreements with local rulers, the Kingdom of Dahomey became a protectorate of France. The Second Franco–Dahomeyan War lasted from 1892 to January of 1894; France once again emerged triumphant. As a result of the Second Franco–Dahomeyan War, the Kingdom of Dahomey became, on June 22, 1894, a French colony under name of the "Colony of Dahomey and Dependencies" (*Colonie du Dahomey et Dépendances*). It was by French decree that the territory received the name Dahomey.

During the second war, the Dahomeyan king, King Béhanzin—the last independent ruler who fought against the French colonization of his country—was captured and sent to exile on the Caribbean Island of Martinique, then also a French colony. There was, however, a legal problem. Even though the French attained the surrender of Béhanzin, they did not procure Béhanzin's signature on any document of national surrender or treaty. Thus, following Béhanzin's exile, the French general, Alfred Dodds, was willing to offer the throne to every one of the immediate royals in return for a signature legalizing the establishment of a French protectorate over the kingdom. All the royals refused except for Agoli-Agbo, Béhanzin's army chief of staff and relative of the deposed king. He agreed to sign the treaty, but instead of being appointed to the throne as the head of a sovereign nation, the French made him a "traditional chief."[1] He ruled until 1900 and was considered to have been the twelfth, and chronologically last, official king of Dahomey.

Soon after, in 1904, Dahomey was incorporated into French West Africa, a federation of eight French colonial territories in Africa, including Mauritania, Senegal, French Sudan (now Mali), French Guinea (now Guinea), Côte d'Ivoire (the Ivory Coast), and Upper Volta (now Burkina Faso). Post–World War II, French African colonies, including the Colony of Dahomey became the overseas territories with its own parliament and representation in the French national assembly.

Along with many other African colonies, Dahomey attained its independence in 1960—a year therefore referred to as the Year of Africa. Unlike other European colonies of that time, however, Dahomey gained independence as a non-settler French colony; this happened not through military struggle of pro-independence national liberation movement, but through political and administrative reforms introduced by France starting in the 1920s and 1930s, accepted by the Dahomeyan population as a goodwill gesture toward French colonies. After World War II in the 1940s, and France's defeat at Dien Bien Phu in 1954, which demonstrated the weakness of colonial France and the myths of her as a powerful country, France had been seriously diminished and local politicians of then-colonies, among others of Dahomey, were increasingly favorable to the idea of more autonomy eventually leading to their independence.[2]

Between the Brazzaville Conference[3] in 1944 and the proclamation of independence in 1960, Dahomey followed the same development course as its African neighbors under French protection: in 1946, suffrage was introduced and elected assemblies were established; then, following the *loi-cadre* (the French Reform Act, which increased self-governance across African territories) of 1956, which was interestingly presented to the French Parliament by a Dahomean politician, universal suffrage was introduced and the first ministerial cabinet of Dahomey was constituted.

On May 29, 1957, Sourou Migan Apithy (Migan Apithy), chairman of the Partie Republicain of Dahomey and deputy to the French National Assembly since 1945, was called upon to form the first government. In September 1958, the Dahomeyan approved by a great majority the Constitution proposed by General de Gaulle. In December 1958, the territory became the Republic of Dahomey (République du Dahomey), a self-governing political entity within the French Union created to replace the old French colonial empire system. The new French constitution provided that there were no longer French colonies, but that metropolitan France, the overseas departments, and the overseas territories combined constituted one France. On July 11, 1960, the agreements for the transfer of powers making Dahomey a fully independent State, endowed with all the attributes of internal and external sovereignty, were signed in Paris. Finally, after more than half a century of French rule, on August 1, 1960, the Republic of Dahomey gained full independence from France.

An important role in this process was played by General Charles de Gaulle. "It is thanks to France and its leader, General de Gaulle, that we have acquired independence in a way that still astonishes the world, since it was done smoothly and without bloodshed," later declared Dahomey's first ambassador to France, and future Dahomeyan president, Dr. Émile Derlin Zinsou (Émile Zinsou).[4] Another Beninese source would add that "this did not happen without the fierce battle of the African elite and the political class that existed" independent from Paris African territories.[5]

Upon independence, like many other newly independent African nations, Dahomey found itself lying within artificial boundaries imposed by its colonial ruler, encapsulating forty-two, often traditionally rival ethnic groups. The pre- and post-independence borders of Dahomey enveloped the territories of three historic tribal kingdoms, each with ambitions for exclusive rule over the new state. Historically, two were considered the most politically influential: the largest tribe in Dahomey, the Fon, many of whose members converted from their traditional Vodoun (also spelled Vodun, Voudou, Voodoo, etc.) beliefs to Christianity or Islam under colonialism; and the "Brazilians," who the authors of the *Historical Dictionary of Benin* explain to have been "people of mixed African-European parentage exiled at the time of Kingdom of Dahomey, and slaves' descendants taken to Brazil and returning back to Dahomey in the nineteenth century."[6] The "Brazilians" were notably the cultural elite during the 1930s, a decade later becoming an influential element of the Dahomeyan political elite. One of them was Dr. Émile Derlin Zinsou, short-time president of then-Dahomey and an important player in Opération Crevette.

Regionalism fueled by the artificially drawn colonial borders encompassing rival groups struggling for power permeated the Dahomeyan armed forces, which were then characterized by education-based cliques of military officers. On the other hand, Samuel Decalo has stressed, in reference to the contemporary history of Dahomey/Benin, that: "Benin's social and political life has been marked by fragmentation, patron-clientelist relationship. . . . The regional schism arise out of intense and exclusive sub nationalism of the many ethnic groups artificially compressed into the territorial unit established by treaties between France, England, and Germany at the outset of the colonial era."[7] With these factors at play, the political stability of the country was, as one might assume, negatively affected.

Within roughly its first decade post-independence (1963–1972), the country experienced extreme political instability rife with political, economic, and social experiments. These included regime changes, serial coups d'état, the amendment or adoption of approximately five constitutions, diarchy, and rule by ten successive civilian or military councils. This political turbulence, including the highest number of coups d'état of all African nations, led to the branding of Dahomey as "the sick child of Africa."

Despite the number of military coups d'état, post-independence Dahomey stood out from other newly independent African countries; astonishingly, the coups d'état of Dahomey, although serial, were always bloodless. The Beninese people continue to stress this fact with pride, regardless of political opinion. Further, apart from presence of the "Brazilians," post-independence Dahomey found itself uniquely populated with locally or foreign-educated young people, primarily from France. Due to "[t]he number, behavior, and attitudes of the Dahomeyan modern elite of the 1930s have been outstanding among the French-speaking African elites and have earned for Dahomey fame as the Latin Quarter of West Africa."[8] Many of these educated youths had found themselves working in the colonial administrations of Benin and other French African colonies. There, they gained experience in running both state and military affairs. The prospectus of a newly independent state, however, stimulated the return to Dahomey of these individuals, bearing an array of ideological and political views and eager to join a new political scene.

Upon return from abroad, however, these eager minds would face four conservative, long-term Francophile politicians, still dominating the political stage. These included: Coutoucou Hubert Maga (Hubert Maga), the country's first president; Migan Apithy, the second president; Justin Ahomadégbé, an acting president and later chairman of the Presidential Council; and Dr. Émile Zinsou, the fourth president and a major political player in Benin's history. Already well-known across Dahomey, these four had been active in the French colonial administration, representing Dahomey as diplomats to France as well as other countries, and serving years as deputies or senators in the French National Assembly. The first three, Maga, Apithy, and Ahomadégbé, each represented different regions of the country, different ethnicities, and often-conflicting ethnic political and economic interests. Little did they know, a soon-to-be political player representing the younger generation, Mathieu Kérékou, would make a much more far-reaching political career and would impact the history of the country more meaningfully than any of his predecessors.

The political instability of Dahomey in the early years of its independence became legendary. The first nine years of this period were marked by one coup d'état after another. This is best illustrated by a simple fact: between 1960 and 1972, the military organized twelve coups d'état, five of which (1963, 1965, 1967, 1969, and 1972)[9] were successful. In the span of the fourteen years encompassing these coups (1963–1977), Dahomey had fourteen governments, nine presidents, and five changes to the Constitution.

The leading political figures in the 1950s and 1960s were Migan Apithy and Justin Ahomadégbé in the south and Hubert Maga in the north. Untamed political ambitions leading to uncompromised personal rivalries between those three politicians resulted more often than in other African countries reaching for power by the Dahomeyan military.

On September 28, 1958, the Dahomeyan people approved by a great majority the Constitution proposed by General de Gaulle. On December 4, the Republic was proclaimed, and the Assembly was transformed into a Constituent Assembly with Mr. Apithy as head of the provisional government. On February 14, 1959, the Constitution of the Republic of Dahomey was adopted, and General Legislative Assembly election were held between April 2 and 23, 1959.

The country's first presidential and National Assembly elections were held on December 12, 1960, and were won by a party alliance forged between the parties of Hubert Maga and Migan Apithy. Hubert Maga played a role as flexible man-in-the-middle between two feuding southern politicians, Migan Apithy and Justin Ahomadégbé. He became the head of government and then first president of the republic with Migan Apithy as a vice president. Hubert Maga, who was called *l'homme du Nord* (the Northerner), represented the northern tribes of the country. The former colonial elites, mostly from the south of the country, soon embarked on the conquest of power with both Migan Apithy and Justin Ahomadégbé, and it was their rivalry that subsequently opened the Pandora's box of a series of coups d'état orchestrated by the army. When Migan Apithy withdrew to solve the parliamentary crisis, the Chamber unanimously chose as his successor Hubert Maga. A coalition of the three parties took office, with Maga as prime minister. In November 1960, after losing a vote of confidence, the Dahomeyan Democratic Union (*Union Démocratique Dahoméenne*, UDD), ministers resigned, and Migan Apithy's the Parti Républicain du Dahomey and Hubert Maga's the Dahomeyan Democratic Rally (*Rassemblement Démocratique Dahoméen*, RDD) united first in the Dahomeyan Nationalist Party (*Parti des Nationalistes de Dahomey*) and later in the Dahomeyan Unity Party (*Parti Dahoméen de l'Unité*, PDU), again under Maga as prime minister. At the end of 1960, the PDU's single list of candidates won overwhelmingly over the UDD and thereby gained complete control of the executive and the legislature. In 1961, the UDD was banned, and Dahomey became a one-party state.

During his presidency, Hubert Maga faced moribund economic problems, vast unemployment, and well-organized and government-hostile labor unions. In May 1961, tribal and sectional conflicts that spread disorder through the country and culminated in a failed assassination plot against him led by his prominent opposition leader, Justin Ahomadégbé. Ahomadégbé and eleven other individuals were put on trial and subsequently sentenced and jailed,[10] and his party, the Dahomey Democratic Union, was disbanded. After the fall of the Maga government in October 1963, the PDU was disbanded and replaced by the Dahomeyan Democratic Party. As a result, the Dahomeyan Unity Party, the presidential party, became the sole legal party in the country. But not for long. When, in October 1963, union strikes, massive demonstrations, and riots took place in a southern region of the country, the army moved in. It was first direct military intervention in Dahomeyan politics. On October 28, 1963, Dahomey's First Republic collapsed[11] thanks to a coup d'état conducted under leadership of General Christophe Soglo.

NOTES

1. Mildred Europa Taylor, "How a Benin Royal Sold the Mighty Dahomey Kingdom to the French for a Title in 1894," *Face2Face Africa*, January 17, 2019, https://face2faceafrica.com/article/how-a-benin-royal-sold-the-mighty-dahomey-kingdom-to-the-french-for-a-title-in-1894.

2. Bernard Droz, *Histoire de la décolonisation au xxe siècle* (Paris: Éditions du Seuil, 2006), 63, 69, 245–63.

3. The Brazzaville Conference (French: Conférence de Brazzaville) was a meeting of prominent Free French leaders held in January 1944 in Brazzaville, the capital of French Equatorial Africa, during World War II. The conference recommended political, social, and economic reforms and led to an agreement called the Brazzaville Declaration. The French empire would remain united. Semi-autonomous assemblies would be established in each colony. Citizens of France's colonies would share equal rights with French citizens.

4. Marlène Panara, "Indépendance du Bénin: Vous avez dit démocratie?" *Le Point Afrique*, August 1, 2020, https://www.lepoint.fr/afrique/independance-du-benin-vous-avez-dit-democratie-01-08-2020-2386323_3826.php#11.

5. "L'Indépendance du Bénin," *Vister le Benin* (blog), https://visiter-le-benin.com/l-independance-du-benin/.

6. Mathurin C. Houngnikpo and Samuel Decalo, *Historical Dictionary of Benin*, fourth edition (Lanham, MD: Scarecrow Press, 2012), 87.

7. Samuel Decalo, *Coups and Army Rule in Africa: Motivations and Constrains*, second edition (New Haven, CT: Yale University Press, 1990), 91.

8. It was French intellectualist Emmanuel Mounier who in 1948 described Dahomey as the "Latin Quarter" of Africa. The Latin Quarte area of Paris, on the south bank of the river Seine, has been a hub of learning for centuries. It was a university district where teachers and students spoke Latin until 1789, hence the name Latin Quarter or, in French, Quartier Latin. It remains a student neighborhood today as home to the Sorbonne, France's oldest university.

9. Interesting detailed political and social analysis of the coups d'état in Dahomey could be found in monography by Ebénézer Korê Sedegan and Olivier Djidénou Allocheme, *Histoire des coups d'état au Dahomey (1963–1972)* (Paris: L'Harmattan, 2021), 170; and Samuel Decalo, "Regionalism, Politics, and the Military in Dahomey," *Journal of Developing Areas* 7, no. 3 (April 1973): 440–78; Decalo, *Coups and Army Rule in Africa*, 99–131.

10. On May 26, 1961, Information Minister Albert Tévoédjrè notified Hubert Maga that Justin Ahomadégbé had plotted to assassinate the president. A public trial was held in December 1961, and Justin Ahomadégbé received five years for his role in the conspiracy, and the others were dealt from one- to ten-year sentences. Maga ultimately released them in November 1962, saying in a broadcast that it was not only due to their good behavior in jail but also to reconcile with his former enemies ("Libération de l'ancien président de l'assemblée du Dahomey," *Le Monde*, November 5, 1962).

11. Decalo, *Coups and Army Rule in Africa*, 98. The author explains that following French practice each major constitutional change since independence is given a number (Ibid., 309).

Chapter 2

"Sick Child of Africa"

OCTOBER 1963 COUP D'ÉTAT

Hubert Maga was deposed in October 1963 by a coup d'état conducted by his military advisor, Colonel Christophe Soglo. Soglo's coup, also referred to as the *Revolution d'Octobre 1963* (the "October Revolution of 1963"), would be the first of a series of coups d'état (in the recent history of Dahomey/Benin) that ended in 1972 with the establishment of a seventeen-year Marxist dictature. This dictature would eventually lead to Opération Crevette in 1977.

Among the various factors that led to the coup was the collapse of Dahomey's economy, left by France after years of colonial exploitation. There was little foreign investment, and unemployment rose. In response, Hubert Maga launched a four-year plan in January 1962, which was to increase agricultural production by encouraging the nation's youths to work in the fields. Widespread social protests and disturbances stemming from poor living conditions led to trade union strikes organized by the main union: the Union of Workers of Dahomey (*Union Générale des Travailleurs du Dahomey*, UGTD). With an estimated ten thousand UGTD members and a total trade union membership in Dahomey of roughly twenty-one thousand concentrated in the main cities, the voice of trade unions could not be ignored by political or military centers of power. A 10-percent cut in the salary of civil servants and talks of a planned austerity program sharpened a country's political debate atmosphere.[1] Personal power struggles between Hubert Maga and its vice president, Migan Apithy, only fueled the explosive political and social atmosphere in the country. This was "a quarrel" that dated from the colonial period with conflicts between the political actors, and particularly the elites of the south and the north of Dahomey.[2]

Hubert Maga and his political associates were accused of living a "luxurious lifestyle"[3] while making an "abusive increase in the number of ministerial posts" and failing to satisfy social demands or keep promises. Maga was further criticized, among others, for enjoying foreign travel and building a $3 million presidential palace in the capital city, Cotonou, whose reception rooms allegedly resembled the film set for *Cleopatra*. The president's administration was also blamed by the opposition for taking antidemocratic measures in response to social disturbances that "martyrized the people and reduced them to nothing."[4] But the "straw that broke the camel's back" was apparently a criminal case: *Bohiki affair*.[5]

Christophe Bohiki was a well-known PDU and National Assembly of Dahomey member. Bohiki had murdered (poisoned) a member of the Dahomeyan administration on the pretext that the latter was courting his wife. Arrested, he was quickly released due to parliamentary immunity to continue to enjoy his freedom as if nothing had happened. This "woman skirt affair,"[6] as it was called by some, was also referred to as the "small incident that unleashed the storm" by others.[7] This incident was taken over by the political forces of the southerners, led by Justin Ahomadégbé, to protest Bohiki's release without prosecution as an alleged murderer.

The street demonstrations in Cotonou and Porto-Novo in protest against the release of Bohiki began on October 21, 1963. On one occasion, the civilian protesters approached military headquarters at Camp Guézo demanding that the military take over the country's rule. In the account of an eyewitness the night of October 20/21,1963, gunfire erupted on the streets of Dahomey's capital. "In Cotonou, and nearby Porto-Novo, the ragged crowds carried black-draped coffins and chanted war songs as they ransacked government offices, burned cars, hauled down the green, yellow and red national flag from public buildings, and demanded Maga's ouster. Bariba tribesmen from Maga's native northern region leaped into the fray in his defense and killed two demonstrators with bows and arrows."[8]

In an attempt to resolve the crisis, Colonel Soglo dissolved the National Assembly, suspended the Constitution. He nominated a provisional government with only three cabinet members presided over by Hubert Maga with Justin Ahomadégbé and Migan Apithy, each of them with a title of minister of state. The latter two, however, refused to work with Hubert Maga as the leader.[9]

In this context of sociopolitical crisis, the army came out of its hinges to take the side of the agitated populations. Without the solid support of the military, Hubert Maga, who a few years earlier tried to suppress the trade union movement, found himself personally and politically defenseless.

On October 28, 1963, the president was arrested in his office of the presidency of the republic and forced to resign by an armed commando from the Camp Guézo in Cotonou. Colonel Christopher Soglo remained as head of such provisional government for the three months between the coup in October of 1963 and January 1964. In January of 1964, Migan Apithy,[10] whose Dahomeyan Democratic Party (*Parti Démocratique Dahoméen*, PDD) won the legislative elections, replaced Colonel Christophe Soglo as the head of state with Justin Ahomadégbé as prime minister. After acceding to power, both ministers signed the decree by which they nominated Colonel Christophe Soglo as a general.[11]

On December 4, 1963, the army placed Hubert Maga under house arrest and charged him with corruption and "embezzlement and bad administration of public funds," but he was never prosecuted. After his release in 1965, Maga left Dahomey and lived for a short time in Togo and then five years in exile in Paris.

At the end of November 1965, Migan Apithy resigned, leaving Ahomadégbé and Maga as two co-presidents.

According to one description of the events, "While President Apithy was in Paris, Vice-President Ahomadégbé passed a law concerning the appointment of the members of the supreme court. On his return Apithy refused to sign the law."[12] The single political party in which both leaders were members, but controlled by Ahomadégbé, asked Apithy to resign from the presidency. He refused, and Ahomadégbé decided to remove Apithy himself. He donned a military uniform and wanted to lead an army detachment to remove Apithy from the presidential palace. Colonel Soglo met Ahomadégbé accidentally in the outskirts of Porto Novo and was angered by the sight of him in uniform. Soglo returned to Camp Guézo in Cotonou, the major military camp, called together the senior officers, and together they decided to demand the resignation of both Apithy and Ahomadegbe. Those two acting presidents would govern for a cumulative twenty-five days. Following growing dissension between President Migan Apithy and Vice President Justin Ahomadégbé, both men resigned on November 29, 1965.

1965 INTERIM PRESIDENCY

Justin Ahomadégbé held power from November 27 to 29, 1965. This highly brief two-day term was forcibly terminated again by General Soglo, who instated to the presidency—as provided for in the Constitution—then speaker of the National Assembly, Tahïrou Congacou, who took office as the acting president. He had the particularity of being the first civilian to come to power, without an election and without a coup d'état. His cabinet consisted of only four ministers—technical experts. Tahïrou Congacou would govern for twenty-three days, from November 29, 1965, to December 22, 1965. Congacou's presidential term was cut short when he was removed on the official grounds of failing to form a national coalition government. There seemed to be, however, more real reasons behind his removal: the continued, unresolved economic and financial crisis, opposition activities of trade unions, open rivalry between Migan Apithy and Justin Ahomadégbé, mass demonstrations against both, and a dispute between the president and the National Assembly over the appointment of members of the Supreme Court added only to the reason the additional arguments.

DECEMBER 1965 COUP D'ÉTAT

On December 22, 1965, Christophe Soglo "unilaterally withdrew Tahïrou Congacou's mandate and assumed full powers setting his own administration."[13] Again, the main source of public protest and disturbance was the country's extremely difficult economic and financial situation. And again, like in the past, trade unions were in front of opposition, this time to the government supervised by the military.[14] General Christophe Soglo spent nearly two years as president unsuccessfully coping with the social and economic problems before being ousted in yet another military rebellion organized by a group of junior officers.

1967 COUP D'ÉTAT OF COLONEL
MAURICE IROPA KOUANDÉTÉ

The coup was preceded, again like in earlier years, by trade unions that organized a wave of strikes across the private and public sectors, with the general strike in Porto Novo and Cotonou by December 13, 1967. Two young, blood-related, ambitious officers led this rebellion: a graduate of the prestigious French military academy Saint Cyr, former commander of general Christophe Soglo's security unit, Presidential Palace Guard, and former head of the country's security services, Major Maurice Iropa Kouandété (Maurice Kouandété); and his French-educated cousin, Captain Mathieu Kérékou, former *aide-de-camp*[15] to president Hubert Maga between 1961 and 1963.

Likely unaware of brewing coup d'état preparations, Soglo paid a state visit in France from November 21–24, 1967, where he was greeted with all state honors by French president Charles de Gaulle.[16] There he was praised by the press as a democratic leader because he allowed three ousted former leaders—Migan Apithy, Justin Ahomadégbé, and Hubert Maga—"to leave the Dahomeyan territory without difficulty to settle in Paris."[17] Obtained during a visit in Paris, the French promise of granting Dahomey financial aid did not impress Dahomeyan trade unions, and strikes continued after Christophe Soglo's return home. In the middle of December, the government cut off telecommunications with neighboring Togo, suspended mail communication, closed Cotonou airport, and, finally, the police and army took over strategic points in Cotonou.[18] Even the trade unionists released after being arrested during protests would not quiet the political atmosphere in a country.

At 7:30 a.m. on Sunday, December 17, 1967, two paratroop commando units that were brought into the capital during the industrial disturbances to help police maintain public order, led now by Major Kérékou and Colonel Maurice Kouandété, surrounded the residences of prominent army commanders: General Christophe Soglo, Leuitenant Colonel Alphonse Alley, Lieutenant Colonel Philippe Aho, and Commandant Major Benoît Sinzogan. They took over strategic points in the city.[19] Colonel Alley and Major Sinzogan were placed under house arrest. When General Christophe Soglo noticed sixty commandos putschists surrounding his house, he, allegedly, in a cartoon-like fashion, scaled the wall of a compound adjacent to the US embassy, escaping apprehension by the rebelling soldiers. From there, Christophe Soglo was secreted into diplomatic protection by a French diplomatic mission in Cotonou, later fleeing through Abidjan in the Ivory Coast for exile in Paris. General Soglo retired from politics after this incident.

The presidential seat was open once again. In the middle of December 1967, Captain Jean-Baptiste Hachème and Major Maurice Kouandété formed a short-lived interim government prior to the anticipated presidential elections in May of 1968. Captain Hachème was appointed as a one-day (December 19–20, 1967) transitional chairman of the military government,[20] with Major Kouandété becoming the one-day (December 20–21,1967) head of state. When France refused—after earlier warning that he should not try to overthrow General de Gaulle's favorite Christophe Soglo—to recognize him as a head of state and threatened to withhold financial aid to Dahomey, he handed over power to Lieutenant Colonel Alphonse Alley, the former army chief of staff during Soglo's presidency, who on December 21, 1967, was named a de facto head of state. Major Mathieu Kérékou was elected chairman January 22, 1968, of the fifteen-member Military Revolutionary Committee (MRC) (*Comité Militaire Révolutionnaire*, CMR), a provisional government after the coup d'état. Alphonse Alley remained in power for the next six months thereafter, until July 17, 1968. His leadership would end as a result of political chaos after an electoral boycott called for some politicians—among them former presidents Hubert Maga and Migan Apithy—that resulted in a low voter turnout and the subsequent cancellation of the election results by the military. Under pressure from Paris, Lieutenant Colonel Alley stepped down, and the army turned over the combined position of president and prime minister to a civilian politician, Dr. Émile Derlin Zinsou.[21] The decision was immediately protested as unconstitutional by, living in exile in Paris, three "old enemy brothers"—Justin Apithy, Hubert Maga, and Justin Ahomadégbé.

"POISONED GIFT": THE PRESIDENCY
OF ÉMILE DERLIN ZINSOU

Although a medical doctor by training, Zinsou was already a seasoned "old-timer" politician with a conservative curve. He was well known not only in his own country but also in the broader political scene of Africa. He had extensive friendly contacts with French politicians, an essential factor at that time for any success-oriented local African politician.

Born in Ouidah (a city in the southwest of present-day Benin) on March 23, 1918, Émile Zinsou was educated at Porto Novo (the present-day official capital of Benin) and the École William Ponty in Senegal; throughout the French colonial period, the latter trained almost all the executives of French-speaking Africa. Zinsou later studied medicine at the Dakar Medical College (also in Senegal). After brief service as a physician in the French army from 1939 to 1940, Zinsou opened a private practice, became involved in Dahomeyan politics, and was one of the founders of Dahomey's first political party, the Dahomeyan Progressive Union (*Union Progressiste Dahoméenne*, UPD). During his early years in local politics, he was an assistant to Migan Apithy in 1945 and a deputy to the French national assembly. Between 1947 and 1953, he was vice president of the assembly to the French Union (the French Union being a political entity created to replace the French colonial system). Subsequently, he became a senator in the French Senate (1955 to 1958) and a deputy in Dahomey's territorial (later national) assembly, also serving as the minister of commerce. After August 1, 1960, when Dahomey achieved independence, Zinsou became the first president of the Supreme Court, the first ambassador to France, and briefly, the minister of foreign affairs (1962 to 1963) when he got involved in inter-African political relations and was a candidate for the role of the secretary general of the newly established Organization of African Unity (OAU). Although Zinsou's candidature failed, another Dahomeyan diplomat, Gratien Pognon, was elected deputy secretary general of that organization.[22] As the history of Benin's political life seems to show later, one can only assume that such a situation could adversely affect the personal relationship between these two ambitious politician-diplomats.

After the first coup d'état in Dahomey, Zinsou again became (1965 to 1967) the foreign minister in General Christophe Soglo's military government. Following the electoral boycott in 1968 called for by some Dahomeyan politicians and subsequent army leadership to annul the elections, Zinsou was the military pick for a new president. In his memoirs, he recounted how he was notified about the army designation of him to the presidency—with one phone call during his lunch at home.[23] Zinsou became the third (after Hubert Maga and Tahïrou Congacou) Dahomeyan civilian to take over the presidency without elections or a coup d'état. However, to justify his ascent to power in an unconstitutional way, Zinsou sought widespread approval in a nationally held referendum. In 1968, after being approved by more than three-quarters of voters, he was formally invested as president on July 17, 1968. On July 31, 1968, the Military Revolutionary Committee (CMR) was dissolved, and Zinsou held power as an independent. Well aware of the intricacies of Dahomeyan politics, the new president, on his first state visit to Paris, soberly observed: "the position of head of state, in Africa, is very uncomfortable and, in Dahomey, more than elsewhere."[24] In an interview with *Jeune Afrique*, he described the army's decision to designate him a president a "poisoned gift."[25]

Addressing the country's military leadership,[26] Zinsou made his understanding of his relationship with the army's leadership clear: "If you wanted to choose a puppet, a puppet that would be a toy in your hands, you are at [the] wrong address. . . . But if you wish to give this country a leader, a leader who commands all, and who is obeyed by all, beginning with you, gentlemen of the military, then I could be your man."[27]

Like most of his presidential predecessors, Zinsou did not last long in office.[28] He remained in power for only eighteen months (July 17, 1968, to December 10, 1969) before being ousted in a yet another, fourth for Dahomey since independence, coup d'état.

Although Zinsou was warned by the head of the country's security service, Robert Johnson, about a brewing coup, he still continued to believe in the loyalty and faithfulness of the chief of staff, Colonel Kouandété. He even shared his suspicions about a conspiracy to conduct another coup d'état with members of his cabinet expressing opinion that the planned coup might be directed not against him but against Colonel Kouandété to punish him for his fidelity to him as a president.[29]

As it soon turned out, his trust of the army leadership was misplaced. The coup was, in fact, conducted by the top army officers: leading them was Chief of Staff Colonel Kouandété, who had originally elevated Zinsou to presidency, and Lieutenant Colonel Paul-Émile de Souza, both of whom decided that the latter would replace Zinsou as head of state. Colonel Koffi Benoît Sinzogan was the third leader of the putschists. The reason for this coup was Colonel Kouandété's alleged discovery of President Zinsou's plans to replace him as chief of staff of the army and cut the size of the armed forces, all in effort to repair the state budget. Officially, Kouandété justified his coup by claiming that President Zinsou had failed to reconcile the country politically, and further failed, despite taken efforts, to improve Dahomey's economic conditions.

Thus, on December 10, 1969, the putschists, under Kouandété's command, seized the Cotonou radio station at 8:00 a.m. and stormed the presidential palace. However, at that time the President Zinsou did not arrive yet for the meeting. The soldiers took the ministers who were there to meet with the president hostage. When the presidential two-car motorcade approached the palace entrance, the soldiers fired upon it from a military jeep and blocked the president's car from entering the palace driveway.

Recalling the coup, Zinsou noted that on that particular day, the usual itinerary of the presidential motorcade had been changed upon his request. In his memoir, he provided the following details of the events: "I arrived at the palace by the great gate which I did not usually take. At the same time, a jeep of armed soldiers arrived from the side gate. Our two cars arrived almost at the same time on the steps. The soldiers jumped to the ground and opened fire on my car without further ado. They emptied their magazines. By the miracle, while eleven bullet holes riddled my car, I was not hit."[30] Two of President's Zinsou bodyguards, however, had been killed in action.

Uninjured, President Zinsou was apprehended, transferred to an armored vehicle, and driven off to the airport from which he was flown to the then small garrison town of Natitingou, located more than four hundred miles northwest from Cotonou. There, he remained in the army custody. After three days, Dr. Zinsou was released from custody and safely brought back to Cotonou. Reminiscing a few decades later on his short presidency, Zinsou made a bitter observation: "It wasn't a good gift."[31]

To Colonel Kouandété's disappointment, the rest of the military command refused to recognize the overthrow of President Zinsou or acknowledge Kouandété, the leader of that coup, as a new, even temporary, head of state. As a compromise between the coup leaders, a three-member Military Directorate[32] was established with Paul-Émile de Souza as its chairman. After three days in power, the three-member Military Directorate consisting of the coup leaders, Colonel Maurice Kouandété, army chief of staff; Lieutenant Colonel Paul-Émile de Souza, chairman of the directory; and Colonel Koffi Benoît Sinzogan, head of the gendarmerie; agreed that its chairman, de Souza, should become the interim head of state (December 13, 1969, to May 7, 1970). He immediately ordered new presidential elections to select a civilian president. Although the three "old guard" political candidates, Hubert Maga, Justin Tomêtin Ahomadégbé, and Migan Apithy each won more than 25 percent of the votes in each of their native regions, the army nullified the results in Maga's region on suspicion of electoral fraud. The fourth candidate in this election, Dr. Zinsou, who had received only 3.2 percent of the popular vote, admitted electoral defeat and "for personal reasons" refused to participate in any future presidential coalition.

In response to the invalidation of elections, Maga threatened to secede with his northern region from unitary Dahomey unless he was declared president. On his part, Apithy announced that if Maga took the presidency, he would lead his region, the central part of the country, to join neighboring Nigeria.

Bloody confrontations between supporters of the leading presidential hope-fuls occurred in various parts of the country. In order to avoid a prolonged political crisis and yet another election to prevent a civil war and the general disintegration of the country, the Military Directorate pressed all four presi-dential candidates (Ahomadégbé, Apithy, Maga, and Zinsou) to meet and reach a political agreement. The two, Ahomadégbé and Maga, accepted the Directorate's advice, while the other two declined. Thus, during the meeting on April 16, 1970, in the village Savé, Ahomadégbé and Maga reached a compromise to create, based on the triumvirate of the Military Directorate, a Presidential Council. Migan Apithy who initially declined to meet in Savé with the other two, later joint their agreement. Dr. Zinsou decided not to part in this endeavor. Three weeks later all three signed a charter establishing a presidential triumvirate, the Presidential Council.[33] The three politicians would rotate as part of a Presidential Council, each for a term of two years. This, however, as it soon became clear, did not sit well Zinsou, who now lived in a self-exile in France, but who had not given up his political ambitions or buried his political hatchet yet. Dr. Zinsou refused to participate, arguing that "the country was not a cake that we would share as we pleased."[34]

One of the first moves of President Maga during his term (1970–1972) of the triumvirate was the promotion of his former *aide-de-camp*, Captain Mathieu Kérékou, to the ranks of major and deputy chief of staff, as well as commander of the elite paratrooper unit in Ouidah garrison. Maga likely counted on Kérékou's continued loyalty as protector of his presidency against an always-possible coup d'état by his two political adversaries.

When in May of 1972 Ahomadégbé took his turn as a rotating president, rumor of yet another military coup d'état hatching had already circulated. According to an eyewitness account, Ahomadégbé received fair warning not to take his official tour. A couple of months before President Maga finished his tour, Colonel Kouandété cautioned Ahomadégbé on the escalator at the presidential palace saying, "as long as I live, if you accept your presidential tour, I will kill you."[35] Ahomadégbé allegedly returned the courtesy by declar-ing: "I will serve my tour and it will be me who will kill you."[36]

Soon after, in February of 1972, army units in fact attempted an unsuc-cessful military coup accompanied by an attempt on the life of army chief of staff, General de Souza, who just recently had taken the place of Colonel Kouandété as a head of the army. The coup attempt failed after Kouandété's former deputy, now Lieutenant Colonel Kérékou, had refused, this time, to support the mutiny. The failed coup leaders, among them Kouandété, were tried and received severe sentences, including the death penalty. Although death sentences were soon commuted and Kouandété's life was spared, it looks like it was Ahomadégbé, not Kouandété who correctly predicted, at least for a while, the development of events (see appendix A for a detailed table of presidents and heads of state).

NOTES

1. Staffan Wiking, *Military Coups in Sub-Saharan Africa: How to Justify Illegal Assumptions of Power* (Uppsala, Sweden: Scandinavian Institute of African Studies, 1986), 82, https://www.jstor.org/stable/484479?origin=crossref.

2. Josaphat Dah-Bolinon, "Ces putschistes du Dahomey," *24 Heures au Benin*, n.d., https://www.24haubenin.info/?Ces-putschistes-du-Dahomey-14414.

3. Military spokesmen cited the extravagant lifestyle of a number of ministers as another reason for the takeover. See: *Analysis of the Causes of Military Coups d'Etat in Sub-Saharan Africa*, 1960–1982. Final Report. April 1983. Prepared for: Defense Intelligence Agency. US Department of Defense. Benin. Appendix B: *Description of Sub-Saharan Military Intervention Events*, 1960–1982, B–2. Declassified report available at https://apps.dtic.mil/sti/pdfs/ADA151943.pdf.

4. Dov Ronen, *Dahomey: Between Tradition and Modernity* (Ithaca, NY: Cornell University Press, 1975), 193.

5. Ebénézer Korê Sedegan, and Olivier Djidénou Allocheme, *Histoire des coups d'état au Dahomey (1963–1972)* (Paris: L'Harmattan, 2021), 58–59.

6. Ruben Abadagan, "Les coups d'état au Dahomey: Le point coup d'état du 28 octobre 1963," Facebook, posted November 22, 2018, https://www.facebook.com/groups/yehoutotche/posts/2582828608410557/.

7. Terray Emmanuel, "Les révolutions congolaise et dahoméenne de 1963: Essai d'interprétation," *Revue française de science politique* 14, no. 5 (1964): 926.

8. "Dahomey: Sounds in the Night," *Time* 82, no. 19, November 8, 1963.

9. Sedegan and Allocheme, *Histoire des coups d'état au Dahomey*, 60.

10. "Interview du general Soglo apres son coup d'etat de 1965," YouTube video posted on August 19, 2010 by Jomalick1, 2010, https://www.youtube.com/watch?v=JKFgQxNup08. "Dahomey: Sounds in the Night," 36; "Coup d'Etat au Dahomey," *L'INA éclaire l'actu*, December 22, 1965, https://www.ina.fr/ina-eclaire-actu/video/caf96065107/coup-d-etat-au-dahomey.

11. Decret No. 5/PR dated February 3, 1964.

12. Dov Ronen, *Political Dynamics in Benin*, Center for International Affairs Harvard University, April 1984, 22.

13. *Historical Dictionary of Benin*, fourth edition, by Mathurin C. Houngnikpo and Samuel Decalo (Lanham, MD: Scarecrow Press, 2013), 122.

14. The role of the Dahomeyan trade unions in 1960s and military response to their demands: W. A. E. Skurnik, "Can the Military Modernize?" *Africa Today* 15, no. 2 (1968): 5–6.

15. *Aide-de-camp*, in French military nomenclature, an officer, usually a captain who acts as a personal assistant to a general.

16. "Le général de Gaulle a accueilli mardi matin le général Soglo, chef de l'etat du Dahomey," *Le Monde*, November 22, 1967. De Gaulle greeted visiting general by

saying: "The France warmly welcomes, Mr. President, to welcome in your person the President of the Republic of Dahomey."

17. "Le général Soglo a Paris," *Le Monde*, November 22, 1967.

18. Philippe Decraene, "Situation politique tendue au Dahomey," *Le Monde*, December 15, 1967.

19. "Analysis of the Causes of Military Coups d'état in Sub-Saharan Africa, 1960–1982,"

Final Report, April 1983, Prepared for: Defense Intelligence Agency, US Department of Defense, Appendix B: Description of Sub-Saharan Military Intervention Events, 1960–1982, B–4: [Declassified report—authors] https://apps.dtic.mil/sti/pdfs/ADA151943.pdf. Also: Sedegan and Allocheme, *Histoire des coups d'État au Dahomey (1963–1972)*, 80.

20. Africa Info, "Bénin: Quelques Repères Historiques et Différents Présidents Depuis 1960," *Africa News* (blog), December 26, 2015, http://infoafricanews.blogspot.com/2015/12/benin-quelques-reperes-historiques-et.html.

21. "Qui etes vous Docteur Zinsou?" *Jeune Afrique*, no. 396, August 11, 1968, 28–31; Émile Derlin Zinsou, *En ces temps là . . .* (Paris: Riveneuve, 2013); Mathurin C. Houngnikpo and Samuel Decalo, *Historical Dictionary of Benin* (Lanham, MD: Scarecrow Press, 2012): 37375.

22. Gratien-Lazar Pognon held this office from 1964 to 1972.

23. Zinsou, *En ces temps là . . .* , 185–87.

24. Quoted in: [Portrait] "Émile Derlin Zinsou, le vétéran qui n'était pas pressé," http://www.ortb.info/index.php/info/politique/4141-portrait-emile-derlin-zinsou-le-veteran-qui-n-etait-pas-presse.

25. "Coup d'etat pou loi," *Jeune Afrique*, no. 392, July 1968, 24.

26. Andre Sabas, "Coup d'etat au Dahomey," *L'INA éclaire l'actu*, December 12, 1969, https://www.ina.fr/ina-eclaire-actu/video/caf96065113/coup-d-etat-au-dahomey; "L'élection présidentielle est annulée," *Le Monde*, May 15, 1968, https://www.lemonde.fr/archives/article/1968/05/15/l-election-presidentielle-est-annulee_2503546_1819218.html.

27. "Qui etes vou Docteur Zinsou," 30.

28. For an excellent, detailed description of stormy period of Dr. Zinsou presidency, see Samuel Decalo, "Full Circle in Dahomey," *African Studies Review* 13, no. 3 (December 1970): 447–57.

29. Zinsou, *En ces temps là . . .* , 31.

30. Zinsou, *En ces temps là . . .* , 224.

31. Quoted in: [Portrait] "Émile Derlin Zinsou."

32. Two other members of the Military Directorate were Colonel Kouandété and Colonel Benoît Sinzogan, head of the Gendarmerie. The two had a very inimical relationship.

33. Ordonnace no. 70–34 / CP du 7 mai 1970 portant Chartre du Conseil Présidentiel: https://sgg.gouv.bj/doc/ordonnance-1970-34/.

34. Zinsou, *En ces temps là . . .* , 230.

35. Christophe D. Agbodji, "Coup d'etat du 26 octobre 1972: Les troublantes révélations de Pascal Chabi Kao (Première Partie)," *Le Benin vu par un jeune*

(blog), October 25, 2011, http://actudubenin.over-blog.com/article-coup-d-etat-du-26
-octobre-1972-les-troublantes-revelations-de-pascal-chabi-kao-87267329.html.
    36. Ibid.

Chapter 3

Enough Is Enough

When, in May of 1972, Ahomadégbé took his turn as rotating president, rumor of yet another military coup d'état hatching had already circulated. According to an eyewitness account, Ahomadégbé received fair warning not to take his official tour. A couple of months before President Maga finished his tour, Colonel Kouandété cautioned Ahomadégbé on the escalator at the presidential palace saying, "as long as I live, if you accept your presidential tour, I will kill you."[1] Ahomadégbé allegedly returned the courtesy by declaring: "I will serve my tour and it will be me who will kill you."[2]

Soon after, in February of 1972, army units attempted an unsuccessful military coup accompanied by an attempt on the life of army chief of staff, General de Souza, who just recently had taken the place of Colonel Kouandété as a head of the army. The coup attempt failed after Kouandété's former deputy, now Lieutenant Colonel Kérékou, had refused, this time, to support the mutiny. The failed coup leaders, among them Kouandété, were tried and received severe sentences, including the death penalty. Although death sentences were soon commuted and Kouandété's life was spared, it looks like it was Ahomadégbé, not Kouandété who correctly predicted, at least for a while, the development of events.

Unresolved disputes between the army leadership and civilian politicians regarding how to eradicate widespread corruption and how to deal with the pervasive demands for commuting the death penalty sentences, meted against the February 1972 failed coup attempt, constant quarrels between three co-presidents, led to yet another, the sixth since independence, bloodless military coup d'état.

According to the account of an American *charge d'affaires* (a diplomat who temporarily takes the place of an ambassador to serve as an embassy's chief of mission) accredited in Cotonou, he had learned that the French were "very worried" given indications of an impending coup d'état in Dahomey during his visit in September 1972 to Quai d'Orsay in Paris (where the Ministry of Foreign Affairs and other French government offices are located).[3] The

SDECE (*Service de Documentation Extérieure et de Contre-Espionnages*, or French External Documentation and Counter-Espionnage Service) sources were right. Another military coup d'état in Dahomey was forthcoming.

Although this coup is commonly referred to as "Kérékou's coup d'état," the Beninese debate as to who actually inspired this coup continues to this day.[4]

Some behind-the-scenes details of the coup were kept confidential for fifty years. Most detailed information, although certainly subjective (as any personal memoires would be), were revealed in 2010 by an eyewitness, a long-term politician, political insider, and co-president Hubert Maga's loyalist Pascal Chabi Kao.[5] In his view, the October 1972 coup was the result of political discord between the two co-presidents, Justin Ahomadégbé and Hubert Maga. Early in 1972, toward the end of President Maga's term, Ahomadégbé became increasingly concerned that he might be prevented from coming to power, especially after the February army mutiny. The most recent bone of contention between the two co-presidents was supposedly the issue of the exemplary execution of former chief of staff Lieutenant Colonel Iropa Maurice Kouandété, the organizer of three earlier coups d'état—two successful (1967 and 1969) and one failed (1972). The failed one, on February 23, 1972, resulted in a short trial before the Military Tribunal, which handed down death sentences for him and two his closest associates. Twenty-one soldiers, civilians, and Maga bodyguards received lighter sentences. Forthcoming co-president Ahomadégbé was allegedly pushing for the execution of the convicted rebels while co-president Maga, whose term was just ending, was against such executions. As aforementioned, Ahomadégbé and Kouandété had already, at an earlier occasion, promised each other death. It looked like when Ahomadégbé had presidential power, he wanted to realize his promise. Among those high-level officers who opposed the execution of convicted officers was Major Kérékou. During the February coup attempt Kérékou, then chef of battalion in Ouidah, had shown his loyalty to the government, rallying a large fraction of the army that was undecided. It was he who had obtained the surrender of the mutineers entrenched in Cape Guézo of Cotonou, saved the term of ending presidency of Hubert Maga and secured the peaceful transfer of presidency to Justin Ahomadégbé. But not for long.

On October 26, 1972, the group of young officers, led by captains Janvier Assogba, Michel Aikpe,[6] and Michel Alladaye,[7] staged yet another military coup d'état.[8] The coup was initially planned for Wednesday October 25, 1972, the day the government regularly met under the chairmanship of a current president. However, on the evening of Wednesday October 25, 1972, former-president Maga held a separate meeting with some of his ministers and the regular meeting of whole council was postponed to Thursday, October 26, 1972.

During the Wednesday meeting, around midnight, one of the ministers received a phone call with information that the parachutist unit from garrison in Ouidah were on their way to Cotonou, most likely in order to conduct a coup d'état the very next day. In fact, around 2:00 p.m., a column of several tanks and armored vehicles left the Ouidah Support Subgroup for Cotonou. At the head of the column, Captain Janvier Assogba, commander of this unit, in an army Jeep car. Since coups d'état were frequent at that time, a column of tanks and armored vehicles leaving the Ouidah Military Camp did not surprise many people.

Some members of the council present at the meeting head over to the residence of Major Kérékou to warn him about the possible military coup. As related by Chabi Kao, Kérékou allegedly responded by saying: "Oh good! They want to make a coup without me! Let them come, I'm waiting for them! Go to bed, let them come!"[9] So, nothing happened that evening and all they went home.

Also, the putschists later asked their superior officer Commandant Mathieu Kérékou to join them as their leader. Kérékou, at this point only thirty-nine years old, was their senior officer, a deputy chief of staff, the battalion chief, and commander of main Dahomeyan paratrooper unit stationed in Ouidah.

MATHIEU KÉRÉKOU

Mathieu Chaad Kérékou's career is a prime example of a young male military professional's career advancement in pre-independence Francophone African countries. Born in 1933, at the young age of fourteen, Kérékou joined a military school for boys and was reared by the French colonial army. He subsequently studied at the military academy École d'Enfants de Troupe de Kati (EETS) in then–French Mali, and successively at École d'Enfants de Troupe de Saint-Louis in Senegal. In Senegal, young Kérékou caught the eye of his future military and political patron, Maurice Robert, a former principal of EETS. and later resident of the French intelligence service station SDECE (Africa division) in Dakar. In 1953, as a twenty-year-old soldier, Kérékou joined the French colonial army stationed in Dahomey. As promising career soldier, Kérékou was appointed corporal first category on January 13, 1954, and a few years later, on January 1, 1958, was advanced to staff sergeant first category. Later, he continued his military education in continental France at the Training School for Officers from Overseas Territories (*École de Formation des Officiers Ressortissants des Territoires d'Outre-Mer*, EFORTOM) at Frejus, France, attended by many future military leaders in Francophone African countries.

After Dahomey gained independence from France on August 31, 1960, Kérékou served as a second lieutenant in the nascent air force of Dahomey and as an *aide-de-camp* of then-president Hubert Maga. Soon after, in 1962, he was promoted to lieutenant, reaching rank of a captain merely three years later. At thirty-four, he entered the Dahomeyan political scene for the first time, joining as its chairman the Revolutionary Military Committee (*Comité Militaire Révolutionnaire*, CMR) in 1967, set up after the coup d'état of Major Kouandété that resulted in bringing by the putschists to presidency Dr. Émile Zinsou. At that time, as most of these young military putschists and Dahomeyan civilians supporting them, Kérékou was under the strong leftist and communist ideological influence from French intellectual and political elites and propagating as a political and socioeconomic ideal the Communist revolution of Mao Zedong (Tse-tung) in People's Republic of China that was very popular in some West European countries, including France. Like all other young cadets in French military schools, Kérékou was exposed to political indoctrination and the glorification of the French revolution of 1789 with its ideology of revolutionary change of governments and methods of governance. No wonder these graduates were ready for revolutions, military coups d'état, and exercising dictatorial power to impose Communist-oriented political, social, and economic systems on their countries. Many of them would pattern their revolutions in postcolonial Francophone African countries on examples of Communist China, Castro's Cuba, or Kim Il-sung's North Korea. Captain Mathieu Kérékou turned to be one of them, at least temporarily.

Transferred to First Mixed Battalion of Dahomeyan Armed Forces (FAD) and assigned to the Command and Support Company (CCS), he would be seconded to the presidency of the republic to serve as *aide-de-camp* of President Hubert Maga, his mentor who has since become prime minister, then president of the Republic of Dahomey on August 1, 1960. Promoted to the rank of lieutenant on September 1, 1962, he left the presidency of the republic and took command of the Centre Training Parachutist (CIP) of Bembèrèkè. He would then be appointed at the head of the Pioneer Company (CP) of OKPARA.

In January 1965, he was promoted to captain, and a year later in February 1966, he was appointed deputy officer to the commander of the First Intervention Battalion at the position of commander of the command company. Soon after Kérékou was advanced to commander of the support sub-group, one of the most equipped units based in Ouidah on which he remained for next three years.

Mathieu Kérékou's exposure to politics began in 1967 when he was appointed a member of the *Comité Militaire de Vigilance* that supervised General Soglo's policies. After Kouandété's coup d'état in 1967,

Kérékou became vice president and then president of the *Comité Militaire Révolutionnaire*.

In 1969, Kérékou received the rank of major and, seemingly leaning more toward a military than a political career, Kérékou was sent to attend a training program for non-commissioned officers of the army in order to receive future higher army officer training at National Active Non-Commissioned Officers School (*L'École Nationale des Sous-Officiers d'Active*, ENSOA) at Saint Maixent, France. Two years after his return home, he was appointed (on August 31, 1970) the assistant chief of staff of the army of Dahomey and was given the command of a major elite unit of paratroopers stationed in Dahomey's main military camp in Ouidah, located twenty-five miles (forty kilometers) west of Cotonou. His military education was crowned with completion of course at the Staff School (*École d'état-major* de Paris, EEM).[10]

Such fast advancement within FAD was to some extent dependent on the positive evolutions he received from the French officers charged with selecting young promising (from the French point of view) African officers for advanced, specialized training at French military schools. They were seen as future military or political leaders in French *pré-caré*, the reserved domain of each French president from Charles de Gaulle to Sarkozy, "subject to special monitoring for fifty years through the African cell of the Elysée and men of shadow and trust" like for most of the time was Jacques Foccart.[11]

POWER SHARING, OCTOBER 1, 1972, COUP

In the middle of 1970s, it looked like a power sharing agreement that was reached by civilian politicians the country facilitated a period of some political stability. Two years later, however, Benin would be the scene of the next, fifth, military coup d'état. This coup would be led captains Janvier Assogba and Michel Aikpé who had organized the fifteen-member Military Revolutionary Committee (*Comité Militaire pour la Révolution*, CMR) with Major Kérékou as its chairman. Kérékou's decision to join the putschists in 1972 turned out to be the beginning of his important role in the political history of Benin.

The next day, October 26, 1972, the members of President Ahomadégbé's cabinet held a postponed regular weekly meeting of the Council of Ministers at the palace of the republic; this meeting was attended by the presidential council member Hubert Maga and members of the government. The third member of the presidential triumvirate, Migan Apithy, had been on vacation in France since September 27, 1972.

At 2:30 p.m., using elements of the Third Combined Battalion composed of the detachment of parachutists under the command of Captain Michel Aikpe; the company of command and support; and the First Squadron of Armored Vehicles led by Janvier Assogba,[12] set off from the Ouidah Military Camp—the largest military camp in the country at the time, in the direction of Cotonou. "In Cotonou, near the Bon Pasteur Church in Cadjèhoun"—according to one author—"not far from the presidency, the procession split into two: one group continued on its way to the palace, while the other headed for the headquarters of the national radio station."[13]

The arteries leading to the presidential palace were closed to traffic by tanks and jeeps whose weapons were pointed at the presidential palace. Military vehicles broke the palace's gate, and soldiers occupied the premises of the palace. According to some accounts, the soldiers were firing their weapons, but the putschist quickly took control of the presidential palace.

According to reports at the scene, soldiers busted abruptly into the cabinet room of the presidential palace and started firing bullets, but no one was injured. When they entered the meeting room, Hubert Maga turned to President Ahomadégbé requesting that he take action to stop the soldiers, but the president remained silent.

According to an American diplomat accredited in Cotonou and other eyewitness statements, the arteries leading to the presidential palace became intentionally blocked to city traffic by tanks and jeeps whose weapons were pointed at the palace. Convoy of armored cars that drove from Ouidah stopped in front of the presidential palace (*Palais de la Marina*), the lead armored car turning into the driveway and breaking through the big wrought-iron gates onto the grounds to open machine gun fire.[14] The company of twenty soldiers under Captain Philippe Akpo directly attacked the palace. Some shots were fired back from the palace, but rebel soldiers soon burst into the cabinet room and opened fire inside. The Presidential Guard detachment was "neutralized," immobilizing any effective defense for the members of the council.[15]

For a while the members of the governing council participating in the meeting were uncertain who was conducting the coup. If it were Akipe or Major Kérékou, Maga's supporters would be safe and Ahomadégbé's presidential term would end. If supporters of Ahomadégbé had undertaken the coup, Ahomadégbé would be safe and could continue his presidential term that had begun in May 1972.

As usual in case of the coups d'état undertaken across Africa, the country learned about the thirty-minute-long successful coup from a communication broadcasted on the national radio. Around 3:00 p.m., a voice that many Dahomeyans recognized as that of Mathieu Kérékou read on a public radio already renamed to the "Voice of the Dahomey Revolution" a broadcast proclamation announcing the dissolution of the Presidential Council and the Revolutionary Military Government led by Commander Kérékou took power.

In the proclamation, Mathieu claimed that the *Kovacs affair*[16] (detailed in chapter 4) was the primary reason for the president's removal from of the office. The *Kovacs affair*, rife with corruption, provided an alibi for the military to overthrow the Presidential Council, to prevent Ahomadégbé from executing Kouandété, and to prevent a civil war from ensuing.[17] It was in this speech when Mathieu Kérékou used his famous description of the Presidential Council as "the hideous three-headed monster, pompously baptized: Presidential Council which served as a support for imperialist foreign domination" and his no-less-famous quote from the Dahomeyan proverb: "The branch will not break in the arms of the chameleon" adding that "Dahomey will be wisely commanded and directed by a revolutionary military regime." Kérékou also ensured Dahomeyans that "[t]he army solemnly undertakes to give the Dahomeyan people the hope of a truly new dawn."

No one was injured during this coup, but both politicians present were detained. Subsequently, all three members of the Presidential Council—Hubert Maga and Justin Ahomadégbé immediately, and later also Migan Apithy—were placed under house arrest in a military camp in the northern city of Parakou. At the same time, special commissions opened investigations of their activities while in office. An American embassy report described the three presidents' living quarters as "comfortable." They were never brought to trial or even criminally charged. Eventually, they were released[18] from custody without prosecution and only allowed to leave the country in 1981. All left for France from where they continued oppositional political activity, earning in Dahomey the moniker the "Paris spoilers" due to their continued attempts of obstruction of local politics.[19]

As noticed some time after the coup by foreign visitors, "Were it not for the numerous statements of the new President, which are broadcast at regular intervals over the local radio, a visitor would hardly realize that a military coup had taken place only a few weeks ago."[20]

The young putschists had entrusted the country's leadership to their senior officer and deptuty chief of staff, Mathieu Kérékou, whom they considered "the best" among them and who had "the image of a brave and honorable man."[21] The three coup leaders took crucial ministerial positions: Captain Michel Akipe became minister of internal affairs, Commander Michel Alladay became minister of foreign affairs, and Captain Janvier Assogba became minister of civil service. Thus, in 1972, Kérékou became the Dahomeyan president, head of the Revolutionary Military Government (*Gouvernement Militaire Révolutionnaire*, GMR), and an army chief commander. In an interview with French TV, Kérékou stated that the coup d'état took place because the triumvirate was "truly a monster" that showed an "unpardonable incompetence"; further, he stated, "Dahomey is too small for three presidents." Comparing his country with France, Kérékou argued that France, with fifty million people, has one president while Dahomey with a population of three million, had three.[22]

Figure 3.1.   1960 - Colonel Mathieu Kérékou, President of Dahomey. Credit: Keystone Press / Alamy Stock Photo.

The October 1972 coup was, most probably, conducted without the knowledge of the French special services. After all, the three leaders removed from power represented pro-French political views and remained under French influence during their political activity. Paris had pushed them during the conference in Savé in April 1970 to agree to a power-sharing agreement that resulted in the establishment of the Presidential Council. During his June 1972 official visit to Paris, President Ahomadégbé—when he met President Georges Pompidou, Jacques Foccart, secretary general for African and Malagasy affairs, Yvon Bourges, secretary of state for foreign affairs, and Prime Minister Jacques Chaban-Delmas—there was no indication that France would be considering a change of the power sharing agreement imposed by Paris on the presidential system of Dahomey, not to mention allowing for the creation of a new military dictatorship in the country. A sign of French disapproval of the October coup was the cancellation of President Pompidou's state visit in Cotonou where he planned to meet in November 1972 with President Justin Ahomadégbé. The details of Pompidou's visit were worked out only two weeks before the coup during Jacques Foccart's stay in Cotonou.

The October 1972 coup d'état was the last successful military coup in Dahomey before democratic changes were introduced in its political system at the beginning of 1990s. Despite the subsequent changes in Benin's political and economic systems and despite terrible socioeconomic consequences of that coup, it is still recognized as an important event in Benin's history. The date of the coup, October 26, is annually celebrated in Benin as a Day of Beninese Armed Forces. It led to an almost seventeen-year failed experiment of a Marxist–Leninist dictatorial revolutionary, political, economic, and social system imposed on the country by young ideologized political activists and radicalized members of the higher army command. In consequence, the country was falling under the influence of the so-called socialist countries, such as the Soviet Union, Communist China, and North Korea. Benin also established a close relationship with several African countries led by radical anti-West leaders experimenting, like Mathieu Kérékou, with socialist-type economies and building political ties with the Eastern Bloc and non-alignment movement countries. This, in turn, made the French want to reverse these changes and return Benin into Paris's sphere of influence—to what was called *Françafrique*.

While during the presidency of Georges Pompidou (1969–1974), the events in Dahomey were somehow tolerated by Paris, during the presidency of his successor, Valéry Giscard d'Estaing (1974–1981), the policy toward former French African colonies radically changed. He wanted to make France the "Western and anti-Communist sword" on the black continent where we no longer speak of the "Cold War" but of "fresh war." One of the changes was a policy of containment of the rise of Marxist regimes and to return those countries into Paris's sphere of influence—to *Françafrique*. This was the reason for Paris's support for Bob Denard's Opération Crevette.

NOTES

1. Christophe D. Agbodji, "Coup d'etat du 26 octobre 1972: Les troublantes révélations de Pascal Chabi Kao (Première Partie)," *Le Benin vu par un jeune* (blog), October 25, 2011, http://actudubenin.over-blog.com/article-coup-d-etat-du-26-octobre-1972-les-troublantes-revelations-de-pascal-chabi-kao-87267329.html.

2. Ibid.

3. Association for Diplomatic Studies and Training, "The 1974 Coup in Benin (Dahomey)," Huffington Post, December 6, 2017, https://www.huffpost.com/entry/the-1974-coup-in-benin-da_b_8302874.

4. Charly Hessoun, "Bénin: Le voile se lève sur le coup d'Etat du 26 octobre 1972," *La Nouvelle Tribune* (blog), December 15, 2015, https://lanouvelletribune.info/2015/12/benin-le-voile-se-leve-sur-le-coup-d-etat-du-26-octobre-1972/. In 1975, was sentence to death for his opposition to Kérékou. Forty-three years later, after death of Kérékou, Assogba minimized the role of his coup associates and claimed that it was mainly his idea to launch that coup.)

5. Pascal Chabi Kao served in the cabinet of president Hubert Maga from 1960 to 1963. After the presidential election in 1970, that would have reinstated Maga, was annulled, he threatened secession of northern Dahomey. He was named minister of labor and finance after the Presidential Council was established in May 1970. He was accused of irregularities, such as bribery, influence peddling, and embezzlement in the *Kovacs affair* of 1972. Justin Ahomadégbé attempted to fire him but was blocked by Maga. Later, Chabi Kao was accused of planning a coup against Kérékou on February 28, 1973, and was imprisoned with twenty years of hard labor but was released before serving the whole time and remained active in politics until 1990s.

6. According to some it was Aikpe who "spearheaded" the 1972 coup. He was later appointed a minister of interior. In 1975, Aikpe allegedly caught *in flagranti* with Kérékou's wife, was killed on a spot by members of the Presidential Guard.

7. Michel Alladaye (born 1940) is a former Beninese politician. He was the foreign minister of Benin from 1972 to 1980.

8. Hessoun, "Bénin." Forty-three years later, after death of Kérékou, Assogba minimized the role of his coup associates and claimed that it was mainly his idea to launch that coup.

9. Binason Avèkes, "Pour l'histoire: Coup d'etat du 26 Octobre 1972 et Affaire Covacs: Le Roman Crépusculaire de Pascal Chabi Kao," *Babilown*, February 12, 2012, https://babilown.com/2012/02/12/coup-detat-du-26-octobre-1972-et-affaire-covac-le-roman-crepusculaire-de-pascal-chabi-kao/.

10. Biography of Mathieu Kérékou is based on Mathurin C. Houngnikpo and Samuel Decalo, *Historical Dictionary of Benin*, fourth edition (Lanham, MD: Scarecrow Press, 2013), 223–24; Amadou Osumane, *Notre ami Kerekou* (Cotonou, Benin: Éditions Assuli, 2016), 298–301.

11. François Bost, "France, Afrique, mondialisation: Le 'pré carré' français à l'épreuve de la décolonisation et de la mondialisation de l'économie" [Africa, France, Globalization. France's "private reserve" and the challenges of decolonization and economic globalization], *Bulletin de l'Association de géographes français* 87, no. 1 (2010): 133, https://www.persee.fr/doc/bagf_0004-5322_2010_num_87_1_8186.

12. Philippe Akpo, *Role et implications des forces armees beninoises dans la vie politique nationale: Temoignage, ma part de vérité sur les faits et les non-dits* (Cotonou, Benin: Editions du Flamboyant, 2005), 70 and 73.

13. Serge Ouitona, "Bénin: Il était une fois . . . le 26 octobre 1972," *Afrik.com*, October 26, 2020, https://www.afrik.com/benin-il-etait-une-fois-le-26-octobre-1972.

14. "Windshield Tour of a Military Coup in Benin," Association for Diplomatic Studies and Training, September 30, 2015, https://adst.org/2015/09/windshield-tour -of-a-military-coup-in-benin/.

15. Charly Hessoun, "Janvier Assogba: 'Le coup d'etat du 26 octobre 1972, personne n'était demandeur,'" *La Nouvelle Tribune* (blog), December 11, 2015, https: //lanouvelletribune.info/2015/12/janvier-assogba-le-coup-d-etat-du-26-octobre-1972 -personne-n-etait-demandeur/.

16. Pascal Chabi Kao served in the cabinet of president Hubert Maga from 1960 to 1963. After the presidential election in 1970 that would have reinstated Maga was annulled, he threatened secession of northern Dahomey. He was named minister of labor and finance after the Presidential Council was established in May 1970. He was accused of irregularities, such as bribery, influence peddling, and embezzlement in the *Kovacs affair* of 1972. Justin Ahomadégbé-Tomêtin attempted to fire him but was blocked by Maga. Later in 1973, Chabi Kao would be accused of planning another coup against Kérékou on February 28 (1973) and would be imprisoned with twenty years of hard labor; he would be released before serving the whole time and would remain active in politics until 1990s.

17. Avèkes, "Pour l'histoire: Coup d'etat du 26 octobre 1972."

18. Formally dissolved on the same day by Ordonnance no. 72–39 du 26 octobre 1972 portant abrogeant l'Ordonance no. 70–34/CP du 7 mai 1970, portant Chartre du Conseil Presidentiel: https://sgg.gouv.bj/doc/ordonnance-1972-39/.

19. "Situation au Dahomey après le coup d'etat: Interview du Président Kerekou," *L'INA éclaire l'actu*, October 29, 1972, https://www.ina.fr/ina-eclaire-actu/video /caf92015518/situation-au-dahomey-apres-le-coup-d-etat-interview-du-president -kerekou; Andre Sabas, "Coup d'etat Au Dahomey," *L'INA éclaire l'actu*, December 10, 1969, https://www.ina.fr/ina-eclaire-actu/video/caf96065113/coup-d-etat-au -dahomey.

20. The World Bank Group Archives, Folder title: Travel briefs, Dahomey (Benin) (01/01/1973–31/01/1973), Folder ID: 1772664, ISAD(G) Reference Code: WB IBRD/IDA 03 EXC-10–4540S, Records of President Robert S. NcNamara, Digitized May 16, 2013. http://pubdocs.worldbank.org/en/319281391204515496/wbg-archives -1772664.pdf.

21. Hessoun, "Janvier Assogba."

22. "Situation au Dahomey après le coup d'etat: Interview du Président Kerekou" INA Histoire, YouTube video, posted July 23, 2012, https://www.youtube.com/watch

?v=ZJWT0khnRaM; "On October 26, 1972 in Benin, Mathieu Kérékou Took Power by Coup d'état," ORTB, YouTube video posted October 26, 2015, https://www .youtube.com/watch?v=jq2UNZCXy_M; "Rappel historique des trois glorieuses," ORTB, YouTube video posted on December 1, 2014, https://www.youtube.com/watch ?v=sq8CZVYEpao.

Chapter 4

Revolutionary Changes

With the new president came a new political vision that evolved from initial trend on the African continent in 1970s of the "Africanization"[1] of political, economic, and social life after period of colonial European domination to turning to the choice between to concurring European born systems: capitalism and socialism. Thus, from 1972 onward, there were two major phases of political, economic, and social structuring and restructuring in succession: the first seventeen, from 1972 to 1974, was a short period of nationalism, and the second, from 1974 to mid-1977, was the radicalization and institutionalization of Mathieu Kérékou's regime.

Upon his ascension into presidency, Kérékou made a political declaration regarding the policies of a new Dahomeyan government: "we do not want communism, capitalism, or socialism. We have our own Dahomeyan social and cultural system."

Kérékou would wait out the next two years, rife with internal political debates between his young acolytes in the army and radical leftist hardliners (*Ligueur*), influenced by Marxist ideologies, before proclaiming in a keynote speech delivered at Place Goho at Abomey on November 30, 1974, a second anniversary of the 1972 coup d'état, that Dahomey would become a socialist state with a mixture of a Soviet and Chinese version of Marxist ideology.[2] Kérékou stated he was "convinced that these [were] the profound aspirations of our militant people," that the new society, where it will be good to live for each Dahomeyan and every Dahomeyan, will be a socialist society."[3] This would become the newly imposed official state ideology. "Our choice is scientific Socialism, our guide is Marxism–Leninism," could be later found proclaimed on banners hanging from the public buildings.

After the government adopted Marxism–Leninism as its official ideology, it embarked on a vast program of "revolutionization" of society that was to symbolize the change of name of the country. In 1975, to reduce the political influence of the south, the name of Dahomey was abandoned for that of Benin,[4] the name of the kingdom that had once flourished in neighboring

33

Nigeria. In November 1975, the country took the official name of People's Republic of Benin, the name that beyond the historical meaning harked also to its new political system: socialist republic.

Nationalization of all sectors of the economy, reform of the education system, establishment of agricultural cooperatives and new local government structures (local revolutionary committees), prohibition of political and trade union activities, launch of a violent campaign to eradicate "feudal forces" (chiefdoms and traditional religions): the power locked all activities and institutionalized the dictatorship with the creation, in 1975, the Party of the People's Revolution of Benin (PRPB), a solely legal political party and leading political force in the country, the election of a National Revolutionary Assembly (ANR) and the adoption of a new Basic Law in 1977.[5]

Kérékou's critics mocked the system due to the enormous plague of unrestrained corruption, calling it "laxism[6] Beninism" (French: *laxism-beninisme*) or "Kérékisme" (French: *Kérékouism*). Kérékou liked to call it Marxism--Beninism. In the eyes of the West, Benin at that time had earned the label of "Africa's Cuba."

Thus, Kérékou's revolutionary regime, like the regimes of other socialist or communist countries, imposed on Dahomey society a one-party system, effectively eliminating any legal political activity outside his PRPB. Any other party, even those more radical than PRPB, such as the Communist Party of Benin (*Parti Communiste du Bénin*, PCB) founded in 1977 by the Union of Communists of Dahomey were considered illegal by the government. Paradoxically, in a country with a political, economic, and ideological system mirroring other Communist regimes, the PCB was excluded from any political influence and acted clandestine from its creation until its legalization in 1993. The party—more radical than PRPB, ideologically communist, anti-revisionist, Marxist–Leninist, and Hoxhalst[7]—would act rather as an ideological than political opposition against Kérékou's regime. Its members were aggressively critical of Kérékou's regime, referring to it as "military-Marxist deviationists" and were often prosecuted during his presidency. No wonder that he was described by Dahomeyan Communists as "an incorrigible, cynical, Machiavellian autocrat who sets, like the chameleon, the color of the moment and of the environment to quench its thirst for the absolute power and the advantages which are bound to it."[8] Throughout his time in power, Kérékou would be thereafter associated with the nickname "Chameleon."

In the first years of the revolutionary regime, Kérékou enacted radical changes in Benin's foreign policy. Relationships with France were severely and adversely affected by the nationalization of foreign—mainly French—banks and companies that had business in or with Benin. Revolutionary authorities renounced several bilateral treaties signed with France in 1961, among them an agreement on military cooperation. France, however, wanted to maintain influence in Benin, as it failed to do after Sékou Touré's social-ist revolution in Guinea. Paris, trying to accommodate Kérékou's regime, included Benin in a round of Franco–African negotiations regarding the revision of treaties that Paris had concluded with its former colonies in the early 1960s. The accords on military cooperation with Francophone African former colonies often included secret clauses regarding the possible political and intervention of France when an African party to such accord requested it. These clauses often served as a legal basis for French intervention in a par-ticular country upon an African leader's request. Typically, this secret clause would provide for direct Franco–African defense or military cooperation treaty assistance to the African party of the agreement. The French military may be called to intervene in a particularly serious situation if demanded by the interested head of state would be directed to the president of French Republic through an intermediary of ambassador.[9]

Such clauses were also often used by African leaders afraid of losing their grip on power or, in some cases, by an opposition that wanted to remove a current leader from power but was too weak to do so. In the early 1970s, upon demands of many of radical Francophone African countries, among them Benin, France agreed to renegotiate their old agreements with the aim of "normalizing" her relationship with former colonies that demanded a more balanced relationship with the Hexagon,[10] otherwise, due to the characteristic shape of her European part, known also as France.

In the case of Benin, despite Cotonou's critical attitude of France, fifteen newly revised agreements concerning political, economic, and military coop-eration were signed in Cotonou in February 1975. The new treaties provided fundamental changes in bilateral relations between Paris and Cotonou. Thus, the French ambassador to Benin would not be—as prior under Article 1 of the Treaty on Cooperation between the Republic of France and the Republic of Dahomey of 1961—automatically recognized as a dean of diplomatic corps in Cotonou. The parties also abandoned the principle of regular mutual consultations between both capitals in matters of foreign policy and, most importantly, revised a provision that under earlier military cooperation agree-ment allowed Paris to intervene militarily in Benin in the case of political or military instability.[11] When in 1978 France finally ratified these agreements, the country was still referred to as Dahomey even though it was formally changed to Benin three years earlier. Further, and rather notably, France aban-doned its secret clause, thereby depriving France of legal grounds for military intervention in Benin upon the more or less voluntary request of any current, or overthrown, president or head of state. Therefore, if France ever wanted to intervene in Benin against, for instance, Kérékou, France could only do so through the involvement of her other African allies or the clandestine use of mercenaries.

What Paris, however, considered unacceptable regarding its political and economic interests in Francophone Africa was Benin's close cooperation with Marxist-oriented African governments—such as Guinea or Tanzania—as well as with Communist countries, such as the Soviet Union, Albania, Cuba, North Korea, and China. Benin's relationship with Communist China developed not only in the political sphere but also in cooperation in domains of technology, economy, military, culture, and ideology.[12]

The first three years of revolutionary changes in Benin, from 1972 to 1975, are still called by some Beninese as the "Three Glorious Years." In the opinion of others, they deserve nothing but severe criticism. An interesting assessment of the revolutionary changes made under the leadership of President Mathieu Kérékou was given during an international scientific conference organized on the occasion of the fiftieth anniversary of the October 1972 coup d'état at the University of Abomey-Calavi in Benin.[13] Noting that the revolutionary decisions made a "profound effect" on the country's history, the introduction to the conference offers the following:

> The latter affected the social, societal, political and economic order. On the social and societal levels, the GMR advocated national unity, engaged in a struggle against a supposed feudalism of traditional authorities, witchcraft, vodun priests with the closure of many convents, set in motion a new curriculum called the "New School," etc. Economically and ideologically, the GMR set the country on the path to scientific socialism in the light of Marxism-Leninism. In this wake, the banks and production units were nationalized, and some sixty state-owned companies were created. It was a complete takeover of the country's economic apparatus by the state. Socialism banishing the exploitation of man by man, the GMR, through its actions and its discourse, was resolutely anti-imperialist and anti-colonialist. All of this initially had aroused popular support among many Beninese. On the other hand, however, very quickly, the people became disillusioned. The PRPB regime was transformed into a repressive, police power, which confiscated all democratic freedoms, and engaged in an unprecedented witch hunt. Serious infringements of freedoms were made. In the absence of public debate on political and economic questions, the revolutionary regime prospered in a solitary and calamitous management of state affairs. The mismanagement and plundering of the economy became a feature of this phase of national history. During this period, the plundering of the economy reached unprecedented proportions.[14]

Increasing radicalization of the Beninese political life on top of the strong personal rivalries between revolutionary military elites and dramatically failing economic conditions resulted in the absence of any organized local civilian opposition, in three thwarted military coups d'état attempts against

Mathieu Kérékou that proceeded Opération Crevette. Two coups d'état were attempted, according to Benin's government, in January and October of 1975.

In the first case, Captain Janvier Assogba attempted to use the armed division stationed in Ouidah to stage the removal of President Kérékou from power on the grounds that Kérékou was implicated in the corrupt practices associated with the *Kovacs affair*.[15] The attempt described as "a murky ill-prepared assault" failed.[16]

On January 17, 1975, a handwritten document signed by Captain Janvier Assogba, the co-organizer of 1972 putsch and later Kérékou's minister of finance who became disappointed with Marxist policies of President Kérékou, was put into circulation. It brought together various letters addressed to Mathieu Kérékou by Louis Kovacs; a Hungarian businessman accused of bribing the president to obtain economic privileges in Benin. As minister of finance, Captain Assogba was made aware of the existence of this case of bribery. Using evidence available to him, Captain Assogba tried to influence the president to change the radical course of Marxist-oriented changes. But to no avail. Then he publicly blamed the head of state for corruption.[17]

Subsequently, on the night of January 21, 1975, a plan was hatched for fraction of the Dahomeyan Armed Forces (*Forces Armées Dahoméennes*, FAD) and heavily armed group commanded by Captain Janvier Assogba, to move in the direction of Cotonou to overthrow the regime and its leader, Mathieu Kérékou. The plan of a coup, however, was revealed to the authorities, most likely by Major Alladaye. Seventy officers from military garrisons in Cotonou, Ouidah, and Porto-Novo had been summoned to appear on January 21 at 5:00 p.m. for a meeting at Camp Guézo on initiative of Captain Assogba. When the officers appeared at the appointed hour, they were arrested, punished by sixty days of fortress arrests, and then relieved of their duties—with one exception: Captain Assogba, who failed to show up, instead moved the same afternoon with the Supporting Subgroup Units of armed vehicles based in Ouidah on Cotonou.[18] Dissuaded by one of his companion officers, he halted the operation and returned to camp in Ouidah where, the next day, he was arrested and sentenced to a ten-year prison term for "plot against the revolution."[19]

Then minister of information Martin Dohou Azonhiho asserted that the putsch attempt was neither because of the *Kovacs affair* nor the bad reputation of President Kérékou, "but it is because of our program of new politics of national independence and our socialist orientation."[20] Such an opinion was confirmed years later by none other but Assogba when, in interview with French media, he confirmed that it "was clear that I rebel against this way of arguing of our intellectuals" who were influenced by French Communist Party.[21]

It seems that based upon information about such dissent within the Beninese army officer's corps and the willingness of some army units to change the regime by force, the exiled politician gathered in the Front for Liberation and Rehabilitation of Dahomey (*Front de Liberation et de Rehabilitation du Dahomey*, FLERD) and their backers in French intelligence circles came to the conclusion and later passed it to Bob Denard that his operation will easily find the support of army personnel disillusioned with Kérékou's Marxist orientation, who would join mercenary assault on governmental buildings and institutions.

The authorities accused a number of military officers and civilians charged with support of the foiled coup with the intent to bring to power Dr. Zinsou, who was living in self-exile in Paris.

In March 1975, Zinsou and six others of his alleged co-conspirators, including his brother, René Zinsou, also a physician, received *in absentia* death sentences for their alleged support of the Assogba failed coup d'état. This would be the first, but not last, death sentence meted against Zinsou by the Beninese courts.

The second foiled attempt to remove Mathieu Kérékou and his associates from power took place in October of the same year, 1975, when authorities announced suppression a "gigantic plot" accusing, again, "Zinsounistes" as its instigators, among them many high-level actual and former state functionaries. The Cotonou government reported that it had foiled an attempted coup by former president Zinsou and "foreign mercenaries supported by 'financial powers.'"[22]

The plot, informed minister of information Martin Azonhiho, was "organized by the traitor Émile Zinsou, included plans to murder members of the National Council of the Revolution and the Military Government headed by Lieutenant Colonel Mathieu Kerekou." Azonhiho specified also that according to Benin authorities the "plotters," backed by "international imperialism," had sought to make use of Dahomeyan "reactionaries" to overthrow the Government in a coordinated plan of sabotage and murder.[23]

The government accused Zinsou again of instigating the attempted coup with the support of a host of foreign mercenaries and Togolese minister of foreign affairs Joachim Hunlede, who had served as ambassador to France at the same time as Zinsou.[24] Hunlede was accused of trying to overpower the revolution of the Beninese people by exterminating its leaders using weapons fitted with silencers. Dr. Zinsou denied his involvement and questioned whether any such coup attempt happened at all.[25] Hunlede, on his part, in a televised interview, rejected Beninese charges as lacking any evidence and ridiculed that Togo was too busy with its own development to be bothered with plotting against its neighbors.

Subsequently, the eleven "Zinzounists" were charged for their presumed participation in conspiracy against Kérékou. In February 1976, they received sentences from death to twenty-year imprisonment meted by the Revolutionary Tribunal.[26]

On his part, Zinsou commented a month later at a public press conference on the recent events in his home country. These included comments on the death of one of Kérékou's associates who had been accused of having an affair with president's wife, making references to Beninese authorities as a "Dahomeyan military regime composed of assassins, criminals, and thieves," and he expressed opinion that "no Dahomeyan would have to imagine, that there are still a few years, that this country can undergo what it undergoes now." He further did not hide his political agenda when he declared: "I am a resolute opponent, and, if there is only one left, I shall be that one. I am, and I remain a politician. I have big ambitions: it is, whatever office it is, to participate in the developing of my country."[27] However, since it was common knowledge that Beninese authorities, under international pressure, had not executed anyone sentenced for political offenses, a death penalty for the alleged patronage of the October 1975 plot had not discouraged Dr. Zinsou from plotting against Kérékou once again. Zinsou, who described himself, then, as a "humanist socialist," as opposed to Marxist radicals represented by Kérékou's associates and advisers, considered himself the best alternative to Marxist regime in Cotonou, and he intended to prove it, with help from Bob Denard and company.

NOTES

1. The "Africanization" has been applied in various contexts. According to *A Dictionary of African Politics*, "Africanization" is the process of Africanizing government and society following independence, at which point colonial officials, norms, and values continued to exert considerable influence. This involved a range of different strategies in different countries, such as replacing European officials with African ones, nationalizing foreign-owned companies, promoting African languages, and changing the names of roads, cities, and in many cases the country itself. Africanization was often explicitly invoked as a policy goal by postcolonial leaders in order to demonstrate that they were bringing about social and political transformation. *A Dictionary of African Politics* (online), Nic Cheeseman, Eloïse Bertra, and Sa'eed Husaini, (Oxford: Oxford University Press, 2019), https://www.oxfordreference.com/display/10.1093/acref/9780191828836.001.0001/acref-9780191828836-e-103?rskey=RVyAsz&result=1.

2. "Notre nouvelle société sera une société socialiste: Discours d'orientation nationale du 30 novembre 1974," in Marius Loko, *la politique étrangère du Benin: D'hier à aujourd'hui* (Paris: L'Harmattan, 2022): 234–38.

3. *Daho-Express*, December 1, 1974.

4. The colony was at first called Benin (from the Bight of Benin), not the preco-lonial Kingdom of Benin, which is in Nigeria), but in 1894 it was renamed French Dahomey. In 1958, French Dahomey became the self-governing colony called the Republic of Dahomey. It was renamed, in 1975, the People's Republic of Benin and, in 1991, the Republic of Benin.

5. "Le régime révolutionnaire de Mathieu Kérékou," *Encyclopaedia Universalis* (online), https://www.universalis.fr/encyclopedie/benin/3-le-regime-revolutionnaire -de-mathieu-kerekou/.

6. Defined as the lack of strictness; synonyms include indifference, indulgence, and negligence.

7. The ideology is named after Enver Hoxha, an Albanian Communist leader. Hoxhaism was developed in the late 1970s due to an ideological dispute between the Communist Party of China and the Party of Labor of Albania in 1978. It is a variant of Marxism–Leninism. See *Communism for Know-It-Alls* (Minneapolis, MN: Filiquar-ian Publishing, 2008).

8. Sébastien Coutu, "Chronique de la vie d'un autocrate, Kerekou," accessed November 23, 2021, Https://Docplayer.Fr/72524996-Chronique-De-La-Vie-D-Un-Autocrate-Kerekou.Html.

9. Michel Debré and Jean Foyer, "Projet de Loi," Reunion de plein droit du Par-lement en application de l'Article 16 de la Constitution, mai 1961, https://www.senat .fr/leg/1960-1961/i1960_1961_0226.pdf. (See, for example, "Accord de défense entre les Gouvernements de la République française, de la République de Côte-d'Ivoire, de la République du Dahomey et de la République du Niger," 24 avril 1961).

10. The Hexagon (l'Hexagone) is an epithet of Metropolitan France, owing to the shape of its European mainland.

11. Michel Houndjahoué, "Notes sur les relations internationales du Bénin sociali-ste: 1972–1986," *Études internationales* 18, no. 2 (1987): 371.

12. Diplomatic relations with the People's Republic of China are good example of France's influence on Dahomey/Benin foreign policy. Established in 1964, under pressure from Paris, Benin, during short presidency of Émile D. Zinsou, recognized Taiwan and in 1967 withdrew diplomatic relations with PRC only to re-establish them two months after the 1972 coup d'état when it adhered to the "One China Policy" promoted by Bejing. Kérékou's paid a state visit to PRC in 1976.

13. Colloque Scientifique, Cinquantenaire de la Révolution du 26 octobre 1972, 26 au 28 octobre 2022, Campus d'Abomey-Calavi, Bénin, http://www.prointer.ufpa .br/images/CasaBrasilAfrica/Appel_communication_cinquantenaire_Revolution.pdf.

14. Ibid.

15. Houngnikpo and Decalo, *Historical Dictionary of Benin*, 128–29.

16. Ibid., 128.

17. A more detailed description of Captain Assobge's attempt to use Kovacs affaire to compromise Mathieu Kérékou can be found in K. Honoré Banidje and Çağatay Benhür, "The Instrumentalisation of the History: The Benin's Aggression on 16th January 1977 and the Memory of the Victims," *The Pursuit of History International Periodical for History and Social Research* 19 (2018): 134.

18. *Daho-Express*, no. 1588, January 24, 1975, 6.

19. P. J. Franceschini, "Le régime militaire a célébré son troisième anniversaire dans un climat politique tendu," *Le Monde*, October 29, 1975.

20. *Daho-Express*, no. 1588, January 24, 1975, 6.

21. A. da Silva, "Bénin / Coup d'etat du 26 octobre 1972: Le Témoignage du Colonel Janvier Assogba," *Journal Adjinakou Benin* (blog), June 18, 2017, https://www.journal-adjinakou-benin.net/benin-coup-detat-du-26-octobre-1972-le-temoignage-du-colonel-janvier-assogba/.

22. "Smashing of a Plot Reported by Dahomey," *New York Times*, October 20, 1975, 10.

23. Ibid.

24. "Découverte d'un Vaste Complot Ourdi Par Le Dr Zinsou," Le Monde, October 21, 1975.

25. "African Land, No Stranger to Coups, Repulses an Attack by 'Mercenaries,'" *New York Times*, January 17, 1977, 1.

26. "Onze personnes sont condamnées à mort pour avoir participé au complot d'octobre 1975," *Le Monde*, February 5, 1976, https://www.lemonde.fr/archives/article/1976/02/05/onze-personnes-sont-condamnees-a-mort-pour-avoir-participe-au-complot-d-octobre-1975_2960450_1819218.html.

27. "L'ancien Président Zinsou dénonce la repression," *Le Monde*, November 6, 1975.

Chapter 5

The French Connection

HATCHING THE COUP

The Opération Crevette regime change strategy was either the brainchild of, or at least discreetly supported by, the French intelligence service (SDECE; since 1982, *Direction générale de la sécurité extérieure*, DGSE), working together with two ambitious Beninese émigrés: Dr. Émile Zinsou and former Beninese ambassador Gratien Lazar Pognon. These two co-conspirators, upon French insistence, were supported by the heads of state of France's former African colonies, including Gabon, Morocco, Togo, and, possibly, the Ivory Coast. Interviewed years later about France's involvement in Opération Crevette, the long-term director of the African division of the SDECE, Jacques Foccart, maintained that he "didn't know anything about the project" and was "surprised" to learn about Denard's commando."[1] However, according to Foccart, the other high-level member of French president's African Celle, Réne Journiac, "was informed" and also named other French officials, like Maurice Robert and ambassador to Gabon Maurice Delauney (1965–1972, 1975–1979) who maintained close relationship with Bob Denard and played some role at different stages of preparation for Opération Crevette.[2]

An experienced diplomat, Gratien Pognon would be one of France's many links to Opération Crevette. Throughout his political career, Pognon served as Benin's ambassador in various European capitals and the United States, as well as a deputy secretary general of the Organization of African Unity (OAU)[3] in the early 1960s. Pognon was later on the advisor of foreign affairs to President Kérékou. In 1975, however, he refused to continue working for Kérékou's military government and, instead, settled down in France where he joined the Front for Liberation and Rehabilitation of Dahomey (*Front de Libération et de Réhabilitation du Dahomey*, FLERD). Zinsou had created this front three years earlier (1974) with the support of the Beninese exile

43

communities in France, Gabon, the Ivory Coast, Senegal, and Togo. As an opposition movement, FLERD claimed to have secret supporters within Benin[4] and later admitted that it was behind the organization of Opération Crevette.[5]

Benin's authorities alleged that Ambassador Pognon had been recruited through his wife into the French intelligence agency SDECE while in France, further stating that both Pognon's resignation from his ambassadorial post in Brussels and his active engagement in anti-Kérékou opposition was instigated by the SDECE.[6] Other sources reported, however, that his resignation was preemptive and occurred upon learning that he had been slated for recall along with various other ambassadors connected to the Dahomeyan *ancien régime*; they would be replaced with new "revolutionary" diplomats.

Gratien Pognon would soon find himself working with Robert Denard. While operating in the Congo, Bob Denard caught the eyes of two French intelligence service men who had particular interests in Africa: Maurice Robert, then director of the SDECE, and Jean Mauricheau-Beaupré, intelligence advisor to various African heads of state. Although he would only personally meet Denard in 1963, the former became his handler on behalf of the French intelligence service in 1961. It was Maurice Robert who, according to his personal account, offered the SDECE a promising soldier of fortune; Denard was to inform the SDECE about anything happening in the Congo and other wars within the international theaters in which Denard would play his part. In exchange, Maurice Robert promised Denard that the SDECE would provide him with the most effective protection to cover his mercenary activities.[7]

In early 1968, on the recommendation of Maurice Robert, Denard met with Jacques Foccart to offer his services to the *Cellule Africaine*. Denard's close relations with the SDECE remained the subject of speculation and denial until a 1999 interview with French magazine *Le Figaro*. During his interview, Denard finally answered the question, "Are you a soldier of fortune or an agent of secret services?" Denard replied, "I was never an agent of a secret services but I often and for a long time worked with them." In a surprising reveal, Denard continued, stating, "you are the first to whom I am revealing that I had four handlers: Colonel Robert, General Jeannou Lacaze and two others . . . whom I will not name."[8] As one observer later noticed, "The world of the mercenary has finally offered Denard the dreams of career which Navy and French police had refused him."[9]

Denard's activity in Benin would be just one of the many, often anti-Communist conflicts he would engage in on behalf of himself and France, who he quietly backed as it attempted to maintain influence across *Françafrique*, France's realm of her former African colonies.

According to Denard, in case of Opération Crevette, his contacts in the SDECE initiated the offering of his services to Dr. Zinsou, as France was interested in stripping Kérékou from power.[10] When the two met in Paris, Émile Zinsou proposed that Denard conduct an operation doing just that. Denard recounted that Zinsou justified the need of a coup by referring to the death sentences meted on individuals involved in the 1975 failed coup attempt. Zinsou claimed, "this tyrant Kérékou intends to liquidate eleven of my supporters. You need to help me to overthrow this Marxist regime."[11] It was Pognon who apparently acted as an intermediary between Zinsou and Bob Denard, promising Denard, on top of his contract pay and covering of all coup-related expenses, a one-million-dollar award upon the success of the operation.[12]

Denard was recommended to Émile Zinsou through the "Moroccan agent." Representing "a friendly head of state" whom he identifies as King Hassan II and whom he allegedly personally met twice to discuss the plan of a coup d'état's details.[13] Denard presented himself "as the man for the situation." "His assurance as to success—recalls Zinsou—had impressed me."[14] Denard "already knew what to do and where the training of men would take place." "I told him—continues Zinsou—of my position: to liberate my country without loss of human life, on either side." He described the intent of his conspirators as "liberation" from Marxist government acting on appeals for conducting a coup d'état coming from inside Benin.[15] "All the signals (French: *echos*) coming from the inside begged those from the outside to make every effort to free the country."[16] In Zinsou's opinion, "to achieve this . . . intervention must be done in such a way that the Dahomean troops, some of whose high officials were in on the secret, having promised to help, would only have one desire: to lay down their arms."[17]

Zinsou would staunchly deny any involvement in Opération Crevette for over thirty-six years, even claiming that the "fable of the Zinsouist coup" was a "diversion" invented by the Beninese authorities to turn public attention away from the country's deep economic crisis. Years later, after he returned to Benin from emigration and the revelation of many details regarding Opération Crevette to the public, Zinsou formally repeated his denial of association during a news conference at the Sheraton Hotel in Cotonou. Only in his memoires, published in France in 2012, did Zinsou finally admit to his involvement, stating, "In the preparation of our action, I was not only informed, but also involved. We were a group of Dahomeyan fellow countrymen to prepare an action of a liberation of our country of the government which reigned in the name of the Marxism there—hardly read and not digested Leninism—an unbearable power."[18] His admission also confirmed that Pognon acted as a leader during, euphemistically called by him, the "events of January 16, 1977."[19]

After the failed coup attempt in October 1975, FLERD leadership realized that due to the climate of suspicion and police surveillance in Benin,[20] a coup d'état launched from inside the country "would be extremely dangerous, because of the possibility of information leaks and lack of enthusiasm on the part of opponents of the regime inside the country to be first to become involved."[21] Thus, in view of the opposition, the only way to conduct the coup appeared to be by use of foreign mercenaries, or "intervention from outside."

What would soon become Opération Crevette was more precisely defined as a plan of action "[to] eliminate the present regime and install the new team from the Front for the Liberation and Rehabilitation of Dahomey"; If this was not done "Benin, like Equatorial Guinea, Sao Tome and Principe, will soon be another stronghold on the Algiers–Conakry–Brazzaville–Luanda axis, to mention just a few examples in this large area making up West Africa."[22] This is in reference to those African countries that in 1970s were govern by most dictatorial leftist or Marxism-oriented regimes that were considered by France as a threat to her influence and interests in her former colonies. Additionally, there was a psychological aim to the operation that was certainly in the cards for SDECE: "An action in Benin aimed at putting an end to the slide of the current regime towards the East would . . . have a psychological effect, perhaps direct on some African heads of State inclined to compose very far with the Marxists whatever their reasons: prudence or ideological conviction. A victorious action would give the Marxists themselves the notion of a limit to their thirst for expansion."[23]

Looking for a solution, Zinsou admitted, omitting names, "we got in touch with some of our friends—the heads of state—soliciting their advice and their help."[24] Who might those friends with expertise on how to execute a coup d'état have been? Who had good reason to get rid of the Marxist regime in Cotonou without direct involvement? The answer to their problems: France.

France had good reasons stemming from economic as well as foreign policy interests for regime change in Cotonou. Paris hoped that the new Beninese authorities would reverse the Beninese nationalization of French-owned businesses and allow for unrestricted French investments in the country. In regard to her foreign policy, Paris was critical of Benin's support of the Comoros Islands who demanded the return of the island Mayotte from French administration to remain part of independent Comoros. Just a year before Opération Crevette, in February 1976, Benin, as a rotating, non-permanent member of the United Nations (UN) Security Council, joined the group of states calling for the opening of negotiations between France and Comoros. These negotiations would consider revising the status of Mayotte, which were both claimed by the Comoros as part of its geographical and historical territory but considered by France as its own overseas department.

UNHOLY ALLIANCE: BANALIA, MOANA, ZANGARO

The plot to remove Kérékou from power also seemed to be in the interest of some African governments, primarily former French colonies still closely connected with France by a web of political, economic, and military ties; these former colonies were parts of *Françafrique*.

As with all clandestine mercenary operations, the organizers of Opération Crevette assigned one another code names. Each of the African countries directly involved in supporting this operation has its respective name. Benin received the code name "Banalia," Gabon was called "Moana," and Togo was named "Zangaro." No code name was assigned to Morocco, although, according to the United Nations documentation published as a result of the international investigation conducted after the operation, the country also played an important role in the execution of Opération Crevette.

Although Bob Denard claimed that he knew Moroccan King Hassan II from a prior assignment, later cancelled, from 1970 to remove Colonel Mouammar Kadhafi, the Libyan head of state,[25] and even met Hassan II twice in person in preparation for Opération Crevette, it is doubtful whether Moroccan monarch would get involved in such risky mercenary operation without French insistence on his assistance. The same seems with Gabon's involvement in Opération Crevette. Since Denard served in President Omar Bongo's Presidential Guard,[26] he had to maintain some personal contacts with the president. However, only a behind-the-scenes push by SDECE leadership and French ambassador to Gabon could lead to Bongo's decision to allow Denard to use the territory of Gabon for purposes of Opération Crevette.

Gabon's president and Morocco's king seemingly readily complied with the French request for assistance in removing "Great Comrade" Kérékou, not only due to their close long-term relationship with Paris but also in their own interest to contain the spread of Marxist ideology on the African continent. In a similar situation was Togo's president, whose country was in conflict regarding the border with Benin and, as an immediate neighbor, was seriously "annoyed by the adoption of over-radical position" represented by Benin's regime.[27]

It seems that the planners of Opération Crevette at the preparatory stage of the operation had consulted, among others, two African presidents. The first was President General Gnassingbé Eyadéma of Togo (born Étienne Eyadéma), a veteran of two military coups in his country that successfully removed two presidents from office; these included a coup in 1963—the first coup d'état in the history of post-independence Africa—which resulted in Togolese president Sylvanus Olympo being killed, and a second coup in 1967 that resulted in the exiling of then-president Nicolas Grunitzky and

Eyadéma's assumption of the role of the presidential role for next thirty-eight years. President Eyadéma's motivation for giving a hand to Kérékou's opponents was, in the opinion of the deeply embedded chief African policy advisor to France as well as co-founder of unit specialized in covert African operations, Jacques Foccart, that Eyadéma "considered himself the most directly threatened, because of the permeability of the Togolese-Benin border."[28] The other "consultant" to Dr. Zinsou was then–Gabonese president El Hadj Omar Bongo Ondimba, the closest ally of France in black Africa. Both Presidents, Eyadéma and Bongo, were eventually named by an international inquiry mission as the foreign supporters of *Opération Crevette.* Further, Zinsou's later admission of his arrival in Rabat, Morocco, on January 15, 1977, "a day before"[29] the attack in Cotonou indicated that oppositionists were also in intimate contact with Moroccan allies.

Faced with another controversial issue on the African continent, Cotonou supported the move for independence by Western Sahara, which Morocco, Paris's close ally in Northern Africa, claimed to be part of its territory. Benin, however, recognized the region's Sahrawi Arab Democratic Republic as an independent country on the territory of the former colony Spanish Sahara, as well as actively supported POLISARIO (*Frente Popular de Liberación de Saguía el Hamra y Río de Oro*), the liberation organization of Western

Figure 5.1. Heads of States during the OAU Conference in Nairobi, 1972: from left, President David Dacko of Central African Republic, Omar Bongo President of Gabon, Lt Co. Mathieu Kérékou President of Benin, President Hassan Gouled of Djibouti, Sir Dawda Kairaba Jawara President of Gambia, General Gaafar Mohamed Nimeiri President of Sudan. Credit: ZUMA Press, Inc. / Alamy Stock Photo.

Sahara. Because of this, a regime change in Benin also seemed to be in the interest of Morocco. As such, Kérékou's positions in international affairs only strengthened the Paris and Rabat alliance aimed at removing him from power. Later, the motivations of Morocco's King Hassan II were suggested to be more strategic. Jacques Foccart stated, "The king wanted to manifest himself like the ally on heads of State African who considered themselves threatened by a Soviet penetration."[30]

To those who were responsible for planning and executing France's policy toward her former African colonies, the plan of Opération Crevette was known from the start. Among them was René Journiac, French president Valéry Giscard d'Estaing's (in office May 1974 to May 1981) advisor, a role that positioned him within the African Cell. A secretive and powerful organization, the African Cell consisted of French presidential advisors who "overs[aw] France's strategic interests in Africa, holding sway over a wide swath of former French colonies."[31] These advisors included Maurice Delaney, then-ambassador to Gabon (1965–1972 and 1975–1979), and former SDECE head Maurice Robert. Among others, these members of the African Cell were tasked with planning and coordinating regime changes across Francophone Africa. Although Journiac always maintained that he had nothing to do with Opération Crevette, his mentor and predecessor in the African Cell, French presidential advisor Jacques Foccart, claimed that it was specifically Journiac's idea "to replace" Kérékou with "someone closer to French point of view."[32] However, Maurice Robert would later present Journiac's role in the operation as a passive supporter who only learned about the plan of the operation from the former director of intelligence service SDECE; Director General Jeannou Lacaze at time of Opération Crevette was the commander of Eleventh Parachute Division (1976–1979) (commonly the "onzième choc" and known as the elite parachute regiment of the French army serving as the armed branch of the SDECE).

As for General Lacaze's involvement in Opération Crevette, "[Lacaze] had received Bob [Denard] after the refusal of his case officer . . . to give him a green light. Lacaze was favorable to an orange [yellow] light, the one we have already spoken about, which is reflected in an absence of opposition but also of formal acquiescence, which means: 'I do not want to know anything, I am not aware. I do not forbid you to do so, but if you do, it is under your responsibility. Journiac told me that he had agreed to this position.'"[33] Although Journiac confirmed that he was aware of the planned operation, he categorically denied his support because it was badly conceived and executed.[34] Maurice Robert, however, claimed in an interview for French TV broadcasted in 1994 that it was Rene Journiac who had organized the operation at the request of five rulers: President Omar Bongo of Gabon, President Gnassingbé Eyadéma of Togo, President Houphouet Boigny of the

Ivory Coast, and President Léopold Sédar Senghor of Senegal, with financial and logistic assistance King Hassan II of Morocco.[35] Jacques Foccart was even more specific in his recollections, stating, "The king of Morocco played a more important role than Journiac."[36]

In 1976, President Kérékou publicly accused the Gabonese government of harboring Beninese exiles who had attempted a number of failed coups d'état against him with the purported support of both the Gabonese and French authorities. The special relationship between France and Gabon was best illustrated by President Bongo of Gabon's famous declaration, referring to France's dependence on his country's oil: "Gabon without France, it's a car with no driver. France without Gabon, it's a car with no gas." Further, as of the mid 1970s, Bob Denard was officially working as a security advisor to Gabon's president, Bongo, therefore having direct and confidential access to him. Denard also personally knew Bongo's French military, intelligence, and business entourage, who formed the so-called Gabonese Clan.

In the case of Togo, the organizers of Opération Crevette undoubtedly counted on President Gnassingbé Eyadéma's readiness to support the coup in Benin due to animosity resulting from disputes between those two countries. Specifically, Togo accused Benin of intent to invade its territory and Benin accused Togo of support for anti-Kérékou activists. President Eyadéma considered himself also directly threatened with Marxist influence because of the porous Togolese–Benin border.[37] As mentioned above, in March of 1976, when the Beninese court sentenced eleven participants of the October 1975 "Zinsounist" coup attempt against Kérékou, it criticized the government of Togo for fomenting Beninese opposition and "open interference by Togolese government in internal affairs of Benin." Togo naturally denied any such involvement, and in a gesture of good will, expelled from its territory twenty-five Beninese citizens suspected of anti-Kérékou activities. In an attempt to improve their bilateral relations, presidents Eyadéma and Kérékou, acting upon an invitation of Guinean president Sékou Touré, met in 1976 in Togo's capital, Lomé, where they decided to open the joint border between their countries and to "formally and definitively" ban any subversive activities directed from a territory of one of them against the territory of other.

Later-discovered plans of Opération Crevette showed, however, that there was likely another group of GEI (*Group Etrangère d'Intervention*)[38] mercenaries in Togo, separate from those organized by Denard for the operation. As of October 15, 1976, this group was improving the combat-readiness of Togolese soldiers in order to dispatch a battalion of Togolese infantry, accompanied by the mercenary commandos who trained them, in support of the final phase of Opération Crevette in Benin. They were purportedly to enter Benin in order to repel any alleged Beninese aggression against Togo;

their true mission, however, would be to quash any civilian opposition to the removal of Kérékou.[39]

The other two Western-oriented African countries, and the closest allies of Paris within *Françafrique*, were the Ivory Coast and Senegal. Although not actively cooperating in Opération Crevette, the leaders must have been aware that France would appreciate their assistance in the operation against Kérékou. Contrary to these beliefs, however, according to Jacques Foccart, Leopold Senghor, the president of Senegal, was not involved.

Denard claimed that only one person gathered the intelligence needed for executing Opération Crevette: his comrade from earlier mercenary adventures, Gerard.[40] Traveling to Benin under the guide of a tourist, he was tasked with collecting vital intelligence on the political and economic situation of the country. However, given that the operation was instigated by the French SDECE, Denard must have had its full intelligence support, especially as to details regarding military, paramilitary, and police forces, their size, weaponry, and location. Although France staunchly denied involvement in Opération Crevette, the Beninese authorities accused French intelligence and the newly accredited French ambassador in Cotonou, Jean Meadmore, of "active support of subversive activities directed against Benin."[41]

What happened next depends which interpretation of facts one chooses to believe. Benin claims that it recognized Ambassador Meadmore as a *persona non-grata* and requested her departure. On its part, Paris claimed that it recalled ambassador Meadmore from Cotonou "for consultations" due to the "vexatious decisions" taken by Beninese authorities against him. Those "vexatious decisions" were described by the French Ministry of Foreign Affairs, Quai d'Orsay, as the failure to invite French ambassador to the ceremony of presentation of the New Year's wishes to the head of state, Mathieu Kérékou.[42] Such polite, diplomatic references were simply used to describe the former colony's decision to expel its colonial power's diplomat suspected of meddling in internal affairs of the former. Regardless of interpretation, there was no action on either side to suspend or break bilateral diplomatic relations. The French *charge d'affaires* represented Paris until December 1978 when a new French ambassador experience in African countries, Pierre Decamps, was accredited.[43]

Years later, the facts about France's direct involvement in Opération Crevette were confirmed by French officials who either had been personally involved or had knowledge of such involvement due to their then positions within French government. "Sometimes France closes its eyes but supports an operation when it serves its interests,"[44] Maurice Robert, former head of the SDECE, later acknowledged.

In fact, Denard prepared the plan of Opération Crevette relying on "the various studies" and encouragement by opposition leaders who indicated that the necessary and adequate prerequisites for the defeat of the Kérékou's regime were present. "In summary of the various studies made, the opposition officials concluded that almost all the necessary and sufficient conditions are now met to bring down the current regime with the *maximum chance of success; the means at their disposal have been the subject of a complete analysis,* only a small 'push' would be necessary to forge the instrument of victory."[45] This "push" was supposed to be executed by Denard's Omega Force commando. According to reports received by Denard, this should have been an easy task. "[T]he loyalty of the armed forces as a whole is uncertain and . . . First Company and . . . First Squadron are ready for an uprising"; "the elements a priori faithful to the present regime do not seem very strong, either in men or in equipment."[46]

It remains unclear why, as it would later turn out, Denard had received incomplete, inaccurate, and even misleading information about Benin's sociopolitical situation and defense capabilities if he was acting in cooperation with French intelligence agencies. At the time of Opération Crevette, there was a French embassy in Cotonou with a French military attaché. French intelligence agencies at home had access to information collected directly in Benin, as well as gathered by the special services of Benin's neighbors, such as Togo, who cooperated closely with Paris. Why Denard allegedly sent his underling for the collection of crucial intelligence for operation planning instead of obtaining such information directly from the SDECE, we will never know.

NOTES

1. Jacques Foccart, *Foccart Parle, Entretiens avec Philippe Gaillard,* vol. 2 (Paris: Fayard/Jeune Afrique, 1997), 260.

2. Ibid., 260–64.

3. Since May 26, 2001, it is known as the African Union.

4. Émile Derlin Zinsou, *En ces temps là . . .* (Paris: Riveneuve, 2013), 233. Zinsou admitted in his autobiography that he not only knew about but was also "implicated" in Opération Crevette.

5. Mathurin C. Houngnikpo and Samuel Decalo, *Historical Dictionary of Benin,* third edition (Lanham, MD: Scarecrow Press, 2012), see 176, 249, and 284.

6. Benin, "Letter Dated 77/04/04 from the Charge d'Affaires a.i. of Benin to the United Nations Addressed to the President of the Security Council: Addendum" (New York: United Nations, April 5, 1977), see 56.

7. *Maurice Robert, Maurice Robert, "ministre de l'Afrique,"* essais H. C. édition (Paris: Seuil, 2004), 222–34.

8. Jean Francois Mongbibeaux and Bernard Sidler, "Bob Denard nous dit tout," *Le Figaro Magasin,* April 1999, see 44.

9. Martin Barnay, "Mémoire présenté à la Faculté des arts et sciences en vue de l'obtention du grade de maître ès arts en histoire" (MA thesis, Université de Montréal, 2014), https://papyrus.bib.umontreal.ca/xmlui/bitstream/handle/1866/12478/Barnay _Martin_2014_memoire.pdf.

10. Bob Denard and Georges Fleury, *Corsaire de la République* (Paris: Robert Laffont, 1998), 288.

11. Ibid., 287–88.

12. "Bob Denard et les 'services' au banc des accusés," *L'Humanité*, March 12, 1993, https://www.humanite.fr/bob-denard-et-les-services-au-banc-des-accuses -51832.

13. Denard and Fleury, *Corsaire de la République*, 287 and 289.

14. Zinsou, *En ces temps là . . .* , 233–34.

15. Ibid., 233.

16. Ibid.

17. Ibid., 234. Original quote: "Pour y parvenir, disais-je, il faut que intervention déploie des moyens tels que les troupes dahoméennes dont certains hauts cadres étaient dans le secret, avaient promis leur concours, n'auraient qu'une envie: déposer les armes."

18. Ibid., 233.

19. Ibid.

20. Ibid.

21. Benin, "Letter Dated 77/04/04," 27.

22. Ibid., 5.

23. Ibid.

24. Émile Zinsou, *En ces temps là . . .* , 233.

25. Denard and Fleury, *Corsaire de la République*, 264–65.

26. Ibid., 258–63.

27. UN, Special Mission of the Security Council Established under Resolution 404 (1977), "Report of the Security Council Special Mission to the People's Republic of Benin Established under Resolution 404 (1977): Addendum" (New York: United Nations, March 8, 1977), 8.

28. Foccart, *Foccart parle, entretiens avec Philippe Gaillard*, 26.

29. Ibid.

30. Ibid., 260–61.

31. David Gauthier-Villars, "Colonial-Era Ties to Africa Face a Reckoning in France," *Wall Street Journal*, May 17, 2007, sec. A, 1.

32. *Foccart, Foccart parle, entretiens avec Philippe Gaillard*, see 231. Original quote: "le remplacer par quelqu'un de plus proche des vues françaises."

33. Robert, *Maurice Robert, ministre de l'Afrique*, 238. Original quote: "Je ne veux rien savoir, je ne suis pas courant. Je ne vous interdis pas de le faire mais, si vous le faites, c'est sous votre responsabilité."

34. Kaye Whiteman, "The Man Who Ran Françafrique," *National Interest*, no. 49 (1997): 97.

35. See *Foccart, Foccart parle, entretiens avec Philippe Gaillard*.

36. Ibid., 260.

37. Ibid., 260–61.

38. Foreign Intervention Group (*Group Etrangére d'Intervention*, GEI).

39. Report of the Security Council Special Mission to the People's Republic of Benin Estabilshed under Resolution 404 (1977)," S/12294/Add. 1, Annex VI, 29–30; "Benin: L'affaire du 16 janvier Selon l'ONU," *Jeune Afrique*, no. 850, April 22, 1977, 28.

40. The name Gerard is likely a pseudonym for one of Denard's associates, to which no surname is associated.

41. *Le Monde*, January 10, 1978.

42. *Le Monde*, January 5, 1978.

43. *Le Monde*, October 23, 1978; *Le Monde*, December 18, 1978.

44. "Au tribunal correctionnel de Paris Bob Denard, mercenaire ou corsaire?" *Le Monde*, March 12, 1993.

45. Benin, "Letter Dated 77/04/04," 25; UN, Special Mission of the Security Council Established under Resolution 404 (1977), "Report of the Security Council Special Mission to the People's Republic of Benin Estabilshed under Resolution 404 (1977)," see Annex IV, 133.

46. UN, Secretary-General and Gabon, President, "Letter Dated 77/04/04 from the Secretary-General Addressed to the President of the Security Council" (New York: United Nations, April 4, 1977), see Annex VI, 15.

Chapter 6

The Doctor's Orders

A CHANGE OF REGIME

The aim of Opération Crevette was "to neutralize the present authorities" and, more specifically, to "size or destroy" Mathieu Kérékou and his close political entourage.[1] This entourage included Colonel Martin D. Azonhiho, described in the operation's plans as "the real leader, the eminence grise"[2] of Mathieu Kérékou's administration. Azonhiho was the prime ideologue of Kérékou's regime who served as minister of interior, the head of gendarmerie, and minister of information since 1974.[3] "It is true"—wrote *Le Monde* correspondent on the occasion of the third anniversary of Mathieu Kérékou's ascent to power—"that Gendarmerie Lieutenant Martin Dohou Azonihiho [*sic*!] is considered one of the main guarantors of the 'Marxist–Leninist' orientation of the regime established by a coup d'état three years ago, on October 26, 1972."[4] Because of the important role of Martin Azonhiho in Kérékou's Marxist regime, the plan of the operation provided for his physical liquidation.

Thus, accommodating the wishes of his French patrons, some foreign supporters, and specific request of his Beninese opposition sponsors,[5] Denard prepared the plan of the Opération Crevette, who's goal was "to eliminate the present regime, to install the new team from the Front for the Liberation and Rehabilitation of Dahomey."[6] This goal would be reached in the following manner: "To intervene in the Republic of Banalia [the People's Republic of Benin] with a view to dismantling its offensive system; By depriving the EM [the General Staff] of the Banalian armed forces of its leadership; By destroying a maximum of forces in order to diminish the morale of the country and its army; To create conditions favorable to the establishment of a government not hostile to Zangaro [the Togolese Republic] and, if possible, having a similar ideology."[7]

But the operation should, according to its planners, have a wider than local, internal effect on political system of Benin. If successful, it should halt "the swing to the East" of not only Benin but also "perhaps [have a] decisive, psychological effect on certain African Heads of State who are all too willing to compromise with the Marxists, whether as a precaution or from ideological conviction."

In a post–World War II era, between the 1950s and the mid-1980s, thirty-five African countries adopted a Marxist or socialist ideology alongside a corresponding political and economic system. The leaders of these countries believed socialism offered their best chance to overcome the many obstacles these new states faced at independence. Initially, African leaders created new, hybrid versions of socialism, known as African socialism, but by the 1970s, several states turned to the more orthodox form of socialism—scientific socialism.[8]

Turning toward a socialist economic and political system meant the nationalization of foreign economic assets, mainly owned by individuals or companies belonging to former colonial powers. It also often meant cutting off economic relations with former colonial states and substituting them with relations with socialist or communist countries of Eastern Europe, Asia, or Cuba, or other socialist-oriented countries of Africa. All of this led also to political affiliations with a block of socialist and communist states in international relations resulting in voting with them in international organizations, like, for example, the United Nations (UN).

What worried France at that time was that Benin, if not prevented by a forcible change of regime would, like Equatorial Guinea and Sao Tome and Principe, become "another stronghold on the Algiers-Conakry-Brazzaville-Luanda axis," a group of West African states that had Marxism-oriented political and economic systems. So, the change of regime in Benin was suppose give the Marxists an "occasion to reflect on the limit to their expansionist aims."[9]

THE PLAN OF OPÉRATION CREVETTE

The plan of the operation code-named Opération Crevette was prepared by Denard himself. It was the first plan of a mercenary coup d'état operation drowned up by Denard himself. His earlier mercenary experience in the 1960s mainly in Congo was concentrated on commanding of smaller or bigger mercenary units taking part in often unconventional military hostilities against various rebel groups and separatist Congolese armies. Such activities usually did not require any extensive planning and were, in most cases, concentrated on combat in response to a particular field situation. Even Denard's

1975 operation of support for the overthrowing of President Ahmed Abdallah by Ali Soilih and FNU, did not required any pre-planning. The Denard commando just arrived in the Comoros and helped the FNU putschists to apprehend President Ahmed Abdallah who took refuge on island of Ajouan. The operation in Benin required a detailed plan outlining the many stages of the mercenary operation; this was not limited solely to combat.

The operation is commonly known—although Denard did not use this name in any of the operation's preparatory documents or, later, in his biographies—under a French language code name: Opération Crevette. The name Opération Crevette has also been used in Beninese media and publications dedicated to describing this operation. Denard's acolytes, grouped in the aforementioned association Orbs Patria Nostra, rather, use the code name Operation *Omega*. The latter stems from the code name used by Denard for his mercenary commando involved in the operation: Force Omega. Sometimes, authors describing the event will use the translated French name of Opération Crevette, Operation "Shrimp," in English-language publications.

Initially, the operation was to be executed in the way of two simultaneously conducted "sudden movements": an airborne attack launched from Gabon combined with a land incursion from the territory of Benin's western neighbor, Togo, by a separate group of mercenaries supported by Togolese battalion trained by them for that operation. Thus, Denard's plan of Opération Crevette provided the airborne attack on Cotonou to begin on January 5, 1977, at 6:45 a.m. and the land incursion of the crossing of the Togo–Benin border by the second group "at the same hour." Although the operation's beginning date was later changed, its goal remained the same: the change of regime in Cotonou and "[t]he action itself will necessarily be violent."

To avoid leaks of the operation's plans or any potential exposure of the support of various African countries, the coup d'état organizers initially rejected the option of land infiltration by mercenary commando forces from any of Benin's neighbors, such as Togo, to incite an internal upheaval.[10] Denard considered such actions to be extremely dangerous because of a "lack of enthusiasm on the part of opponents to the regime." On the other hand, assuming based on "all information received," the operation launched from outside would somehow invigorate the passive resistance of most Dahomeyans, turning it to "active and dynamic support" for violent change of Kérékou's regime.[11]

However, Denard and the Beninese and French patrons of his operation, overlooked or ignored the important fact that there was an organized, and illegal, opposition group in Benin at that time: the newly created (in 1976) Union of Communist of Dahomey (*Union des Communistes du Dahomey*, UCD). Any other organized, non-Communist Beninese opposition existed only abroad, mainly in France. Three main political leaders, former presidents

Justin Ahomadégbé, Migan Apithy, and Hubert Maga, were since the October 1972 coup held under house arrest at Avrankou, a small village northeast of Porto-Novo. Thus, they could not, even if they wanted to, mobilize any popular support of their followers for a coup against their jailor, Mathieu Kérékou. Also, it would not be in the interest of Émile Zinsou to count on any support from the followers of his political adversaries and competitors for presidential sit.

The nonexistence of any civilian organized opposition to Mathieu Kérékou's regime was proved when in October 1975, the government in Cotonou announced that it discovered a "gigantic plot" organized allegedly by plotters acting on behalf of Émile Zinsou. In early February 1976,[12] the Revolutionary Council, transformed into the Revolutionary Tribunal, sentenced eleven alleged plotters to death, eight of them *in absentia*, three to life imprisonment (one *in absentia*), and one- to twenty-years imprisonment. Four persons were acquitted. The number of sentences *in absentia* shows that most individuals allegedly involved in the plot on behalf of Émile Zinsou remained, like him, outside of Benin. Not only was this information publicly available in French media, but Denard also received it directly from Émile Zinsou when they were discussing the proposed operation against Kérékou's regime. Moreover, the prosecution and sentencing of Zinsou's supporters seemed to be a crucial argument used by Zinsou in convincing Denard to accept an assignment to conduct Opération Crevette.[13]

The plan of the operation did not mention the role, which in Benin's political system was played by the sole legal party acting under the leadership of Mathieu Kérékou—the People's Revolutionary Party of Benin (*Parti de la Révolution Populaire du Bénin*, PRPB). Since 1975, the sole legal political party and local revolutionary committees acting on each administrative level of the country, or even the youth subjected to ideological Marxist brainwashing, all could be called to the defense of the country against internal and external enemies of socialist Benin. It was young people, often educated abroad (France, Senegal, Eastern European socialist countries, the People's Republic of China, and the Soviet Union), who were members of Dahomeyan youth organizations formed prior to revolutionary changes in their country, such as *Jeunesse Unie Démocratique* (JUD), *Ligue nationale de la Jeunesse patriotique* (LNJP) (called *Ligueurs*) or *Front d'Action commun des Elèves et Etudiants du nord* (FACEEN). Under the influence of these organizations, in 1974, the government, then Dahomey, adopted Marxism–Leninism as its official ideology and embarked on vast program of revolutionizing Beninese society. Those young leftists were behind nationalization of all sectors of the economy, reform of the education system, establishment of agricultural cooperatives, and new structures of local administration and already-mentioned local revolutionary committees.[14] All of them supported

Kérékou's military regime and were willing and ready to defend the Marxist system of their country, not only as the members of the armed forces but also of the Revolutionary Defense Brigades.

So, if Denard counted on massive support from the local population, he should have known better how risky such an assumption was for the success of his operation, especially since he had already rejected the idea of organizing internal strife against Kérékou's regime. One can only assume that Beninese sponsors of the Opération Crevette had either failed to update or purposely misinformed Denard about the real political and social situation in their home country to get his involvement in a coup against Mathieu Kérékou, the first coup d'état in Benin's history not conducted or supported by the country's army.

Thus, after rejection of fomenting a change of regime from inside the country, the organizers of the operation were thus left with two choices: (1) a seaborne landing on a beach close to the presidential complex or (2) an air assault on Cotonou airport.

For Opération Crevette, there were three targets. Two of these included the presidential palace, the official site of the president and Kérékou's private residence considered a presidential complex; and Camp Guézo, a military base located north of that complex. The presidential complex in Cotonou is located about a half-mile from the seashore and separated from it by a strip of a beach, a wide swath of open terrain, and a two-lane Boulevard de la Marina highway. Additionally, a vast sandbar hindered direct access to the portion of the beach closest to the presidential complex. Also, the naval control of coastal waters and customs control of entries to Cotonou's commercial and fishing ports could make impossible an unnoticed approach to the seaside by a vessel carrying on board a mercenary commando hindering any element of surprise required for the success of the covert operation. Thus, the seaborne operation similar to a seven- year earlier Operation Green Sea (*Operação Mar Verde*)—an amphibious attack of Portuguese soldiers on Conakry, the capital of Guinea—the goal of which included, among others, the overthrow of a revolutionary, Marxist-oriented then-president Sekou Touré.[15]

Thus, the choice of attack by Denard's commandos on Benin was narrowed down to an air assault on the Cotonou airport. However, Denard had no experience from his prior mercenary activities in organizing airborne assaults or conducting an airborne operation. Now, he faced logistical and security problems related to covertly bringing to Benin his commando by air and how to land safely enough to secure obtaining of necessary surprise effect. Since neither Beninese nor French patrons of the operation did not guarantee any local support in securing control of the Cotonou airport, he could only count on the inadequate military protection of the airport before its daily opening for regular air traffic alongside an absence of any air tower personnel who could alert authorities of the commando's arrival. There were also serious disadvantages to this choice of attack strategy. Namely, the airport was located approximately a mile and a half away from the operation's two primary attack targets. To reach desired targets, the commando would have to cover that distance through densely populated residential and business areas. On top of this, the early Sunday morning attack plan would mean only a few vehicles, apart from those designated for airport fire protection and maintenance service, would be available for Omegas to reach their targets. None of these circumstances, however, discouraged Bob Denard from launching an airborne Opération Crevette.

Relaying of information provided his close associate Lieutenant Gerard whom Denard allegedly sent to Benin to gather information and probably also advised by his "SDECE contacts," Denard believed that he had obtained for purpose of a planned operation "a precise assessment of the armed forces of Kérékou as well as details on their location.

However, all intelligence information fed to Denard seemed to reflect more anti-Kérékou propaganda of Beninese emigration circles indicating that overthrowing Mathieu Kérékou would render the support of most Beninese citizens than the factual local situation. "The passive resistance of the majority of the Dahomeyan people vis-a-vis the present regime would give way to active and dynamic support for any element likely to bring about such change."[16] The Benineses merely ask "to be allowed to breathe."[17] Denard also believed, probably based on his experience from Congo and a bit of a racist attitude, that the Beninese armed forces "if they were cleverly handled, could become favorable."[18] Based upon such an assumption, the organizers of Opération Crevette specifically counted on the support of specific local army units, such as the First Parachutists company stationed in Ouidah and the First Squadron of gendarmerie from Porto-Novo. Additionally, as previously mentioned, they considered military backup by Togolese parachutists accompanied by a group of foreign mercenaries infiltrating from Togo.

Getting ready for the operation, Denard counted on the Beninese army, *Forces Armées Dahoméennes* (FAD) soldiers' lack of proper training and fighting experience. The plan of the operation described the Beninese military as "very weak; drill training and maneuvers are non-existent; material is generally very old and poorly maintained. Discipline continues to be very variable, including in the Police Force."[19]

The FAD's strongest unit was the Second Company of parachutists equipped with several light armored vehicles, namely AM 8, Panhard AML (*Auto Mitrailleuse Légère*) 60s (or what Denard remembers to be AM Ferret) and half-trucks stationed outside the capital at the barracks in Ouidah, a town about a forty-minute drive from Cotonou (twenty-four miles / forty-one kilometers). FAD units stationed in the capital totaled roughly six hundred men who were concentrated at the main military barracks and security services' headquarters at Camp Guézo, a primary target of the attack. Denard estimated that three to four hundred men of the First Battalion and First Company were stationed at Camp Guézo in Cotonou. Another army unit, such as the Second Battalion, numbering about two hundred men, was stationed far north from Cotonou at the Parakou, Natitingou, and Kandi bases, and were not considered by Crevette's organizers to be any threat during the initial phase of operation.[20]

Since the Camp Guézo was located about mile and a half (2.4 kilometers) from the airport and in close vicinity to the presidential complex, the national radio station, *Voix de la Revolution*, and the residences of political figures central in Kérékou's regime, the element of surprise, including the quick "deactivating" of Camp Guézo, was the most critical part of the operation. Reaching these primary targets quickly and stealthily, however, would require the use of an appropriate number of vehicles ensuring fast transportation and, at least neutrality, if not the active cooperation, of the local army, gendarmerie, and police units.

Relying on information from the aforementioned "various studies" likely provided by the French special services, a Beninese army deserter hired for this operation, and bits and pieces of intelligence gathered in Cotonou by his associate Gerard, "the opposition leaders concluded that there are all necessary and adequate prerequisites for the defeat of the present regime."[21] So, Denard expected the prompt neutralization of army troops, the gendarmerie, and the local police. Further, he wished to use these neutralized units to support the new government created after his successful coup. Most of the information that served as a blueprint for the plan for the attack on Cotonou could be boiled down to one simple actionable fact: "on Sunday, the Beninese army kept on alert for the capital, only a mobile group of 25 men with a few light armored cars and two or three jeeps with mounted cannons." This information was passed down by Denard to his commandos, or at least the European mercenaries taking part, likely to assure them of the relative ease of achieving the operation's goals just before departure for Cotonou.[22]

Surprisingly, the plans for Opération Crevette did not mention any possible role in repelling the Battalion of Presidential Guard (*Bataillon de la Garde Présidentielle*), a four-hundred special unit composed mostly of Kérékou's Fulani tribe members and trained by the North Korean instructors.[23] This turned out to be a serious mistake by Denard.

According to sources, Gratien Pognon was to take power in Benin in the case that Opération Crevette was successful.[24] He was to stand as both the president and prime minister, who, in the name of FLERD, was to direct the rebuilding and restructuring of the country.[25] Others, however, claim that the governing positions were at least for the time until free presidential elections, to be held by ex-inspector of finance (1965–1967) and future president of Benin, Nicéphore Soglo.[26]

A review of the "Situation Report" on Benin used by Denard to plan the Opération Crevette has to lead to conclusion that its content indicated that it must have been cooked up by French intelligence and its political section substantially based upon the wishful thinking of Beninese émigrés and French services' intent to use his operation as a convenient tool for a regime change in the former colony over which Paris lost political and economic control within a frame of the network of *Franceafrique*.

NOTES

1. Benin, "Letter Dated 77/04/04 from the Charge d'Affaires a.i. of Benin to the United Nations Addressed to the President of the Security Council: Addendum" (New York: United Nations, April 5, 1977), https://digitallibrary.un.org/record/564452, see 25; UN, Special Mission of the Security Council Established under Resolution 404 (1977), "Report of the Security Council Special Mission to the People's Republic of Benin Established under Resolution 404 (1977)" (New York: United Nations, 1977), https://digitallibrary.un.org/record/564622, see Annex IV, 133.

2. UN, Special Mission of the Security Council Established under Resolution 404 (1977), "Report of the Security Council Special Mission to the People's Republic of Benin Established under Resolution 404 (1977): Addendum" (New York: United Nations, March 8, 1977), https://digitallibrary.un.org/record/564391, see Annex VI, 95.

3. Mathurin C. Houngnikpo and Samuel Decalo, *Historical Dictionary of Benin* (Lanham, MD: Scarecrow Press, 2012), 69.

4. "Le régime militaire a célébré son troisième anniversaire dans un climat politique tendu," *Le Monde*, October 29, 1975.

5. Bob Denard and George Fleury, *Corsaire de la République* (Paris: Robert Laffont, 1998), 288. Denard will later admit: "my contacts at the SDECE encourage me to put myself at the service of Dr. Zinsou, France having every interest in Kérékou being removed from power."

6. "Letter Dated 4 April 1977 from the Chargé d'Affaires a.i. of Benin to the United Nations Addressed to the President of the Security Council," S/12319. Add. 1, 23.

7. "Letter Dated 4 April 1977," S/12319, Add. 1, 35.

8. See Dieter Lösch: "Socialism in Africa," *Intereconomics* 25, no. 6 (1990): 300–306, https://doi.org/10.1007/BF02928799.

9. "Letter Dated 4 April 1977," S/12319, Add. 1, 24.

10. Ibid., 27.

11. Ibid.

12. "Le régime militaire a célébré son troisième anniversaire dans un climat politique tendu," *Le Monde*, October 29, 1975; "Onze personnes sont condamnées à mort

pour avoir participé au complot d'octobre 1975," *Le Monde*, February 5, 1976; The Amnesty International Report June 1, 1975, to May 31, 1976, London 1976, 57.

13. Denard and Fleury, *Corsaire de la République*, 288.

14. Besides the National Council of the Revolution (CNR), a national political body, relied on the local revolutionary authorities, the Provincial Council of the Revolution (CPR), the District Revolutionary Council (CRD), the Communal Council of the Revolution (CCR) and the Local Revolutionary Council (CRL), to decide, execute, control and coordinate the tasks of the mobilization and organization of the masses. Marcelle Genné, "La tentation du socialisme au Bénin (The Temptation of Socialism in Bénin)," *Études internationals* 9, no. 3 (1978): 393.

15. For some details of that operation see "Guinea Reports Invasion from Sea by Portuguese," *New York Times*, November 23, 1970, 1.

16. "Letter Dated 4 April 1977," 27.

17. Security Council Official Records, 33rd Year. Special Supplement No. III, 132.

18. Ibid.

19. "Report of the Security Council Special Mission to the People's Republic of Benin Established under Resolution 404 (1977)," Annex VI, 71.

20. Parakou is located 260 miles or six-hour drive, Natitingou 350 miles or eight-hour drive, and Kandi 424 miles or ten-hour drive from Cotonou.

21. "Letter Dated 4 April 1977," 24.

22. Alain Chevalerias, "OPS Oméga-Raid sur Cotonou: Témoignage Alain Marc," *Orbs Patria Nostra*, April 1977, https://www.orbspatrianostra.com/ops/ops-benin/temoignage-alain-marc.html.

23. Houngnikpo and Decalo, *Historical Dictionary of Benin*, 75.

24. Ibid., 245.

25. "Report of the Security Council Special Mission to the People's Republic of Benin Established under Resolution 404 (1977)," Annex VI, 29, 161.

26. "Au tribunal correctionnel de Paris Bob Denard, mercenaire ou corsaire?" Le Monde, March 12, 1993.

Chapter 7

Getting Armed and Ready

On November 5, 1976, Denard signed a contract with Gratien Pognon, representing FLERD, in regard to organizing the operation against president Kérékou. In the opening paragraph of the contract, Denard, using the name Gilbert Bourgeaud, stated: "I the undersigned, Gilbert Bourgeaud, undertake by this contract to recruit for FLERD 90 technicians—60 Europeans and 30 Africans—who will serve as the basic element for overthrow the present regime in an operation defined by the annexed OPS plan."[1]

The contract further contained a detailed schedule of the financial arrangements regarding the covering of operation costs, although it did so without naming any specific sources of financing, describing them only as "friendly authorities (H2/OB)." Those sources were later identified in other documents related to the Opération Crevette and by Denard in his later accounts of that operation as Moroccan King Hassan II (i.e., H2) and Gabon's president Omar Bongo (i.e., OB).[2]

For the first three months, during the preparatory stage of the operation, the contract provided that Denard was to receive from the king of Morocco a pre-operational budget in amount of USD $475,000. This money would cover "all the expenses of recruitment, routing, transport, contacts and wage for the group of 90 technicians"[3] ("technicians" referring to the mercenaries). At the end of a three-month period, the Force Omega members were to receive "post-operative leave" in amount of $530,000, which should be paid "by the newly established régime created from FLERD and guaranteed by friendly authorities (H2/OB)."[4] Hassan II who also "guaranteed per contract that Dr. Zinsou [would] allocate on his part [an] additional $400,000 for us." The following payment of $530,000 would come from the new government of Benin, created after toppling Kérékou. The payments were to be deposited into accounts at *Société Intercontinentale de Banque* in Luxemburg and *Banque Bordier* in Geneva. The copy of this contract was signed by Denard, missing Pongon's signature, was made public by the Beninese authorities.[5] Denard also received a down payment of $145,000 from FLERD for arranging of the operation.[6] In the event of success, he was to receive a one-million-dollar bonus. Denard optimistically anticipated, based on his mercenary experience from the Congo and Comoros, that after the success of the operation, at least some of the GEI mercenaries would remain in Benin after the renewal of the initial contract to provide security for the new authorities.

Organizing Opération Crevette, Denard visited both Morocco and Gabon. He boasted that during his visit to Morocco that he even met twice with the Moroccan monarch.[7] His accounts of these personal meetings with Hassan II seem to be somewhat doubtful as the king would not have likely been directly involved in the planning of such an operation. However, through contacts arranged with Moroccan special services and military, Denard was able to secure the Royal Moroccan Air Force base near the town of Ben Guerir for the training of some Force Omega members. Under the command of one of Denard's closest associates, often described as his "right hand," Legrand,[8] basic weapons training was provided to the African members of his commando. This training included the use of automatic machine guns, anti-tank rocket launchers, and mortars.

RECRUITMENT

The Force Omega was to be organized according to the French model for the organization of mercenary troops. This model was patterned on French guerilla organizations, which drew its origins from the experience of colonial wars in Indochina and Algeria and was adopted by Denard for the needs of his operations. Denard had seen this type of mercenary organization in the early 1960s in Congo, where it was introduced by another French mercenary leader of that time, Roger Trinquier.[9]

The basic organizational model was known as *Groupement Mixed d'Intervention* (GMI). The GMI was initially developed by the French in Indochina during the 1950s. In Indochina and Algeria (OAS), GMI groups consisted of forty to eighty native or local men led by French officers or even NGOs (nongovernmental organizations). Denard's Force Omega was of a similar size and further included a number of African members who allegedly held an anti-Communist view—in this case, a viewpoint directed against Benin's president Matthew Kérékou and his pro-socialist administration. In a study of various types of mercenary forces acting across modern Africa, Gerry Thomas named this type of mercenary unit a "coup strike force." This term adequately describes the character of the mercenary units used by Bob Denard in case of coup attempts in Benin and the Comoros. A coup strike force differs from other types of mercenary units in that it is usually "close-knit group of mercenaries hired for one specific goal." It is "usually well-financed, trained, equipped and directed by an exiled opposition leader." Its role is "to spearhead a popular rebellion within the target country."[10] It should be added that in the case of this Beninese coup, the relatively small sizes of the unit alongside the support of the special services of a country interested in the regime change secured the covert character of this particular mercenary coup strike force operation.

Unlike the African recruits, European mercenaries recruited for the operation were expected to have previous military training or experience. For this reason, the recruitment of Europeans began within the circle of Denard's former associates described by him as a "selective and impenetrable" group, like the *Cosa Nostra* Italian Mafia.[11] Among this "mafia" were former personnel of the French army paratroopers and the French Foreign Legion. The problem was that neither Denard nor his close associates had any experience in hiring such a large number of mercenaries. The only other operation Denard had organized had been in 1975 in the Comoros. However, the operation in the Comoros had been conducted with a group of his closest associates who he was able to recruit himself through personal contacts established during his service in the mercenary units in Congo in the 1960s. Those mercenaries recruited for fighting in bigger operation, like civil wars or foreign interventions (e.g., in Angola, Biafra, Congo, or Yemen), were usually recruited by American, French, British, or Belgian special services. This time, Denard conducted the recruitment of a relatively small—a dozen or so "old hands"— group of the European mercenaries by himself.[12]

The initial recruitment of European candidates was initiated by the placing of a newspaper advertisement directed to "responsible individuals," "fully qualified," willing to work for an "overseas company, security and protection" was run in ten French regional newspapers. It specified that applicants' "military experience, preferably in crack units [i.e., elite troops] is desired." It also stated that a "high morality is required,"[13] what sounds like a strange requirement for individuals who, due to their violent behavior during the mercenaries' operations in Africa, were often called *les affreux*, "the Dreadful" or the Dogs of War.

Recruitment of European mercenaries in Paris was conducted through the agency Havas-Contact that arranged meetings with recruits at various Parisian hotels. Recruitment likely also took place in Belgium, Germany (then the Federal Republic of Germany), and Sweden. Out of four thousand European applicants, Denard and his close associates[14] selected a preliminary 150 individuals, finally offering contracts only to sixty of them.[15] All selected men met with Denard in a rented apartment located within Paris's fifteenth arrondissement. Since the majority of men recruited were former mercenaries and special services operators, their contracts would provide merely for a short period of shooting practice.

It is worthy to notice that the French special SDECE service unit responsible for the surveillance of mercenaries under their jurisdiction had not taken any action to curb the recruitment activities of Denard and his associates. Quite the contrary, as he will relate later, it was the French intelligence agency (SDECE) that "encouraged" him to organize on behalf of the Beninese oppositionist Dr. Zinsou a mercenary operation in Benin.[16]

Creating Force Omega according to the described-above French model of mercenary units, coup organizers recruited, from groups of exiled Africans opposed to socialist-oriented governments of their own countries, a number of African mercenaries. Denard claimed that he took the pain to make sure to hire not only exiled Beninese but also Guineans. Such composition of Force Omega helped to craft the cover for Opération Crevette as an internal Beninese (African) coup d'état.

The recruitment of African members of Force Omega took place in Abidjan (Ivory Coast) and Dakar (Senegal). In Abidjan recruitment was conducted by two Beninese exiles: Amadou Assouma (a.k.a. Amadou Tchene or Tchinin), associate and co-leader of Pognon's Movement for Renovation of Dahomey (Mouvement de la Rénovation du Dahomey, MRD), and Beninese former regimental sergeant major Marc Soglo. In Dakar, Denard hired two recruiters representing Guinea's anti-Sékou Touré movement: a Guinean Marxist dictator, *émigré* Regrouping of Guineans Abroad (*Regroupement de Guinéens à l'Extérieur*), Siradiou Diallo, who had already been sentenced *in absentia* to death in Guinea for his participation in the 1970 Portuguese military aggression against his own country; and Oumar Sy Savane. Their contracts provided for forty-five-day service with the commando. Upon signing a contract, each of them received six thousand French francs, an equivalent of his promised monthly mercenary pay.

FORCE OMEGA

Altogether, eighty-nine European and African mercenaries, and two exiled opposition leaders representing FLERD—Gratien Pognon and Pognon's co-leader in the *Mouvement de la Renovation du Dahomey* (MRD) Party, Amadou Assouma (a.k.a. Amadou Tchinnin)—took active part in the operation. Twenty-seven, instead of the planned thirty, Africans—mostly nationals of Guinea and Beninese exiles[17]—alongside sixty-two Europeans of various nationalities—among them fifty Frenchmen, Belgians, Germans, and a Swede—all of whom, including Bob Denard would be later identified by their real names.[18]

Among European mercenaries were individuals of different backgrounds and occupations. Many of them had military experience, such as former

Legionaries from First Foreign Parachute Regiment (French: *Premier REP*) with officer ranks. Others included noncommissioned officers (NCOs) and individuals with no military service experience. Besides Bob Denard, those with the most experience were the European mercenaries, many of whom were former parachutists from *Premier REP* (Green Berets) such as Louis Cabasso (alias Carden), André Cau, Franz Heinmann (alias Eugene François), Alfons Holzapfel (alias Lingen), Werner Kolibius (alias Koli), Istvan Wagner, Hugues de Chivre (alias Sergeant Rucker), Michel de la Contrie de Charette (alias Kermarec), or Van Den Berge (alias Van).[19] The European mercenary detachment was named Foreign Intervention Group (*Group Etrangére d'Intervention*, GEI).[20] The whole mercenary commando team was dubbed Force Omega.

The other, second detachment of GEI formed from the battalion of the Togolese soldiers and French military advisors was allegedly dispatched to the Togolese side of the border with Benin ostensibly to provide military support for the Togolese army against possible aggression by the Beninese military resulting from a long-term border dispute between the two countries or an attempt by the revolutionary forces of Kérékou to topple pro-Western Togolese president Gnassingbé Eyadéma. However, the document entitled "Order from the GEI Commander" authored by "the Colonel" commanding the GEI (a.k.a. Bob Denard) leaves no doubt that the second GEI was stationed in Togo with the mission to render military support from outside for the coup against President Kérékou, to be conducted by the members the first GEI (a.k.a. the Commando). As was expected by the planners Opération Crevette, mutinied elements of the Beninese army would join the mercenary operation. According to the "Order," Denard planned to begin the operation with "two movements simultaneously"—that is, the attack on Cotonou was to be supported by an attack from Togo. Thus, the second GEI was expected by Denard to "cross the frontier in force at the same hour" at which the Force Omega was to commence an attack in Cotonou. It was "[t]o enter the territory of Banalia (i.e., Benin) from the Republic of Zangaro [Togo] with a view of disrupting enemy communications there, destroying a maximum of its forces and bringing back to the Koumea [military base Guezo in Cotonou] attack force." After completion of this assignment, the second GEI should "fall back to across Zangaro frontier and regroup there, prepared to face counteraction."[21] Due to unexpected course of events during Opération Crevette, the second GEI was, however, never sent to action on the territory of Benin.

WEAPONS AND EQUIPMENT

A review of the list of weapons and equipment indicates that the planners of Opération Crevette expected and prepared for a tough urban fight in Cotonou. The plan of the operation also provided for an after-coup presence of the mercenaries with aim to protect, strengthen, and consolidate Benin's new, pro-French administration.

Bob Denard planned to arm members of Force Omega with light automatic weapons and various types of explosives, including hand grenades. In one of the versions of Opération Crevette's plans, the operation organizers planned to arm Omegas with the following weapons:

- eighty-five assault rifles, type FAL G3 or Kalashnikov
- eighty-five automatic pistols, nine millimeters or 11.45 millimeters
- eight machine guns, AA-52 or MG 42
- one machine gun, P 50, caliber 12.7 millimeters
- eight light bazookas, Russian type
- one mortar, eighty-one millimeters
- one mortar, sixty millimeters

The equipment list also called for eighty-five commando type daggers and fifteen walkie-talkies.[22]

THE AMMUNITION

Aside from the ammunition and explosives actually used by the Omegas during the operation, there was a huge volume of various explosives and variety of hand grenades left by them behind at the Cotonou airport. Among them there were 1,256 nine-millimeter cartridges with regular bullets, PA-PM, Lot No. 23–4-SFM75, of French origin; 405 NATO-type nine-millimeter cartridges with regular bullets, of Belgian origin; 33,668 NATO-type 7.62 millimeter cartridges with regular bullets, of Belgian origin; 10,230 NATO-type 7.62-millimeter cartridges on detachable magna-metal belts (one tracer and four regular bullets) of Belgian origin; three thousand 7.62-millimeter cartridges on detachable magno-metal belts (one tracer and nine regular bullets) with Arabic markings; 1,875 12.7-millimeter cartridges on detachable magno-metal belts (one tracer and four regular bullets), of Belgian origin; six offensive hand grenades, D-37, Lot No. SPA-38–60, of French origin; five fuses for offensive explosive hand grenades, Lot No. 42-RYN-60; seven explosive hand grenades, D-37, Lot No. 4-EB-59, of French origin; four explosive hand grenades, D-37, Lot No. 6-TYN-58, of French origin; one explosive hand grenade, D-37, Lot No. 4-TNP-60, of French origin; five fuses for hand grenades, D-37, Lot No. 5-EB-59, of French origin; four fuses for explosive hand grenades, D-37, Lot No. 114-RYN-58, of French origin; fifty-three forty-millimeter explosive rifle grenades, APAV, Lot No. 2-MPA-77, four of which were destroyed, of Belgian origin; ten offensive-defensive hand grenades, M2, with fuses, M-204 AI, Lot No. I MI-6–71, of American origin; eighteen explosive shells, eighty-one millimeters, FA-32 5 BT 36, Lot No. 32, of French origin; twenty propellant cartridges for eighty-one-millimeter shells, Lot No. 44CF-51, of French origin; twenty fuses, DP 24/31 RYG-18, for eighty-one-millimeter shells, Lot No. 9-ATS-62, one of which was destroyed, of French origin; sixty-four relays for eighty-one-millimeter shells, Lot No. 122-CF-51, of French origin; eleven eighty-one-millimeter smoke shells, complete, with fuses, Lot No. 211–71 (fuse, Lot No. 441.76), of British or American origin; five explosive eighty-one-millimeter shells, complete, with fuses, Lot No. 211–71 (fuse, Lot No. 441–76), of British or American origin; four sixty-five-millimeter AC explosive rifle grenades, with Arabic markings, two of which were destroyed; thirty-two sixty-six-millimeter AC explosive rockets, M-72-A-2, Lot No. LS-220-R-8–74,26 of which were destroyed, of American origin; twelve eighty-nine-millimeter AC explosive rockets, BM-66, Lot No. l-73, one of which was destroyed, of Spanish origin.[23]

NOTES

1. UN, Special Mission of the Security Council Established under Resolution 404 (1977), "Report of the Security Council Special Mission to the People's Republic of Benin Established under Resolution 404 (1977)," March 8, 1977, S/12294.Add 1, Annex VI, Document No. 6, 39.

2. Bob Denard and Georges Fleury, *Corsaire de la République* (Paris: Robert Laffont, 1998), 288–89.

3. "Letter Dated 4 April 1977 from the Charge d'Affaires a.i. of Benin to the United Nations Addressed to the President of the Security Council," S/12319/Add. 1, April 5, 1977, 42.

4. Ibid. Abbreviation H2 refers allegedly to then King of Morocco, Hassan II, and OB suggests reference to president of Gabon, Omar Bongo. Both individuals always denied any knowledge of the Opération Crevette.

5. Ibid.

6. Ibid.

7. Denard and Fleury, *Corsaire de la République*, 289.

8. Name "Legrand" is in fact an alias of René Dulac, a former French parachutist who joined him in various mercenary operations. René Dulac used also as aliases "Vincent" and in Opération Crevette "Mercier" or "Commandant Mercier." Alias

"Mercier" as used by Legrand has been de-coded by Pierre Péan, *Mémoires impubliables* (Éditions Albin Michel, 2020), 38.

9. Gerry S. Thomas, *Mercenary Troops in Modern Africa* (Boulder, CO: Westview Press, 1984), 37–38.

10. Thomas, *Mercenary Troops in Modern Africa*, 7.

11. Pierre Lunel, *Bob Denard: Le roi de fortune* (Edition⁰ 1, 1991), 456.

12. Denard and Fleury, *Corsaire de la République*, 288.

13. "Overseas company, security and protection, seeks fully qualified cadres, top physical condition. Preferably served with crack units."

14. Roger Bruni, René Dulac (Legrand), and André Cau.

15. Denard and Fleury, *Corsaire de la République*, 289.

16. Ibid., 288.

17. As to the recruited African mercenaries, their number varying by source. See for example: Lunel, *Bob Denard: Le roi de fortune*, 456, mentions thirty Africans; Philippe Akpo, *Role et implications des Forces Beninoises dans la vie politique nationale* (Contonou, Benin: Editions du Flamboyant, 2005), 181, mentions thirteen Guineans, eleven Beninese mercenaries, plus two leaders of FLERD.

18. "Letter Dated 13 June 1979 from the Permanent Representative of Benin to the United Nations Addressed to the Secretary-General, S/13402," Annex, 2–6.

19. Anthony Mockler, *The New Mercenaries. The History of the Hired Soldiers from the Congo to the Seychelles* (New York: Paragon House, 1987), 243–44.

20. GEI refers throughout only to the European mercenaries. Together with the Africans they are known as the Force Omega.

21. S/12319/Add. 1, 5 April 1977, 36.

22. "Report of the Security Council Special Mission to the People's Republic of Benin Established under Resolution 404 (1977)," March 8, 1977, S/12294/Add. 1, Annex VI, Document No. 8, 47.

23. S/PV. 1986, Security Council Official Records, Thirty-second Year, 1986th Meeting: February 7, 1977, para. 17.

Chapter 8

Bienvenue au Maroc!
(Welcome to Morocco!)

BEN GUERIR AIR BASE

The choice of Morocco as a transit and training point for the Force Omega was not accidental. Denard had long term personal connections with this country. In 1952, when he left French marine service in Indochina, he moved to then French protectorate Morocco where he married a Moroccan woman and became employed in the local colonial French police. During his stay in Morocco, he established important personal contacts within Moroccan intelligence—two directors of the local secret services: General Mohamed Oufkir and his successor, General Ahmed Dlimi. Denard worked for them in various capacities, among other, training the first Moroccan secret agents and assisted in establishing the internal intelligence agency tasked with the monitoring of potentially subversive domestic activities, CAB1.[1] He also became involved with the Moroccan Royal Armed Forces (*Forces Armées Royales*), which at that time were taking part in foreign intervention activities where there was internal conflict in Congo (present-day Democratic Republic of Congo). This was a beginning of Denard's mercenary career. Thus, it was natural that when the organizers of Opération Crevette were looking for a country that could provide them with a safe place for stay and training of the mercenary commando force, Denard's choice was Morocco. Presence at, and use of, the military base by Denard's commando force for training could not have been possible without the consent of highest levels of Moroccan intelligence and military.

The Force Omega rendezvous took place at the Ben Guerir Air Base in Morocco. The base was located a driving distance of about 106 miles southeast from Casablanca. The Ben Guerir Air Base had been owned and operated by US Strategic Air Command since 1951, having been built as part of Operation Storage Sites (1950) for nuclear weapons. It served as a US Air Force base and a Transoceanic Abort Landing (TAL) site for the US Space Shuttle missions. When the Royal Moroccan Air Force took over ownership of the base in 1962, due to changes in the political environment of the country, it was designated as BAFRA No. 6. At this point in its history, the base was often used as a transit base for French military interventions in Africa especially by Thirteenth Regiment of Dragon Parachutist (Treizième Regiment de Dragons Parachutistes, Treizième RDP), a special reconnaissance regiment of the French army, acting hand in hand with the French intelligence service, SEDCE. The base was later deactivated in 2005 due to threats posed by the regional terrorist activities.

In early December of 1976, sixty-one (sixty mercenaries and Denard)[2] European mercenaries departed in groups from France to Morocco. Forty-eight of them flew Air France from Paris to Casablanca; twenty-two flew from Paris to Rabat; and one took a *Union de Transports Aériens* (UTA) flight from Paris to Casablanca with a stopover in Rabat. All of them, accompanied by members of Hassan's II Presidential Guard, were transferred to the Ben Guerir by the Royal Moroccan Air Force. Arriving along with them to the base was Denard using yet another assumed name, this time Colonel Jean Maurin.

MILITARY TRAINING

The initial plan for the mercenary training prepared by Denard provided for a three-to-four-week extensive "all-inclusive" preparation for combat (i.e., open war, conflict as opposed to covert operations) that "should enable each person to reach peak performance by the time set for the operation." It provided, in particular, for middle-distance running, obstacle cleating (combatant's course), grenade-throwing, hand-to-hand fighting, training in firing all weapons: automatic pistol, submachine gun, assault rifle, heavy and light machine guns, rifle grenades, anti-tank rocket launcher and mortars. Training was to be conducted by day and by night. It also included elements such as maintaining order, patrolling, flushing out the enemy in open country, and more. Denard stressed that "these exercises must be performed at all levels."[3]

Although Denard oversaw every detail, including the recruitment and training the Ben Guerir base in Morocco, he delegated responsibility for the technical aspects of the operation to his chief adjutant "Commander Mercier," whom he in his memoir calls "Legrand." In other words, for six weeks Denard "gave him [Legrand—added] *carte blanche* to form a super-trained team"— as detailed by French journalist[4] who participated in Opération Crevette.[5] In reality, the training exercises for some Omegas were not only much shorter than originally planned but also much more limited in their scope. However, one of the European mercenaries, Alain Chevalerias (alias Alain Marc), in his written testimony maintains that he had spent a whole month in training at the Ben Guerir Air Base.[6]

As seen in the example of newspaper advertisements being used by operation recruiters, it was expected that the European applicants be "fully qualified" "for [a] security and protection job." Preferable were former members of crack units ("crack" referring to highly disciplined and overall exceptional troops) in peak physical condition. Such requirements were met by former servicemen of French Foreign Legion, or special parachutists' intervention units. These units were provided extensive military training and had gained experience during French interventions usually in Francophonic African countries. However, what seems to have been overlooked by Denard and his recruiters was the fact that most (if not all) trained European mercenaries had a military background in conventional, as opposed to guerilla, urban type of warfare. Given their oversight, the plan of training at Ben Guerir Base was concentrated mainly on physical fitness exercises and shooting practice.

Training practice was conducted separately for the European and for the African members of the Force Omega. The European mercenaries arrived at the Ben Guerir Base about two weeks before the Beninese and Guinean members of Force Omega joined them at the base. The Europeans practiced in separate parts of the base and, due to their previous experience in the use of weapons, their shooting practice was less extensive than that of the African commando members who had limited or no practical experience in use of various types of firearms.[7]

The shooting practice and related training for Europeans took place between December 11 and 23, 1976. They began with target shooting practice at the hundred-meter range on December 11. Two days later, they practiced shooting at two hundred meters. And on December 14, 17, and 18, they carried out again target practice at two hundred meters with light assault rifles, FAL *(Fusil Automatique Léger)* and MAG (French acronym for *Mitrailleuse À Gaz*, a gas-operated machine gun), for infantry use. Expecting possible armed resistance by the Beninese military, the European members of GEI practiced using anti-tank rocket launchers (RAC) and were trained in the use of signals on December 23. A few days later, on December 30, the day of their departure from Ben Guerir, training was concentrated on the use of nine-millimeter automatic Browning pistols (PA).[8]

On December 23, 1976, a group of twelve Guinean mercenaries arrived in Casablanca on a Royal Air Maroc flight from Abidjan (Ivory Coast). Another group of twelve Guineans and three Beninese exiles arrived on December 30 on flight 984 of Royal Air Maroc from Dakar Yoff International Airport in Senegal. All of them were subsequently driven about 250 kilometers from Casablanca to Ben Guerir. There, they were met by Denard's associate, known by his *nom de guerre*, Commander Mercier, and later also by Denard who was introduced himself to them with his assumed name, Colonel Maurin.

Three days after their arrival, the African commando members began basic their military training. Only at that point did it become evident that a number of trainees lacked fluency in French, which caused communication problems with their French-speaking instructors, members of the European Omegas from GEI 1. As one of the Guinean mercenaries testified later: "most of us were illiterate people" and "[o]nly three of us could speak French."[9] The same mercenary stated that "there were quite a number of us who did not understand French. We needed extra explanations in order to understand."[10]

The training of the African mercenaries at Ben Guerir was initially planned for thirty to forty-five days; it lasted, however, only about ten days. And as would soon be discovered, the entire training proved to be ill suited for the upcoming urban military operation. Shooting practice, for example, consisted mainly of shooting in a prone position (i.e., laying down on the ground, weapon propped up using one's elbows) to a target at about six hundred feet (two hundred meters). It was generic, and rather basic, army training rarely useful in special operations requiring rapid movements and the element of surprise. Since most of the African mercenaries had never previously carried arms, many of them suffered physical injuries during training. The intensity of their training exhausted most of them both physically and psychologically. To make things worse, the results of shooting practice were "rather medio-cre"[11] since in some cases out of ten bullets given to the trainee, he was able to hit the target only with four of them.[12] When the African mercenaries complained about the insufficiency of their short training for the purpose of an armed operation, they were told that they shouldn't worry "because the Europeans would be able to do the job," and they will only carry the ammu-nition as well as carry the radio transmitters.[13] All of this, however, did not discourage Denard to later claim that the African Omegas were well trained with the Guinean Omegas, in particular, being previously trained by him per-sonally in Landes, a southern region of France.[14]

Information about training of the Omegas at the Ben Guerir Base com-ing from the accounts of Denard, Leluc, and documentation collected by the United Nations (UN) Special Mission, shows that their training did not include any rehearsal of the planned attack on Cotonou, nor did it prepare them for an urban military operation. Also, as Leluc observed, without speci-fying whether it related to only European Omega members or all GEI 1 mem-bers, Commander Mercier "used marines' method, breaking his recruits physically,"[15] which unquestionably affected their mental and physical readi-ness for the upcoming assignment Denard expected them to do.

For security reasons, all Omegas were instructed by Denard not to reveal their real names or countries of origin to one another. As described by one of the Africans, "it was completely forbidden to talk about political problems on the base, and everything that was being done there was incognito: nobody was to know our identity or nationality or countries of origin, or what we were doing there; nobody was to know about our training, about what we were supposed to do after we received our training."[16] Their contract with FLERD provided, among other things, that to maintain secrecy, the mercenaries gathered in Ben Guerir would not be allowed to leave the base on their own before the unit's departure to their final destination.[17]

DEPARTURE FOR GABON

The Opération Crevette was initially scheduled to begin on December 31, 1976. Its organizers assumed that New Year's celebrations might cause the defense readiness of the Beninese military to be weaker than usual. However, a last-minute technical problem with their old DC-7 aircraft meant to transport the Force Omega from Gabon to Benin, contrary to plans, forced Denard to re-schedule to January 15, 1977. The Beninese government would later claim that the final date of the mercenary force's landing in Cotonou was set during a secret meeting of presidents of Gabon and Togo, allegedly taking place on January 2, 1977, in village of Kouméa, Togo,[18] located just a few miles from Pya, the Togolese president's birthplace where he supposedly celebrated his birthday. Sometime after the operation, Cotonou radio *Voix de la Revolution* broadcasted a communiqué stating that the both presidents had met in the presence of "certain Colonel Bourgeaud" in the capital of Gabon, Libreville.[19] Both presidents staunchly denied that any such meeting took place, as between December 31, 1976, and January 3, 1977, President Eyadéma of Togo was visiting his native village, Pya, and President Bongo of Gabon, who visited Togo only between January 9 and 12, had remained in the country until January 14 in order to participate in tenth anniversary of President Eyadéma's accession to power. The government of Togo described Beninese accusations as "ranting,"[20] but even according to these schedules, both presidents had enough time between January 2 and 14, 1977, to discuss issues related to Opération Crevette.

Despite documents indicating that Denard had served from 1968 to 1972 as his advisor on security matters, Gabonese president Bongo vehemently denied that he ever met or knew an individual named Gilbert Bourgeaud. He further claimed that any identification documents allegedly issued to him by Gabonese authorities were falsified[21] and denied ever signing a document nominating Gilbert Bourgeaud as his advisor.[22] Interestingly, biography published on the French website *Orbs Patria Nostra*, created in memory of Denard, clearly indicates that between 1969 and 1972, he not only operated in Gabon's capital, Libreville, but that in 1975 he established there with President Bongo a group that would be known as *Clan Gabonais.* "With the help of French secret agents, Freemasons, oil, timber, uranium and manganese magnates, and the mercenaries and hard men, Bongo set up what has been called the *Clan Gabonais*, a group of operators loyal to French political parties, to France, and to Bongo."[23] This "clan" was established with the help of Maurice Robert, and the Gabonese Security Company (*Société Gabonaise des Services*, SGS).[24] as its operator that, among other things, provided protective services for buildings and installations of the French oil company Elf-Gabon. President Bongo owned, through a holding company based in Luxemburg, a controlling packet of 51 percent shares of *Société Gabonaise des Services*.[25]

Robert Maloubier, a veteran of French intelligence services who organized Bongo's Presidential Guard; Louis-Pierre (Loulou) Martin, security chief of President Bongo from 1970 to 1988, and Colonel Edouard-Marie de Bethencourt, former commander of the Gabonese Presidential Guard and co-founder of *Société Gabonaise des Services* and close acquaintance of Denard.

Thus, Denard's choice of Gabon as a base for Opération Crevette, the source of weapon supplies and air transit point, was not accidental. Through influential contacts in local politics, business, military, and security, Denard was able to use Gabon as a springboard for some of his earlier operations; Gabon "facilitated transit" of both his mercenaries and their weapons.[26] Some of those influential contacts returned back to Gabon at end of the 1960s when Denard, along with other European mercenaries, was engaged on behalf of France and with the support of the then-president of Gabon in the Biafra–Nigeria civil war on the side of the Biafran secessionists.[27] In 1976 he was even involved in the restructuring of Bongo's personal Presidential Guard.[28]

The final commando briefing took place around 4:00 p.m. WAT on January 14, 1977, a day before the departure from Ben Guerir. Denard appeared before the Omegas dressed not in the French officer uniform, but in the same uniform as the other commando members. On the top of his right jacket pocket, there were five horizontal stripes indicating the rank of an army colonel, together with the name "Maurin." But he did not wear any other insignia on his epaulet, so it was not clear for which armed forces he had been a colonel. Since Denard never served in the French army, he had never received any French officer's rank. He had, however, been nominated a colonel by President Mobutu of the Congolese army and preferred to not make clear the distinction between being promoted to French and Congolese military ranks neither to his European nor African subordinate mercenaries. Although Denard had never dressed in any French military uniform, all his associates and subordinates addressed him as a colonel.

The myth that Denard had served in the French military or that he had obtained any officer ranks in France is still prevalent in both media reports and academic literature. The fact is, according to various sources, that Denard underwent an eighteen-month training at naval school, briefly served as a gunner, and later as a mechanic in French naval colonial forces in Indochina (*Flottille amphibie Indochine Sud*, FAIS) from 1948 to 1952, where he earned the rank of petty officer of the second class, an equivalent of sergeant in the army.[29]

When two purported African civilians arrived at the base, the commando was lined up in three rows and presented to them was Mr. Wakou, the president of the unnamed African political movement, and his secretary, Mr. Tchènè (UN documents list him as "Tchinnin," an alias used by Amadou Assouma, co-leader of Pognon's party *Mouvement de la Rénovation du Dahomey*, MRD). In fact, the academic-looking Beninese Mr. Wakou was none other than FLERD representative, Gratien Pognon.

Turning to members of his commando, Denard ordered them to get rid of any items that might be used to later identify them or the country from which they came. This included their Moroccan brand cigarettes Casa Sports Olympic that had been distributed to them after arrival in Ben Guerir, instead being given a Western brands of cigarettes such as Gitanes, Pall Mall, Marlboro, and L&M. Commandos anonymized, Denard, accompanied by Pognon and Colonel Ahmed Dlimi, the chief of the Moroccan external intelligence service General Directorate for Studies and Documentation (DGED) and a personal confidant and advisor to King Hassan II (called a "king's hand" and close collaborator of French special services), conducted a military review of the commando. As Denard and Colonel Dlimi stood by, Pognon passed in front of the commando rows, and each mercenary was introducing himself to him by his alias assigned for the operation. Colonel Dlimi's presence during these events constitutes the strongest proof of Moroccan involvement in Opération Crevette.

Saturday morning, on January 15, 1977, ammunition was distributed to the Omegas. Each African Omega was to carry 655 cartridges and five grenades, some of which were incendiary. At 2:30 p.m. WAT (West African Time) the commando team was picked up from Ben Guerir Air Base by Moroccan military trucks for a short drive to the airport. At the Moroccan airport, there was another review in front of "two persons dressed in civilian clothes," the representatives of FLERD. Keeping a tight lid on the operation, the commando unit or, at least its African members, had to this point been left in the dark regarding the country where the Opération Crevette would be taking place, as well as the operation's purpose.[30] It is said, however, they predicted it would be Benin.[31] Only at the airport was it officially confirmed that they would be going to Benin to overthrow the government.[32] Denard, however, would later claim that the Omegas were not provided this information until later on, upon their subsequent arrival in Gabon.[33]

Later that Saturday, the commando and both civilians—Pognon and MRD co-leader, Amadou Assouma—departed on a DC-8–55(F) jet for a nonstop flight from Morocco over the vast landmass of West Africa, directly to Franceville, Gabon. The details of the route that the DC-8–55(F) took from Morocco to Gabon have never been revealed by the organizers of the operation or established by international bodies that investigated circumstances of Opération Crevette. According to Denard, their pilot, Jack Malloch, had previously cleared the flight of the DC-8–55(F) over the territory of Gabon with a change of aircraft at the Franceville airport with Gabonese authorities. On its route between Morocco and Gabon, the aircraft had to fly through a number of airspaces belonging to multiple African countries. It has never been revealed how, if at all, the crew obtained necessary permissions to fly over territories of those countries.

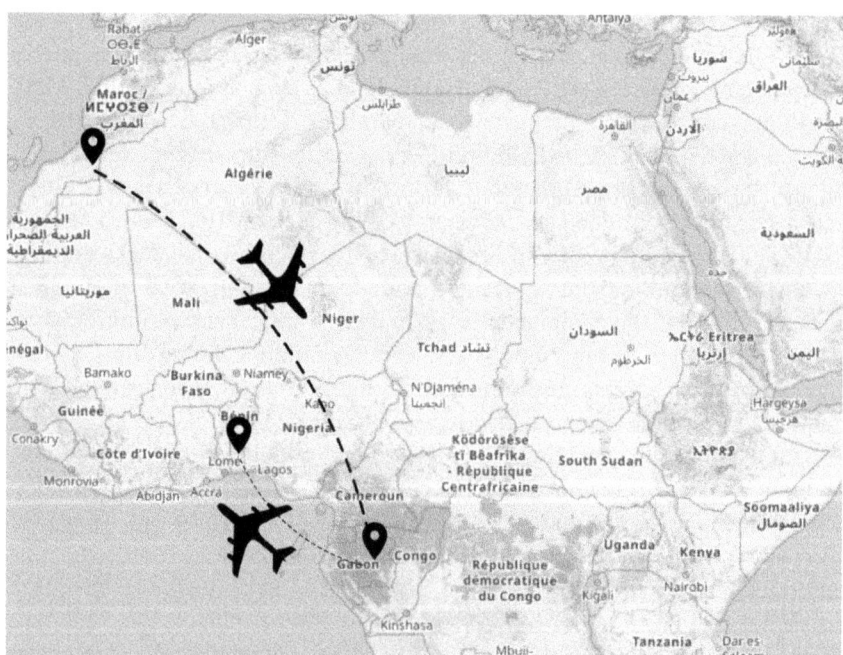

Figure 8.1. Flight path Morocco to Gabon. Credit: Author creation based on Open Source Maps.

After a five-and-a-half-hour flight, the airplane landed about 8:00 p.m. local time (WAT) at M'Vengue El Hadj Omar Bongo Ondimba International Airport at M'Vengue situated near the City of Franceville in the southeast of Gabon. M'Vengue airport was chosen for a stopover and change of the aircrafts because it shared at that its space with a military base that provided discretion and security needed for a clandestine operation. The airport was able to accept DC 8 aircrafts on its runways. There, the commando team changed their DC-8–55(F) for a smaller, four-engine DC-7(F). This change of aircraft was necessary as the runway at Cotonou airport wasn't long enough to allow for the landing of larger planes, such as their DC-8–55(F). This aircraft change in Gabon would later be denied by the Gabonese government in an attempt to avoid exposing their involvement in another African state for Opération Crevette just before the fourteenth annual Organization of African Unity (OAU) Summit Conference of the Heads of States and Governments in June/July 1977. They would maintain, from the start, "the DC-7 aircraft which allegedly transported mercenaries to Benin did not take off from Gabon."[34] Disassociating himself from what would be a failed mercenary operation in Benin was extremely important for President Bongo, as he was hosting the OAU conference of heads of state that was just to adopt the Convention of the OAU for the Elimination of Mercenarism in Africa in his country of Gabon. Article 6, titled "Obligation of States," of the convention calls on the African states to:

a. Prevent its nationals or foreigners on its territory from engaging in any of the acts mentioned in Article 1 of this Convention.
b. Prevent entry into or passage through its territory of mercenary or any equipment destined for mercenary use.
c. Prohibit on its territory any activities by persons organizations who use mercenaries against any African State member of the Organization of African Unity.[35]

As proved by documents about the Opération Crevette alongside the testimonies of the operation's participant, Alpha Bâ Oumarou, and a number of the accounts given by Denard himself, Gabon violated every prohibition against use the of mercenaries provided by Article 6 of the convention. Although the convention was not in force at the time of the events, and therefore did not bind Gabon during Opération Crevette, it was deeply embarrassing for the host of the OAU summit covering the adoption of an inter-African convention against use of mercenaries, to be involved in the operation using mercenaries against another OAU member state. Denard, however, would further recount Gabonese involvement in the series of events, claiming "the military base of Franceville, where I install[ed] them, [was] placed, for the occasion, under the protection of the presidential guard commanded by my friends Loulou Martin and his second [in command], Pinaton."[36]

Both "Loulou" Martin (Louis Pierre Martin) and Hubert Pinaton were former high-ranking French parachutist commanders, veterans of World War II, later of French Foreign Legion, and participants in lost causes in Indochina, Algeria, or Congo. Both previously met Bob Denard, who had seen France losing its war in Indochina up close and served as a mercenary in many internal conflicts in various countries of Maghreb and in Congo. The presence of these two French officers at the Franceville Military Base for providing a security cover for Denard's commando seems to indicate that French authorities either directed them to cooperate at this phase of operation or at least had a full knowledge of its execution by Denard's commando.

Knowing perfectly well that his own special services will not provide foreigners any information about Gabon's involvement in Opération Crevette, President Omar Bongo would later stand his ground, brazenly inviting an international fact-finding commission to Gabon to investigate whether the aircraft used in operation ever took off from Libreville.

NOTES

1. L. Bernichi, "A l'âge de 78 ans, Bob Denard, mercenaire français ayant," *Maghress*, October 19, 2007, https://www.maghress.com/fr/marochebdo/76312.

2. UN, Special Mission of the Security Council Established under Resolution 404 (1977), "Report of the Security Council Special Mission to the People's Republic of Benin Established under Resolution 404 (1977)": Addendum (New York: United Nations, March 8, 1977), Annex VI, 100, names of sixty-one European mercenaries have been listed.

3. Ibid., 62.

4. The authors were unable to find in documents produced as a result of United Nations Security Council Special Mission to Benin any proof of participation of Alain Leluc in the Opération Crevette.

5. Alain Leluc, "Bob Denard: Vingt ans de mercenariat," *Historia*, no. 406 (1980): 12. Leluc also wrote the novel *Mercenaire* (Paris: JC Lattès, 1983), describing his literary vision of Opération Crevette.

6. Alain Chevalerias, "OPS Omega—Raid sur Cotonou: Témoignage Alain Marc," *Orbs Patria Nostra*, statement is dated April 11, 1997, signed by Alain Chevalerias (pseudonym Alain Marc). http://www.orbspatrianostra.com/ops/ops-benin/temoignage-alain-marc.html.

7. "Benin: L'affaire du 16 janvier selon l'ONU," *Jeune Afrique*, no. 850, April 1977, 26.

8. Ibid., 46.

9. See Annex III, 69, testimony of Bâ Alpha Oumaru, a member of the attacking force, given to the Special Mission on February 19, 1977.

10. UN, Special Mission of the Security Council Established under Resolution 404 (1977), "Report of the Security Council Special Mission to the People's Republic of Benin Established under Resolution 404 (1977)" (New York: United Nations, 1977), 58.

11. Ibid., testimony.

12. Ibid.

13. Ibid., 59.

14. Bob Denard and George Fleury, *Corsaire de la République* (Paris: Robert Laffont, 1998), 288.

15. Leluc, "Bob Denard: Vingt ans de mercenariat," 12.

16. "Report of the Security Council Special Mission to the People's Republic of Benin Established under Resolution 404 (1977)," March 8, 1977, Annex III, 25.

17. Benin, "Letter Dated 77/04/04 from the Charge d'Affaires a.i. of Benin to the United Nations Addressed to the President of the Security Council," 43.

18. "Report of the Security Council Special Mission to the People's Republic of Benin Established under Resolution 404 (1977)," March 8, 1977, Annex VI, 154.

19. "Cotonou ne compte plus ses agresseurs," *Jeune Afrique*, no. 854, May 20, 1977, 72.

20. President Bongo allegedly learned about failed Opération Crevette during flight for a visit to Mauretania.

21. "Le président de la République du Gabon: 'Tout est faux,'" *Jeune Afrique*, April 29, 1977, 28.

22. Ibid.

23. Nicholas Shaxson, *Poisoned Wells: The Dirty Politics of African Oil*, first edition (New York: St. Martin's Press, 2007).

24. "Le Colonel," *Orbs Patria Nostra*, accessed November 19, 2021, https://www.orbspatrianostra.com/colonel.html; Societe Gabonaise de Securite, SGS.

25. Douglas A. Yates, *The Rentier State in Africa: Oil Rent Dependency and Neocolonialism in the Republic of Gabon* (Trenton, NJ: Africa World Press, 1996), 120.

26. Pierre Lunel, *Bob Denard: Le roi de fortune* (Edition[0] 1, 1991), 455.

27. Denard and Fleury, *Corsaire de la République*, 258–325.

28. Lunel, *Bob Denard: Le roi de fortune*, 454.

29. Leluc, "Bob Denard: Twenty Years as a Mercenary," 4; Philippe Hugounenc, *Bob Denard, l'histoire d'un homme* (Paris: Philippe Hugounenc Editeur, 2020), 24.

30. Lunel, *Bob Denard: Le roi de fortune*, 458.

31. "Report of the Security Council Special Mission to the People's Republic of Benin Established under Resolution 404 (1977)," March 8, 1977. See testimony of Alpha Ba Oumaru before UN Commission.

32. Alain Chevalerias, "OPS Oméga-Raid sur Cotonou: Témoignage Alain Marc," *Orbs Patria Nostra*, 11 April 1977, https://www.orbspatrianostra.com/ops/ops-benin/temoignage-alain-marc.html.

33. Denard and Fleury, *Corsaire de la République*, 290.

34. Gabon, "Letter Dated 22 May 1979 from the Permanent Representative of Gabon to the United Nations Addressed to the Secretary-General." (New York: United Nations, May 23, 1979).

35. "OAU Convention for the Elimination of Mercenarism in Africa" (Organization of African Unity, 1977). It entered into force only on April 22, 1985. Gabon did not sign the Convention as an original signatory and became its party by an act of accession only on December 6, 2007. Benin and Togo both signed it on July 16, 1978. Morocco has not become the party to the OAU Convention.

36. Denard and Fleury, *Corsaire de la République*, 290; Walter Bruyère-Ostells, *Dans l'ombre de Bob Denard: Les mercenaires français de 1960 à 1989* (Paris: Nouveau Monde, 2014), 75–76.

Chapter 9

Dr. Zinsou Sends the Dirty Ninety

Departure from Gabon was initially scheduled for 11:00 p.m. with an arrival in Cotonou planned for roughly two hours later, well before sunrise. Departure plans, however, were delayed for four hours due to a leak in the oil circuit of one of DC-7(F) propeller engine. This postponed take off from Franceville to the next day, which was Sunday, January 16, at about 5:00 a.m.[1] Before departure from Franceville, the commando members were given pills they were told were intended to keep them awake during the approximately two-hour-long (one hour and forty-six minutes) night flight, as well as throughout the daylight phase of the operation. Apparently, it was only during this flight to Cotonou that the African Omegas were formally informed the mission's specifics: to overthrow Benin's president, Kérékou.[2]

The delayed departure from Franceville caused the Omegas to lose out on the element of surprise necessary for their success, at least at the beginning of the operation. Their aircraft would not be landing in Cotonou at 6:00 a.m. WAT under the cover of darkness, as planned, but rather a couple minutes past 7:00 a.m. when the sun was already rising.[3] To avoid early detection, the DC-7(F)'s lights were off; since no scheduled arrival was expected before 11:15 a.m., there were no lights illuminating the runway that morning. Therefore, in order to land safely, the aircraft crew had to turn on the plane's landing lights, thus making the aircraft visible to any present ground personnel. Moreover, the DC-7(F) was to touch down without establishing of radio contact with the Cotonou control tower and asking for clearance. The plan of the operation provided for arrival at Cotonou before the control tower operators began their morning shift. All these circumstances that would otherwise make it extremely difficult, if not impossible, to safely land a passenger aircraft, would comprise the stealthy approach plan for the DC-7(F).

Although it was delayed due to technical problems before departing Libreville (Gabon), during the DC-7(F)'s approach at 7:00 a.m. WAT (West African Time), there were still no working flight controllers on duty. Their work shift on Sunday mornings would usually begin at 6:30 a.m.; however, the arrival of regular flight 801 of French airline *Union de Transports Aériens* from Paris, scheduled for 6:55 a.m. WAT, had been delayed until 11:15 a.m. This change of the UTA flight route remains one of the unexplained enigmas of Opération Crevette. The crew of UTA DC-10 aircraft received, purportedly from Cotonou control tower, a message that it could not land in Cotonou as scheduled at 6:55 a.m. and had been ordered to continue its flight direct to Abidjan, Ivory Coast.[4] None of the available accounts of Opération Crevette confirm in any way that such message to UTA DC-10 was ever sent from Cotonou airport. The only traffic controller who testified about the events of January 16, 1977, Eugene Acrombessi, testified later that according to the work schedule there was no controller on duty from midnight on Saturdays to 6:30 a.m. on Sundays; that January day, he arrived at 7:03 a.m. instead of 6:30 a.m. "because, on 16 January, no arrivals had been scheduled until 11:15 a.m."[5] It has never been publicly clarified who, in fact, directed the UTA's DC-10 crew to skip scheduled landing in Cotonou and divert the flight to Abidjan, its final destination, before resuming scheduled service to Cotonou. The original timetable of UTA flight provided for a one-hour stop-over at Cotonou's Cadjehoun Airport before departure for Abidjan. The delay of its arrival in Cotonou for four hours was enough time for the Omegas, according to the operation's plan, to successfully complete of the first phase of their operation.

The only remaining explanation for the mystery, however, lies within the Omega's pilot, John Malloch, business relations with UTA airlines person-nel and their pilots. At that time, his Affretair airline's DC-8 was flying cargo from Salisbury to Paris Charles de Gaulle Airport and was serviced there at the UTA's maintenance facility. It is, thus, feasible that an informal arrangement between UTA's personnel in Paris and Malloch, and Denard was reached resulting in change of the UTA's flight number 801's route on that particular Sunday, January 16, 1977, securing the Cadjehoun Airport for the first phase of Opération Crevette.

COTONOU AIRPORT

Cotonou International Airport is located by the sea, west of Cotonou, in the residential area of Cadjehoun District, about three miles from the city center. On Sunday, January 16, 1977, at 7:03 a.m.[6] according to eyewitnesses, or 7:30 a.m. according to Denard, an unscheduled four-engine DC-7(F) aircraft approached, from the seaward perimeter, Cotonou Cadjehoun International Airport's[7] runway 06. Descending after two hours of flight from Franceville, Gabon, over the open Bight of Benin, the aircraft approached at a low altitude of one hundred feet (thirty meters). The ninety members of Force Omega were its passengers, and this was the end of their sixteen-hour exhausting trip from Morocco via Gabon to Benin and beginning of the main phase of the land-leg of Opération Crevette.

Since the DC-7(F) was initially scheduled to land in Cotonou before sunrise on an unlit runway, an experienced crew was critical for both ensuring a safe landing without control tower assistance and obtaining the element of surprise necessary for the success of their clandestine operation. Such safe landing without control tower assistance was possible thanks to two well-experienced pilots, a veteran of World War II, DC-7, Jack Malloch, and pilot-mechanic Björn Leo Isberg.

Jack Malloch was a pioneering aviator who had been involved in numerous clandestine operations across Africa. He was, allegedly, often employed for special missions by both the CIA and the French secret service. Malloch was known for gun running against the encroachment of Communism across Africa. It was Malloch who had arranged both the DC-7(F) and DC-8–55 CF Jet Trader used for Opération Crevette.[8] One of the aircrafts used in Opération Crevette was later established to have been registered in Gabon as TR-LVKM, therefore making it the same airplane used a decade earlier by Malloch's airline, Affretair (*Compagnie Gabonaise d'Affrètements Aériens*) in Southern Rhodesian United Nations' sanction-busting flights. Affretair, headquartered in Libreville, Gabon, was formed in 1969 as a front for Malloch's 1965 commercial airline, Air Trans Africa (Pvt) Ltd. (ATA) based in Salisbury, Southern Rhodesia, after Malloch acquired a DC-8–55(F) Jet

Figure 9.1.   Stamp depicting Cotonou Airport circa 1977. Credit: Author collection.

Trader from the American-aviation-financed company Aerodyne International Incorporated in Chicago. Malloch's ATA had been active in the Rhodesian sanction-breaking operations, during which Rhodesian beef was flown by DC-7(F) to Gabon for re-transfer to European markets; by 1976, Malloch had been reported for these activities three times by Britain to the United Nations (UN). In 1964[9], Malloch gained experience smuggling soldiers when the ATA was contracted to transport European mercenaries fighting under the command of British mercenary Colonel Mike Hoare's in Congo's civil war. In 1967, Malloch's Affretair was chartered as a carrier for the delivery of supplies, mainly armaments, to the General Ojukwu's secessionist in the Biafran Civil War in Nigeria. Cotonou airport was used at that time with the approval of none other than Dahomeyan president Émile Derlin Zinsou acting upon the personal request of the French president General Charles de Gaulle[10] and under pressure from the French and US governments. After receiving a USD $3-million grant toward the country's budget, President Zinsou agreed to allow for such a flight either to originate from or to pass through the Cotonou airport. Since some such night flights to Biafra originated from Gabon, so Malloch was familiar with the flight route between Franceville or Libreville and Cotonou, as was his mechanic, Björn Leo Isberg, of South African and Swedish descent, who became familiar with the Cotonou airport runway from these same stopovers.

Both of Malloch's aircrafts, the DC-8–55(F) and DC-7(F), were now used in Opération Crevette. Since both aircrafts were palletized freighters, neither had seats on board. Thus, during both flights, the commandos sat on the fuselage floors.

In the Beninese "*chargé d'affaires* a.i. [ad interim] letter to the UN Security Council President," evidence provided by "Beninese and expatriate civilians who were present at the scene of the events" provided for the following description of the DC-7 aircraft carrying Force Omega's the landing at Cotonou airport: an "unmarked four-engine DC-7 aircraft landed at Cotonou International Airport without prior authorization from the control tower. It made a short landing on the seaward side of the runway, turned sharply at the civil aircraft taxiway and proceeded to the parking area in front of the technical buildings."[11]

Upon touchdown, the pilot disregarded the orders of airport firefighters who assumed that the unscheduled aircraft was making an emergency landing and were trying to establish radio contact with its crew. The pilots' conduct had alerted the firefighter crew, which had the capacity to contact civil or military authorities over their radio regarding the unscheduled arrival of a foreign aircraft. This would be the next, after delay of departure from Franceville, event in a series of unforeseen events that would affect the course of the operation.

According to another account, it was an airport escort car that first approached the aircraft to show it where it should park, but the pilot of the aircraft chose instead his own parking, which was few meters away from the airport terminal.[12]

During the DC-7 taxiing, the door of the plane had already been opened, and when it stopped, two metal chutes—or according to others a rope—were extended from the plane by which the Omegas slid onto the tarmac. First out from the aircraft slid two men with machine guns. These two, according to eyewitnesses, were speaking English and were dressed in jeans and blue shirts rather than the paramilitary uniforms of the following commando members who communicated in French. One of the mercenaries fired a shot toward the driver of the escort car at which point the driver of the car that was already parked behind the aircraft escaped and drove away to the town to alert the authorities.

Next, a group of white and black men carrying weapons under their armpits slid down on the ground resembling fire fighters during alarm at the station.[13] As soon as they disembarked, some members opened fire at the airport buildings and stormed both the airport control tower[14] and an adjacent airport office.[15] Two eyewitnesses relayed, however, that initial fire was directed in the air. Eugene Acrombessi, a control-tower operator at the airport, noticed that "[o]nce landed they had fired a shot in the air."[16] Similarly, Emil Badou, assistant meteorologist at the airport, saw four armed men who came down from the plane and had "begun shooting in the air and moving in different directions."[17]

Opening fire at this stage of operation was the second event that negatively affected the element of surprise, which was deemed an essential requirement for the successful operation; early in the morning, on a quiet Sunday, the sounds of automatic firearms firing were loudly heard far away from the airport located near the center of Cotonou.

The representative of the European Economic Community (now the European Union) in Cotonou testified later: "On Sunday, 16 January 1977, I heard explosions and automatic weapons fire about 7.05 a.m. . . . . The explosions and firing seemed to me come from the airport area."[18] Similar statements were made by the *chargé d'affaires* of Ghana who, although differed as to the exact time of the event "heard the sounds of heavy gun fire in the direction of the airport."[19] And ambassador of Zaire (present-day Democratic Republic of the Congo) to Benin recalled, later, on that occasion: "I was awakened by firing, an unusual sound in this city."[20] The sounds of fire were heard even further than the embassy row from the airport. Jean Meadmore, the French ambassador in Cotonou, whose residence was located closer to the city center, just on the other side of the presidential palace from the airport, stated he was awakened at approximately 7:00 a.m. by what he thought was "the noise of heavy explosions which seemed to be coming from the area of the area of the airport."[21] Similarly, the ambassador of Egypt was "awakened by the scattered echo of shots which was the result of firing cannons or guns."[22] The ambassador of the Federal Republic of Germany (now Germany) was alerted at 7:30 a.m. by a phone call from his friends "that firing had been heard in the residential area near the airport."[23] Since the Beninese regular forces, except small airport security detachment, organized the resistance efforts almost two hours later, all related above testimonies could only refer to the gunfire opened by the mercenaries after disembarking their aircraft.

Intelligence information about Cotonou's airport security previously fed to Denard indicated that the landing mercenaries should expect no armed resistance. They acted on information that only "one guard with [an] automatic pistol" protected the airport on Sunday morning.[24] However, aside from the one guard, Lieutenant Félicien Dos Santos, a small squadron of Beninese FAP (Forces armées populaires) was also present and equipped with two Panhard AML 60 light armored cars (*L'automitrailleuse légère*, AML)[25] and a jeep.[26]

The Omegas must have been surprised when they noticed Panhards approaching the building from the direction of the sea via the runway with 7.62-millimeter machine guns and sixty-millimeter mortar aimed at them. Although the plan of attack at this phase of operation specifically provided, "if no shots are fired, our chances become greater,"[27] Denard claimed that it was he[28] and "Bruni" (reference to one of the European mercenaries) who fired antitank grenades toward the approaching Panhards and immobilized both vehicles. The cannon of one Panhard had jammed so it could not respond with fire. One of the Panhard drivers had been wounded and the second instantly killed. With 3,800 stored rounds of 7.62-millimeter ammunition and forty-three to fifty-three mortar projectiles each, if sufficiently used, the Panhards could have quickly changed the course of events at the very start of the operation. When both Panhards had been immobilized, their crews "had gone to hide in the bush," but the question remains whether further use of firearms on the side of the mercenaries was, in such case, necessary.

In the meantime, observing chaos developing at the airport, Malloch, an experienced mercenary pilot, turned the aircraft in the direction required for departure. When Denard, concerned about his and his commandos safety, radioed Malloch asking why he made the maneuver, Malloch responded that such positioning would allow for quick take off "in case of disaster." Still suspicious of Malloch's real intentions, Denard blocked the front wheels of the plane by parking a vehicle found at the airport in front of the plane to prevent any premature departure of the DC-7 crew without the members of the Force Omega.

What Denard was unaware of was that an employee of airport meteorological service, Émile Badou, had arrived early to work and observed from the window of his office the group of men dressed in military uniforms dis-embarking from the unscheduled aircraft. Badou immediately alarmed the country's military command headquarters by phone. Similar calls were also allegedly made by Sergeant Major Innocent Jean-Baptiste Favi to the com-mandant of the military aviation and military headquarters to report to them the situation at the airport.[29] This was the next severe blow to the operation's plans. The Omegas were to "cut all telephone communications" and "with a little luck" control the airport telephones,[30] thus preventing any warning of their imminent attack. Unbeknownst to them, since the airport personnel could already make some phone calls to their superiors, it was too late for the Omegas to sever telecommunication between the airport and Beninese civil or military authorities to secure an effect of surprise required for the success of the operation.

As already mentioned in the chapter "Planning the Operation," the com-mando had been divided into four groups plus a command group, known as the General Staff, codenamed in French, *Soleil* (Sun). A command post had been established in the airport's waiting area, located across from the Air Afrique hangar. The General Staff, who remained at the airport to direct the operation by military radio, included Denard and his close associates.[31] Accompanying them were the two civilian representatives of FLERD, Gratien Pognon (a.k.a. Wakou) and Amadou Assouma Tchienien (a.k.a. Tchènè), along with the former Beninese army officer Marc Soglo (a.k.a. Montagne)[32] and Guinean Sy Sawame Oumar (a.k.a. Joseph).[33] All of them waited at the airport for the outcome of the first phase of the operation and, in the case of its success, were to move to Cotonou to replace the Kérékou's administration.

From the very beginning, the conditions at the airport were quite different from the ones envisioned in the plan of the operation. One of the Omegas later described these first moments at the airport:

Once we disembarked from the plane, we took our positions, but there weren't enough cars for everybody—not enough cars to carry all the men and equipment—and some men took the cars that were available, with equip-ment and headed towards the city. But then, since the military staff was only composed of six persons, there weren't enough people to staff the airport, and that's why our group was told not to go ahead with the operation consisting of occupying the road to Ouidah but to stay at the airport and then, further on go to the roof of the airport.[34]

The Red Group was a detachment of three Europeans: Adjutant Garnier, Sergent Webbs, and Sargent Chabert; four Guineans, including Alpha Bâ Oumaru and Alioune Diallo (a.k.a. Rashid); and Pognon's Beninese assistant, Lucien Zogo (a.k.a. Scorpion). The Red Group was to remain at the airport, maintain its control, protect the aircraft,[35] and provide mortar fire cover for the two groups attacking the presidential palace and army headquarters at Camp Guézo.

Faced with the assault of the Omegas, unarmed airport civilian personnel quickly escaped from the building to find safety outside its perimeter; Émile Badou and two gendarmes, Abou Samari and Sergeant Jean-Baptist Favi, however, were taken hostage and forced at gunpoint to help to unload the aircraft. As it turned out later, the fact that it was not the Omegas who unloaded the aircraft contributed to a lot of unexpected troubles for Denard and the members of his commando. Some cases with ammunition were lifted to the terrace of the air control tower, while some were left on the ground. The three Beninese were also forced to carry 12.7-millimeter machine guns and bazookas up to the tower terrace while the Omegas installed a machine gun on the roof of the tower radio transmitter.

Neutralized by the Omega's firepower, the airport security FAP unit was unable to stop the remaining three groups from setting off toward Cotonou on foot and in vehicles found at the airport, or from preventing the Red Group from mortar shelling the presidential palace and Camp Guézo. Initially, the Red Group was also supposed to hinder the movement of any troops into Cotonou trying to repel Denard's commando unit, control traffic passing on the railway tracks on the west side of the airport and adjacent to the northeast corner of the airport road (both connecting Ouidah with Cotonou), and later, to apprehend any politicians who had earlier avoided apprehension by the Omegas and could try to escape to neighboring Togo. However, because fewer Omegas were assigned to the Red Group than planned, these additional assignments were canceled.

NOTES

1. Benin, "Letter Dated 77/04/04 from the Charge d'Affaires a.i. of Benin to the United Nations Addressed to the President of the Security Council." Note: Oumaou testified that it was at 3:00 a.m., not 5:00 a.m.

2. Bob Denard and Georges Fleury, *Corsaire de la République* (Paris: Robert Laffont, 1998), 290.

3. Sunrise on January 16, 1977, was at 7:06 a.m.

4. Jacques Vignes, "Benin: Une mystérieuse agression," *Jeune Afrique*, January 28, 1977, 18.

5. UN, Special Mission of the Security Council Established under Resolution 404 (1977), "Report of the Security Council Special Mission to the People's Republic of Benin Established under Resolution 404 (1977)," 12, para. 53. Neither Acrombessi, nor any other employee of the control tower, was ever prosecuted or brought to trial before the Beninese Special Tribunal in 1979 that condemned all alleged Beninese and foreign participants of the Opération Crevette.

6. See page 5.

7. Since 2008, the International Airport Cardinal Bernardin Gantin de Cadjehoun.

8. A flight crew of three. In passenger configurations, most standard-length DC-7s seated ninety-nine in a high-density single class layout, stretched DC-7Cs seated up to 105 passengers. The capacity of the DC-7F conversion of the DC-7B is 15,700 kilograms (34,600 pounds).

9. "Roy Nesbit, Dudley Cowderoy, Sanctions Busters," *Flight International Magazine*, February 2, 1985.

10. "Le Dahomey autorise la croix-rouge à acheminer des secours à partir de son territoire," *Le Monde*, January 30, 1969, https://www.lemonde.fr/archives/article /1969/01/30/le-dahomey-autorise-la-croix-rouge-a-acheminer-des-secours-a-partir -de-son-territoire_2423063_1819218.html; Émile Derlin Zinsou, *En ces temps là . . .* (Paris: Riveneuve, 2013). In his memoires, *En ces temps la . . .* , Zinsou presents his consent to allow for the landings as a sovereign decision taken upon request from the International Red Cross and after consultations with his friends: a chief adviser for the government of France on African polic,y Jacques Foccard of France, President Bongo of Gabon, and President Houphouet Boigny of the Ivory Coast (216–19).

11. Benin, "Letter Dated 77/04/04," 16. These were the control tower and the meteorological service building.

12. CM/805 (XXVIII) Report of the Administrative Secretary-General on the Events of January 17, 1977, in Cotonou, Republic of Benin. Organization of African Unity/African Union. Council of Ministers Twenty-Eight Ordinary Session, Lome, Togo, February 21–28, 1977, 2, https://archives.au.int/handle/12356789/9824.

13. Denard and Fleury, *Corsaire de la République.* (Some eyewitnesses claimed that Omegas disembarked aircraft using ropes); "Benin: Ou est la verite?" *Jeune Afrique*, March 18, 1977. (This version also found in UN Special Missions reports: two ropes had been hanging down.)

14. Benin, "Letter Dated 77/04/04," 16.

15. Ibid.

16. Ibid.

17. Ibid., 17.

18. UN, Special Mission of the Security Council Established under Resolution 404 (1977), "Report of the Security Council Special Mission to the People's Republic of Benin Established under Resolution 404 (1977): Addendum" (New York: United Nations, March 8, 1977), see Annex II, 3.

19. Ibid., 4.

20. Ibid., 5.

21. Ibid.

22. Ibid., 7.

23. Ibid., 6.

24. Ibid., Annex VI, 92.

25. Denard and Fleury, *Corsaire de la République*, 291.

26. Philippe Akpo, *Role et implications des forces armees beninoises dans la vie politique nationale: Temoignage, ma part de vérité sur les faits et les non-dits* (Paris: Éditions du Flamboyant, 2005), see 216. AMLs were operated at that time

by garrison in Ouidah located forty kilometers from Cotonu. Beninese army (FRAP) lieutenant Felicien Dos Santos, who was present at the airport on January 16, 1977, described the vehicles as *Ferrets* (British-made armored cars).

27. "Report of the Security Council Special Mission to the People's Republic of Benin Established under Resolution 404 (1977)," see Annex VI, 137.

28. Denard and Fleury, *Corsaire de la République*, 291. Quote: "I grasp an assault rifle armed with an antitank grenade, aim at the first intruder and immobilize him in the middle of a cloud of black smoke."

29. CM/805 (XXVIII) Report of the Administrative Secretary-General on the Events of January 17, 1977, in Cotonou, Republic of Benin. Organization of African Unity/African Union. Council of Ministers Twenty-Eight Ordinary Session, Lome, Togo, February 21–28, 1977, 4; https://archives.au.int/handle/12356789/9824.

30. "Report of the Security Council Special Mission to the People's Republic of Benin Established under Resolution 404 (1977)," see Annex VI, 137.

31. Christian Garnier (a.k.a. Alain Fournier), Michel Loiseau (a.k.a. Bosco), Tanguy, and Verdier.

32. Marc Soglo, became, later, *officier supérieur des forces Armées Béninoises*, died July 20, 2008.

33. Benin, "Letter Dated 77/04/04 from the Charge d'Affaires a.i. of Benin to the United Nations Addressed to the President of the Security Council." Described by the Beninese authorities as "Political Commissar of the attack of Sunday 16 January 1977," 57.

34. "Report of the Security Council Special Mission to the People's Republic of Benin Established under Resolution 404 (1977)," see Annex III, 30.

35. Ibid., 59. Bâ Alpha Oumaru described Red Group as composed of four Guineans, one Beninese, and three Europeans.

Chapter 10

The Omegas Are Coming

The execution of the operation on land by the Omegas was to be divided into several stages. Denard claimed that even before signing a contract with FLERD, he instructed "a young officer, Lieutenant Gerard, to make a short reconnaissance trip to Cotonou. He allegedly brought from Benin "a precise assessment of the armed forces of Kérékou as well as details on their location."[1]

It seems that Denard was never shy to claim French intelligence agencies' support or at least, like in the case of Benin, encouragement to conduct a specific mercenary operation, had either not resorted this time to SDECE or had not received accurate information about Beninese military and its defense potential. Thus, based upon intelligence obtained by Lieutenant Gerard, no meaningful resistance by the Beninese army was expected during at least the initial phases of the operation, and especially not before leaving the airport by the assault groups.

One of the most important issues in the planning of a covert operation is the time at which to strike. In this case, it was the choice of proper day and time for landing of the commando at the Cotonou International Airport to obtain a necessary effect of surprise on a local military. Denard initially considered landing his commando in Cotonou on Wednesday, January 5, 1977, at 6:45 a.m., just minutes before sunrise. The date was chosen because, on that day, there used to be a weekly meeting of the Council of Ministers at the presidential palace held between 10:30 a.m. and noon. It is unclear why Denard chose Wednesday instead of Tuesday, a day he knew that they regularly used also meet at the presidential palace, the PRPB Political Bureau, and such meetings were attended by all political leaders who, according to the operation plan, were to be "neutralized" or "eliminated by the Omegas." Also, Denard was fully aware that participants of the Wednesday meeting use to be accompanied by "considerable defense reinforcements (each minister brings two or three guards with him)."[2] Then, the date of the Force Omega in Cotonou was moved to the night of Friday, December 31, 1976, and later changed to Saturday, January 1, 1977. The choice of such a date was dictated by the assumption that, although the Marxists, all Beninese political and military leadership will celebrate New Year's Eve, and the country's defense would loosen more than usual, what would make "that assault will have all chances for success."[3] However, even this arrival date in Benin was finally moved to January 15, 1977. Unforeseen delays forced operation organizers to change, yet again, the date of landing at Cotonou airport to the next day, Sunday, January 16, 1977. First, the aircraft used for transporting of mercenaries to their destination at Cotonou was not ready for operation. Second, the Omegas who underwent military training had not completed their training on time to participate in operation now scheduled for January 15, 1977.

Thus, Denard finally moved the date of landing in Cotonou to January 16, 1977, because he had been informed that "on Sunday, the Beninese army kept a mobile group of twenty-five men on the alert with only a few armored cars and two or three jeeps."[4] Such information about the Beninese army schedule, seems to be almost all what could be obtained in way of observation by Lieutenant Gerard during his brief, one week, visit in Cotonou about size, locations, and readiness of the Beninese army units to be able to repel a mercenary unit assault on the country's capital.

Denard also relied on intelligence information from "various studies" made by the opposition leaders, which suggested that there are "all necessary and adequate prerequisites for the defeat of the present régime, with maximum chances for success." He was assured by the opposition that "the means at their disposal have been thoroughly studied and only little 'push' is needed to ensure victory."[5] Especially encouraging must have been information that "[t]he loyalty of the armed forces as a whole is uncertain" and that some units, such as First Company stationed in Ouidah and First Squadron stationed in Porto-Novo "are ready for an uprising."[6]

Judging from the intelligence information fed to Denard, its primary source was most probably not just Lieutenant Gerard, as mentioned by Denard, but rather various exile opposition activists living abroad, like those accused of working with SDECE and for support of Opération Crevette (i.e., Émile Zinsou, Gratien Pognon, Andrien Houngbédji, Bertin Borna Baliba, Paul Darboux, Idelphonse Lemon, Amadou Fousséni ("Tchinin") or Beninese army deserter, Marc Soglo,[7] who joined the Omegas[8]).

The intelligence service SDECE had prior knowledge of the preparations for Opération Crevette. From the SDECE came, probably, information about regular meetings of Beninese political leadership in a particular location on a specific day and time. Denard himself related that before he decided to run Opération Crevette, he consulted the decision with his anonymous "SDECE contacts," who encouraged him to accept this assignment because France had "every interest in seeing Kérékou removed from power."[9] Information about Denard's consultations with then–SDECE leadership is confirmed by Maurice Robert, former Chef African Sector at SDECE, who reveals that Denard met, looking for approval of his plan, with General Jeannou Lacaze, director of intelligence at SDECE, who allegedly gave his consent to cover operation in Benin.[10]

In a document titled "Mission: To Eliminate the Present Regime—Install the New Team from FLERD," Denard presented a brief description of the fourth phases of an ambitiously planned war-like military operation:

> Firstly, to make a surprise landing of the entire Force OMEGA at the Cotonou International Airport and to control the installations there.

> Secondly, to proceed as rapidly as possible eastward to attack and occupy pre-determined objectives . . . while guarding the northwest (the Ouidah/Calavi/ Cotonou railway axis).

> Thirdly, to control the entire western part of the city, . . . while maintaining coverage toward the west.

> Fourthly, according to developments, to take measures aimed at establishing control over the whole territory of the country.[11]

Even a cursory glance at the above plan tells that Denard was pattering conduct of Opération Crevette on his experience gained during mercenary operations in the 1960s in Congo, where considerable units of European mercenaries, often backed up by Congolese local army units, rebel groups, or militias, were conducting military operations on big, scarcely inhabited swaths of that country. Such operations were also characterized by the training and armament superiority of the mercenary forces over rebel or separatist groups they were fighting against. It seems that, based on the intelligence information provided to him, Denard, without personal knowledge of country conditions, prepared the plan of the operation heavily relying on the active support of both elements of the Beninese army units and, no less important, a simultaneous uprising against Mathieu Kérékou's regime by the local population although, he was already aware of "lack of enthusiasm on the part of the opponents of the regime inside the country."[12] In other preparatory documentation, Denard correctly observes that while the loyalty of the entire population to Kérékou's regime "is not an established fact, it is nevertheless certain that Kérékou enjoys the support of a significant majority of workers in Cotonou, the large majority of youth and *virtually the entire army*" (emphasis added).[13]

Developing the plan of Opération Crevette, Denard was told that armed forces of Benin, *Forces Armées Populaires du Bénin*,[14] consisted of approximately one thousand men, including forty officers. The law enforcement, National Police (*Police Nationale*) had also approximately one thousand officers. This was probably the reason why he recruited ninety men for the operation.

As a result, the first operational stage was planned rather optimistically to take place roughly thirty to sixty minutes after the commando's *surprising* landing. The Omegas were to:

1. Attack and take over the presidential palace.
2. Attack Kérékou's private residence.
3. "Neutralize" the president and the army unit stationed at the military Camp Guézo.

At the military camp, the Force Omega members were instructed to "aim at rapid occupation with, if necessary, destruction of persons, equipment, and installations."[15] During this phase, Denard planned that "we shall need about five minutes to reach the gates of the Presidential Palace or the Military Camp and two minutes at best to reach the house of K [Kérékou]."[16] All three objectives should be dealt with simultaneously.

During the second stage, planned to take place between sixty- and ninety-minutes post-landing, the Omegas were to breach the western part of the town to find and neutralize individuals who might operate telephone and telegraph services, police stations, and the radio station. What remains relatively unclear, however, is how they intended to identify any such individuals during their short window of time except by counting on the public's voluntary support of the operation.

The third stage was scheduled to last 120 to 180 minutes, at which point Denard intended to establish control over the western part of Cotonou. He would consolidate the city by controlling the bridge over the Lagoon de Cotonou that connected two sections of the city; this would prevent access to the port and allow the commandos to keep a watch on the town toward the north, thus guarding against the possibilities of unrest, a national radio broadcast of propaganda material regarding the coup d'état, and the imposing of a city curfew. Denard also intended to train and use any Beninese army units that "would come over to the side of the Force [Omega]"; the coup sponsors assured had assured him that army units would join the Omegas when called to action. With the use of joint mercenary and local Beninese forces, the putschists would then block road access to Cotonou, allowing them to take control of Cotonou's seaport facilities and thus, cut off access for any possible navy forces dispatched to Benin in support of Kérékou's government.

According to Denard's plan, taking control over Cotonou should take Omegas no more than three hours from the time the Omegas land at the local airport.

Following the anticipated success of all the three initial coup operational stages, the putschist hoped to install the representatives of the FLERD roughly five to six hours after their landing. The FLERD representatives were those waiting at the airport for the outcome of the operation, along with Dr. Zinsou, who at the time just so happened to be at a hotel in Rabat, Morocco. The representatives would be protected by a detachment of the Omegas designated responsible for their security. At this point, the putschists expected to obtain the support of Cotonou's civilian population for the regime change. "A new government, made up of new men, would be rapidly accepted," noted the operation's planners.

The final two phases, installation of the new authorities, were planned for lasting several days. The putschists would take control of main population centers and, subsequently, of the whole country.

According to the documents describing preparation for the operation, the Force Omega would operate in four groups directly involved in fighting, and a small command directing the actions of those groups from its post at the Cotonou International Airport.

The division of the Force Omega was planned as follows:[17]

- Command (Staff) (called Sun; *Soleil*) composed of six members: four Europeans—Bob Denard (alias Colonel Maurin), Lieutenant Verdier, and Lieutenant Tanguy; and three Africans—Gratien Pognon (alias Mr. Wakou), Amadou Fousséni Tchinnin (alias Freddy), and Marc Soglo (alias Montagne).
- Fighting groups:
  - Yellow Group—Support Covering Group, composed of twenty-five European mercenaries, assigned yellow (*jaune*) ribbons.
  - Red Group—Covering Group West, nine members, assigned red (*rouge*) ribbons.
  - Blue Group—composed of twenty-nine, mainly European mercenaries, assigned blue (*bleu*) ribbons.
  - Black Group—group of twenty-four Africans, assigned black (*noir*) ribbons.

It was the order in which Force Omega members were soon to meet the reality on the ground in Benin.

NOTES

1. Bob Denard and Georges Fleury, *Corsaire de la République* (Paris: Robert Laffont, 1989), 288.

2. S/12319/Add. 1, 30.

3. Denard and Fleury, *Corsaire de la République*, 290.

4. Alain Chevalerias, "OPS Oméga-Raid sur Cotonou: Témoignage Alain Marc," *Orbs Patria Nostra*, April 11, 1977, https://www.orbspatrianostra.com/ops/ops-benin /temoignage-alain-marc.html.

5. S/12319/Add.1, 24.

6. Ibid.

7. All these individuals were granted on August 30, 1989, amnesty by Assamblée Nationale Révolutionnaire (ANR, parliament) by its decision 89–010. See Francis Kpatindé, "Bénin: Pardon pour les 'impénitents,'" *Jeune Afrique*, no. 1500, October 2, 1989, 38–39.

8. Maurice Robert, *Maurice Robert, "ministre" de l'Afrique*: *Entretiens avec André Renault* (Paris: Seuil, 2004), 238.

9. Denard and Fleury, *Corsaire de la République*, 287.

10. Robert, *Maurice Robert, "ministre" de l'Afrique*, 238.

11. S/12319/Add.1, 26.

12. Ibid., 27.

13. Ibid., 76.

14. On March 25, 1977, the official name of Benin armed forces was changed to Forces Armées Populaires du Bénin.

15. UN, Special Mission of the Security Council Established under Resolution 404 (1977), "Report of the Security Council Special Mission to the People's Republic of Benin Estabilshed under Resolution 404 (1977): Addendum" (New York: United Nations, March 8, 1977), Annex VI, 10.

16. Ibid., 13.

17. Ibid., 51, 55. Anthony Mockler, *The New Mercenaries: The History of Hired Soldiers from the Congo to the Seychelles* (New York: Paragon House Publishers, 1987), 245, show somehow different numbers of the mercenaries belonging to particular groups of the Force Omega.

Chapter 11

Facing Reality

SURPRISE SURPRISE

The plan for Opération Crevette assumed that the Beninese military and the local population would actively support the intervening mercenary forces. The plan therefore provided for, at some point of the operation, joint military action involving both the foreign mercenaries and the local Beninese putschists acting on behalf of an opposition leader who was intending to return to power in Benin.

Denard's military part of the plan of the Opération Crevette was described in one of the documents pertaining to operation in which he listed in order of priority the following objectives. These included to:

1. Seize or destroy President Mathieu Kérékou and, if possible, his friends.
2. Occupy the presidential palace.
3. Surround and deactivate Camp Guézo "with a view to preventing any possibility of immediate or future intervention."
4. Occupy the national radio station in order to use it for their own propaganda.
5. Neutralize and later try to obtain cooperation of local gendarmerie and police.
6. Keep the control of the airport and obtain control over the Cotonou commercial port with aim of blocking to it an access from outside and inside Benin.[1]

All these aims were to be accomplished within the first thirty to sixty minutes after the Omegas landed at the airport. Such an ambitious plan for the coup d'état provided also for the simultaneous, with military assistance for expected local supporters of the coup, the establishment of the new governing team and the spread of putschists' authority over the entire country. In his plan Denard also reckoned with the possibility of a counteraction from the outside, most probably by forces of another socialism oriented African country.

As previously discussed, according to the United Nations (UN) Special Security Council Mission report, the Omegas and local Beninese putschists were supposed to be backed by a unit of Togolese Special Forces called the Second Combat Commando, which would be waiting in Togo for a call to action in Benin. Such a unit was, along with the Omegas, part of the Foreign Intervention Group acting in support of the operation conducted by the Omegas. The Togolese government vehemently denied their presence on the border with Benin on January 16, 1977, and of any such mercenary or Togolese Special Forces unit.[2]

Planners of the operation assumed that garrison in Cotonou would have about six hundred stationed soldiers and policemen. In fact, the number of troops stationed at the Camp Guézo barracks was about three hundred of a total estimated number of country's troops of 1,300 plus police personnel. The rest of the troops were stationed in various regions around the country. The elite 120-member parachutist battalion garrisoned in Ouidah, for example, would not be able, in the case of sudden foreign military attack, to provide immediate support to Cotonou due to the driving distance between the two cities.

The military readiness of Cotonou had been characterized in the plan of the operation with a pinch of disdain. The information, provided by leaders of the Beninese opposition in exile, led Denard to believe that loyalty of the Beninese military to President Kérékou was questionable at best, making some army units ready for rebellion. In a document pertaining to the situation,[3] the planners stated, "The armed forces in the capital would be divided [in] regards [to] their feelings for K. [Kérékou] and his friends. Only the presidential guards would appear to be devoted to him." Whatever loyalty persisted amongst them for Kérékou, Denard counted on the fact that "although these troops have certain bearing, it must be pointed out that they have no combat experience, their training has not been 'Spartan.'"[4]

The Presidential Guard (*Bataillon de la Gardé Présidentielle*, BGB) consisted of 450 Muslim ethnic Fulani minority men supportive of Kérékou's regime, equipped with better weaponry than the Beninese army and trained by North Korean instructors in thwarting military coup attempts and social disturbances. The BGB constituted a counterbalance for the 120-troop battalion stationed in nearby Ouidah, consisting mainly of soldiers recruited from the largest Beninese ethnic Christian group, Fon. Additionally, at Kérékou disposal remained the regular Armed Forces of Benin, the national gendarmerie, special services called Section 2 (*Section Deux*) and units of popular militia.[5]

KOREAN SURPRISE

The most consequential surprise for the Force Omega was the unexpected presence in Cotonou of North Korean military personnel. Denard's various versions of the plan of Opération Crevette had not included any remarks about possible encounters with the North Korean military personnel known to train the Beninese soldiers. It is likely that this is explained by the fact that the number of North Korean military instructors was so few that neither the SDECE nor French military attaché nor chief of a military mission at the embassy in Cotonou considered such information to be essential. One can also exclude the eventuality that the personnel of the French embassy in Cotonou was kept in the dark about the plan to overthrow Mathieu Kérékou and for the regime change in Benin. Whichever might be true, Denard did not consider the element of North Korean military instructors in his plans for Opération Crevette.

As if that was not enough, unbeknownst to Denard—as well as to the other coup organizers (such as Zinsou, for example) and supporters present in Cotonou at the time of the mercenary attack—aside from the military instructors, there was an unknown number of well-armed North Korean military and diplomatic security detachment personnel accompanying a visiting high-level political delegation from Pyongyang. The reason for its presence in Cotonou during Opération Crevette is still disputed: was it pure coincidence, an already scheduled state visit, or a last-minute organized counteraction against a forthcoming mercenary invasion? Neither the government of Benin nor North Korea has released any public explanation for the visit, or any information about the accompanying North Korean delegation armed security detachment. However, there is information in the UN Special Mission report to Benin confirming the presence of the North Korean armed diplomatic security personnel accompanying a North Korean ministerial delegation.

One version of the story prevailing in post-Kérékou era Beninese media is that the deputy prime minister and foreign minister of North Korea, Ho Dam, accompanied by the military security detail, arrived for a state visit on January 14, 1977, two days before Force Omega landed in Cotonou. The decision of the Beninese government to meet with the North Korean delegation was approved by the Beninese Council of Ministers only on January 12, 1977, and published in the official newspaper a day later.

This version of the story supports that public information was published on January 13, 1977, in the official Beninese daily newspaper, *Ehuzu*. The information was buried on page 6 in the text of the press release from the Council of Ministers meeting on January 12, 1977. The paragraph about the North Korean delegation visit reads as follows: "Minister of Foreign Affairs and Cooperation has submitted to the Council of Ministers for approval the program of the visit in our country from 15 to 18 January 1977, Comrade Heu[6] Dam, Deputy Prime Minister and Minister of Foreign Affairs of the Democratic People's Republic of North Korea."[7]

The language of the paragraph suggests that the visit of Ho Dam's delegation to Cotonou had already been scheduled and that, during the January 12 meeting, the Beninese government approved a specific program for that visit. Since both countries maintained diplomatic relations as of 1973, the invitation had probably been extended, and the provisional visit program scheduled earlier through diplomatic channels as a return visit for the February 1976 visit of Mathieu Kérékou in Pyongyang. In such a case, the Council of Ministers only detailed the program that the Ministry of Foreign Affairs and Cooperation prepared. Only then did it become a publicly known timeline of the North Korean delegation's visit to Benin. This could explain why the French intelligence might have been unaware of it and, thus, could not have warned Denard.[8]

Such an explanation of North Korean military detachment presence in Benin had been recently questioned by the Beninese historian, professor Adékpédjou Sylvain Akindes, the author of a three-volume history of contemporary Benin. In his opinion, it is highly impossible that a high-level state delegation from North Korea would be visiting Benin on such short notice without having been officially announced, as generally customary, "unless it is a version invented to justify the presence of foreign soldiers."[9] In his opinion, everything leads one to believe that the presence of the North Korean soldiers this day was hardly due to a chance. Mathieu Kérékou was probably well informed of the attack that was coming and could make arrangements for defense. "It is now certain"—maintains Sylvain Akindes—"that Mathieu Kérékou was informed of the invasion and the date when it was to take place." Allegedly it was Karim da Silva (a Beninese political actor, editor's note) who admitted that he had passed the information about the forthcoming attack to Eustache Prudencio, at the time Benin's ambassador to Lagos. According to the testimonies of certain advisers to the Presidency at the time of the events, the latter had been asked not to appear at the Palace of the Republic on 16 January 1977."[10] This version of events is at least questionable. As much as one could accept that Mathieu Kérékou received an advanced warning about a forthcoming invasion of foreign mercenaries and requested the presence of North Korean dignitaries along with his security detachment, it was apparent even from his personal experience that such detachment would consist of rather limited number of armed men. Ho Dam's security detachment included only fifteen armed personnel. Even unaware of the number of mercenaries involved in the operation, Mathieu Kérékou, a military man, could not reasonably assume that several members of a foreign dignitary security personnel would be able to repel the attack of the unknown number of foreign mercenaries of unknown quality of their military experience or training. Had Kérékou known or expected the arrival of foreign mercenaries, shouldn't he order to reinforce border protection by the Beninese military or gendarmery, especially at the only international airport in Cotonou? Lastly, the Korean diplomatic security detachment would rather have to protect the members of the delegation than get involved in fight with the foreign mercenaries on streets of Cotonou. It should be its main, if not only, assignment.

The North Korean delegation arrived in Cotonou on January 14, 1977, and the official visit was scheduled for three days: from January 15 to 18, 1977. The coincidence of dates between arrival of the North Koreans and arrival by the Force Omega created grounds for speculation that Beninese government scheduled Ho Dam's visit for that specific time. Interestingly, however, in his long speech given at the farewell dinner at Hotel Croix du Sud, Ho Dam condemned the mercenary aggression against Benin, although he did not mention any role of North Korean soldiers, congratulating only "the Beninese people" of defense of the Marxist-Leninist state.[11]

In the statement to the UN Security Special Mission, Ho Dam did not mention any activity of his security detachment, although he did state that "the mercenaries had occupied the building and the area around it."[12] Beninese adjutant Christophe Agossa reported that when passing Omegas noticed a North Korean flag on the *Conseil de l'Entente,* the headquarters of an association of six French-speaking West African states, they entered the building "in an effort to find the Deputy Prime Minister [Ho Dam]," but "they had not succeeded" and only shot Ho Dam's driver who was washing his car outside.[13] Yet another witness, the *maître d'hotel* who came to the building to serve breakfast for the North Korean delegation testified in reference to the mercenaries' presence in the building that he "had been threatened by an armed white man wearing paratrooper jacket and military trousers."[14] Thus, it seems that North Korean security detachment did not participate in any exchange of fire with the mercenaries to protect the residence hosting the North Korean delegation at *Conseil de l' Entente.* The only explanation for that fact might be that the detachment members were for some reason stationed at a location different than *Conseil de l'Entente.* Since they were in the People's Republic of Benin, another friendly socialist state, they could have been accommodated at Camp Guézo, along with the North Korean military instructors already serving at that time in Benin. When President Mathieu Kérékou declared an alert and called for action, they probably joined the military instructors to accompany the Beninese soldiers to repel the Omegas assault on Cotonou.

In two recently published articles in Beninese electronic media, their authors submit yet another explanation regarding the location of North Korean soldiers on the day of the Force Omega assault. Both authors place North Koreans at the presidential palace during the mercenary assault. According to one, the North Koreans supported the president and the Presidential Guard defending the Marina Palace.[15] However, placing the president at the time of Omegas assault at the presidential palace seems to be inconsistent with testimonies of the soldier eyewitness who places Mathieu Kérékou at that time at Camp Guézo. The other author, a Beninese historian, writes, without specifying which North Korean unit he is referring to, about "the presence of North Korean soldiers *at the presidency the same day.*"[16]

Nothing in the intelligence information provided to Denard by his sources or in his plan of Opération Crevette ever referred to the possible presence of North Korean military advisers or soldiers in Benin, some of whom were already present in Cotonou under a military assistance treaty between the two countries.[17] One can only explain it by the customary extreme secrecy of Communist countries regarding any issues related to military matters.

NOTES

1. UN, Special Mission of the Security Council Established under Resolution 404 (1977), "Report of the Security Council Special Mission to the People's Republic of Benin Established under Resolution 404 (1977): Addendum" (New York: United Nations, March 8, 1977), see Annex VI, 9–10.

2. "Le réponse de Togo," *Jeune Afrique*, no. 854, May 20, 1977, 35.

3. Titled "Particular Situation in the Capital."

4. "Report of the Security Council Special Mission," see Annex VI, 132–33.

5. Mathurin C. Houngnikpo and Samuel Decalo, *Historical Dictionary of Benin* (Lanham, MD: Scarecrow Press, 2012), 140; Alan Bryden and Boubaca N'Diaye, *Gouvernance du secteur de la sécurité en Afrique de l'Ouest francophone: Bilan et perspectives*, first edition (Wien: LIT, 2011), 25–29.

6. This original spelling of his name in Beninese media and official documents. The proper spelling is Ho Dam.

7. *Ehuzu*, no. 309, January 13, 1977, 6.

8. François Kouyami, *Affaires d'état au Bénin: Le général François Kouyami parle: Livre- interview, Les grandes interviews* (L'Hay-les-Roses, France: Les Editions IBIDUN, 2011). The Council of Ministers approved the visit program for this individual during their meeting on Wednesday, January 12, 1977.

9. Adékpédjou Sylvain Akindes, *Essai d'histoire du temps présent au Bénin postcolonial. Tome II; 1972–1990; L'équipée révolutionnaire (Problématique d'un engagement politique)* (Cotonou: Star Éditions, 2017), 224.

10. Ibid., 224, 226.

11. *Ehuzu*, January 19, 1977, 3.

12. S/12294/Rev. 1, 10, para. 49.

13. Ibid., 25, para. 106.

14. Ibid., 25, para. 107.

15. Le Souvenir du 16 Janvier 1977: http://newsyoung.fr/benin-le-souvenir-du-16 -janvier-1977/.

16. Emphasis added. Serge Ouitona, "7 décembre 1989–7 décembre 2019: Il y a 30 ans, Mathieu Kérékou virait sa cuti," *Afrik.com*, December 7, 2019, https:// www.afrik.com/7-decembre-1989-7-decembre-2019-il-y-a-30-ans-mathieu-kerekou -ravalait-ses-vomissures.

17. In his book, *Corsaire de la Républic* (1998), published eleven years after Opération Crevette, Robert Laffont writes about the presence of North Korean military personnel in Cotonou and the effect of its presence on the result of the operation.

Chapter 12

A Three-Hour Disaster

Radio monitoring of *Voix de la Révolution* broadcasts showed that at 7:15 a.m.—only a couple minutes after the DC-7(F), carrying the Force Omega, had landed at Cadjehoun Airport and roughly twenty minutes before the radio station informed the public of the mercenary attack—the station sent a call for armed personnel to proceed to the airport in order to destroy the foreign aircraft and create a crater in the runway. Twenty minutes later, this order was retracted for a new one—this time, to build blockades on roads and dams of the Cotonou Lagoon (*Lagune de Cotonou*), which divided the city into two parts, in order to block marine traffic on the Quémé River, bordering Nigeria and flowing into the Atlantic Ocean near Cotonou. About two hours after the Omegas disembarked and launched their attack, the *Voix de la Révolution* commenced broadcasting President Kérékou's appeal to the Revolutionary Defense Brigades (composed of young civilian activists supporting the Kérékou revolution) and Cotonou's residents to repel the attack, block all roads out of the Cotonou, and "track down all the mercenaries and their agents, whether they white or black, flush them out and arrest them."[1] Doctors and nurses were also called to report to Cotonou hospitals. In response, volunteers began gathering in various parts of Cotonou. The Beninese authorities had commandeered all city cabs to deprive the attackers of any additional means of transportation, as well as national lottery vehicles equipped with loudspeakers[2] to reach more city residents with calls for action. Warned over the radio of the foreign attack, Beninese ships anchored in Cotonou port turned on the alarm sirens.

Surprised by the sudden attack at the airport and movement of unknown assailants into the heart of Cotonou, the Beninese military commenced organizing ad hoc defense. Their primary task was allocated to First Mixed Mechanized squadron in Ouidah under the command of Lieutenant Philippe Akpo. Although Akpo's unit was equipped with fast, long-ranged light-armored Panhard AMLs, due to the time needed to arrange an orderly departure from the Ouidah military camp and to cover the nearly twenty-two miles (forty-two kilometers) between Ouidah and Cotonou, it was unable to join the Presidential Guard and other troops offering resistance against attacking mercenaries. Ironically, its move toward Cotonou was also delayed by the necessity of crossing of multiple roadblocks raised on its route by the civilian population responding to radio broadcasts calling for a defense of the capital against an attack by foreign invaders. Colonel Akpo's troops reached the vicinity of Camp Guézo at about 9:30 a.m. By that time, some mercenaries had already been wounded—including a Belgian who was shot in the arm that had to be later amputated—and were forced to withdraw from direct participation in the attack.

OMEGA'S ASSAULT

While the Red Group held their ground at Cotonou's Cadjehoun Cardinal Bernadin Airport, the other three groups advanced toward their designated targets on foot and in a few commandeered vehicles found in the airport parking lot. Since the airport was not yet open for business, there were only a small number of cars available for use by the Omegas. Unable to accommodate all commando members designated to attack the operation's two main targets—the presidential palace and Camp Guézo—two more vehicles were carjacked from French citizens who happen to come to the airport to pick up their mail. One of them recalled that just a few minutes after 7:00 a.m., as they approached the airport, they "were stopped by the soldiers with the rifles in their hands who forced us to give them our cars."[3] Some of these requisitioned cars were found a few hours later back at the airport, covered in blood.

Considering the distance from Cajdehoun Airport to each target of attack, the Omegas would have to move at roughly thirty kilometers an hour via

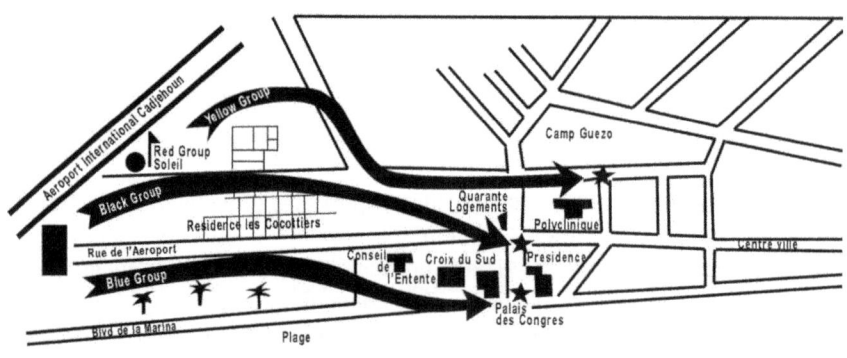

Figure 12.1. Three groups, movements. Credit: Author creation.

Boulevard de la Marina or Route de l'Aéroport to cover the two-mile (3.2-kilometer) distance in their limited twenty-five minutes. The lack of vehicles at the airport, however, meant most of the Omegas were forced to walk on foot, disrupting their timeline of attack. Thus, further impacting any element of surprise that may have been left.

The residents of buildings adjacent to the airport were abruptly awakened around 7:00 a.m. by the sound of gunfire. They observed the squad of about thirty bareheaded European and African paratroopers walk through the coconut grove on the seaside of the street from the airport in the direction of the presidential palace. The Europeans wore camouflage uniforms adored with blue arm bands on their epaulets and had reddish faces, as if they had suffered sunburns during their pre-operational training in the Moroccan Ben Guerir Air Base. Accompanying them, the Africans were dressed in khaki uniforms and were wearing yellow arm bands and bush hats. What astounded eyewitnesses was the strangers' demeanor. They were said to have marched through the coconut grove from the airport to the palace, casually shooting left and right. In a cable from the American embassy in Cotonou to Washington, DC, onlookers reported the Omegas "walked from the airport with guns slung over their shoulders, looking neither right nor left, and certainly showing no signs of alertness to counterattack." The author of the message added, "We can find absolutely no one who saw a battle of any kind with one side shooting at the other. Instead, onlookers from both near and far describe all shooting by the invaders as being either into the air or empty buildings."[4] A European diplomat who had observed the Omegas moving toward the palace related, "They acted as if they didn't have care in the world. It was as if they were on some sort of maneuver."[5] Some of the Omegas went so far as to take long cigarette breaks between randomly shooting at the buildings they were passing.

The Blue Group—comprised of twenty-nine, mainly European mercenaries—was the southernmost advancing group. During the first phase of the operation, they proceeded from the airport, across the beach, and subsequently through the coconut palm groves adjacent to the two-way Boulevard de la Marina. Advancing in a single-file combat formation using the double-lane asphalt road between the Boulevard de la Marina and Interstate Highway (RNIE1) linking Cotonou and Ouidah, they continued on by the single-line, non-asphalt part of the road parallel to Boulevard de la Marina, spaced out over 492 feet (about 150 meters). All of them carried automatic weapons with cartridge belts over their shoulders or bazookas in their hands. They headed toward the main target of their assault: the presidential palace (*Palais de la Marina*). According to the plan, they would need "about five minutes to reach the gates of the Presidential Palace." As soon as the palace was surrounded "a small group [would] be left to guard it while the other forces [would] go to the Military Camp if necessary or to the port and the bridge over the lake, so as to prevent any traffic in both directions."[6]

On their way, they fired at the Nigeria House—the new and not yet occupied complex of the embassy of Nigeria; the chancery building of the embassy of Zaire (present-day Democratic Republic of the Congo); the diplomatic residence of the ambassador of the United States; and the buildings of the Ministry of Interior Affairs and the Treasury, both closed on Sunday.

All these buildings had been more or less damaged by the gunfire. They finally approached the residential Quarante Logements building located within the line of sight of, and approximately two hundred meters across from the palace. A few commando members of the Blue Group entered the building, broke into fourth floor apartments with the windows facing south, and opened machine-gun fire directly at the palace. A French national, resident of the building, described what he had seen going on inside and outside Quarante Logements:

> Suddenly people were knocking at my door, saying, "Open or I fire," knocking louder and louder on the door. So, I opened the door and at that moment . . . in khaki combat uniform and with a green badge on the right shoulder. They pushed me to the floor face down, threatening me with their weapons, and then covered me with a sheet and blankets, however, I could hear the noise they were making. . . . They left my apartment and, firing, climbed up to the fourth floor. . . . Then they came down again, still firing in the direction of the Presidential Palace. . . . The three people who burst into my apartment were white.[7]

The fifteen mercenaries who remained outside the Quarante Logements building were directing machine-gun fire and bazooka projectiles toward both the presidential palace and a structure 328 feet (circa 100 meters) away, which they wrongly assumed housed Beninese soldiers.[8] Some others were directing fire from the building's north-facing windows toward distant Camp Guézo. Both the palace and Camp Guézo were also shelled from eighty-one-millimeter mortars operated by the Red Group who remained at the airport.

The centrally approaching Black Group was composed of another twenty-four African Omegas. The Black Group progressed down the central avenue in Cotonou, Route de l'Aéroport, moving in the same direction as the Blue Group. The Black Group, whose target was also the palace, reached the colonial-style, single story Hotel Résidence les Cocotiers, located a five-minute walk from the airport and occupied by foreigners working in Benin. Its residents were alarmed by gunfire at the airport and observed the commandos passing through their neighborhood.

The blueprint of the Opération Crevette made clear that the Black Group was to take over "occupancy, leave intact, and exploit"[9] Cotonou's national radio station, *Voix de la Révolution*,[10] located in the *Office de Radiodiffusion et Télévision du Bénin* (ORTB) at 366 Route de l'Aéroport, before it commenced its regular daily programming at 6:30 a.m. By the time the group reached the ORTB building, it was well after 7:00 a.m. and regular broadcasting had already begun. For unknown reasons, instead of seizing the building, the Black Group "moved pass the ORTB without any attempt of taking it over." The reports stressed that "[t]he brand new (but unused since it was opened two years ago)[11] television station took one bazooka hit, but the brand-new radio station, broadcasting at the time and completely unwalled on the side from which the invaders came, also came through unscathed.

Failure to seize the radio station had a critical effect on the following sequence of events that morning since it would be later used by President Mathieu Kérékou who would broadcast an appeal to Beninese people to join the army effort repelling the mercenary attack.

The Black Group continued marching down Route de l'Aéroport and, without military necessity, firing at the building of regional African organization, the Council of the Entente (*Conseil de l'Entente*), and the international hotel Croix du Sud, located at Rue 363B in the middle of Boulevard de la Marina and Route de l'Aéroport, even launching incendiary grenades.

According to account of chief warrant officer of the Kerekou's Presidential Guard, El Hadj Sanni Mouftaou, published forty-two years after the Opération Crevette, it was the Black Group that was the Force Omega unit that had an encounter with Beninese military. The encounter took place about 2.3 mile (3.8 kilometers) from the Camp Guézo. It likely took the Beninese unit to reach this area in the early morning on Sunday approximately seven to eight minutes.

This is how he remembered their encounter with the Omegas:

Early in the morning, we started hearing gunshots at the airport, so we took a military truck to go and inquire about the situation that prevailed in order to report. When I reached the level of the Martyrs' square[12] today, I noticed that around seven o'clock the road was completely deserted. There were four soldiers. When we had passed the National Radio (ORTB), the Ministry of Finance, before we got to the place where the Asecna was now built,[13] there were coconut trees all over the place at the time, I noticed that there were people moving towards the city. A few moments later, they saw us and went back to the left side on their way to the airport. When we got to their level, as we were in a military truck, they opened fire on us.[14]

El Hadj Sanni Mouftaou was injured by the mercenaries' fire and, with the rest of his crew, abandoned the vehicle trying to get back to Camp Guézo to notify his superiors about the incident. When asked, "What was going on?" he couldn't give any other answer besides that he "had seen white people shooting and shooting at us."[15] The report of the encounter commanders at the Camp Guézo allegedly "brought then President Mathieu Kérékou, lieutenant-colonel at the time, to the camp to prepare and begin the response."[16] Mouftaou's report purportedly saved the Beninese soccer team from becoming the victims of the Omegas' attack, who were gathered that morning at Camp Guézo before transit by bus to the airport for flight to Lomé, Togo, for a game there.

The last advancing team was the northernmost Yellow Group. Comprised of twenty-five (some sources say thirty-five) European mercenaries, the Yellow Group moved from the airport toward their target, Camp Guézo, through districts Haie-Vive and Cadjehoun and through Route de Lomé, an intercity highway (RNIE 1). They were equipped with two Browning .50-caliber heavy machine guns and two eighty-one-millimeter mortars.

The Presidential Palace

The presidential palace, also called *Présidence* or *Palais de la Marina* due its proximity to the Atlantic coast, was a huge, "ghostly," "sumptuous" stone and glass building. Its construction in 1963 during the presidency of Hubert Maga cost more than 3 million US dollars, which eventually led to its facilitation of the first Dahomeyan coup d'état against the president, then accused of "squandermania."[17]

At the time of the mercenary attack, the palace had three entrances. The main entrance faced the north toward downtown Cotonou but was protected by a closed iron gate and three guards with machine pistols. The other two entrances were guarded by armed personnel of the Presidential Guard. The entrance on the west side faced Route de l'Aéroport and Camp Guézo; it led directly to the palace and was monitored from a guard post with a military vehicle carrying the two AA52 heavy mounted a gun generally carried. Only two soldiers armed with light machine guns guarded the east entrance from *Boulevard de la Marina*. There was also one guard carrying a machine pistol posted on the south side corner of the palace building.[18]

When the Blue and Black assault groups reached the vicinity of the palace from its southeast side, their African members set up a line of mortars and bazookas halfway across the coconut grove between the Boulevard de la Marina and the Route de l'Aéroport. Their other members took over the then unoccupied Congressional palace (*Palais des Congrès*) conference center on the west side of the presidential palace and residential building, and *Quarante*

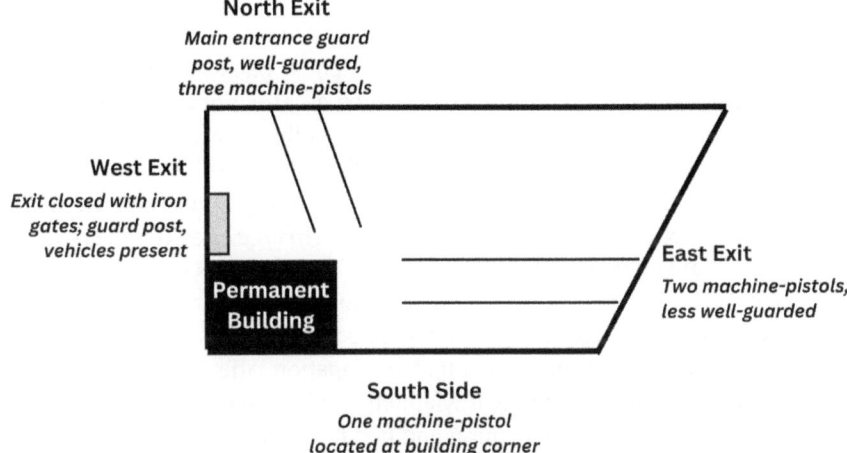

North Exit
Main entrance guard post, well-guarded, three machine-pistols

West Exit
Exit closed with iron gates; guard post, vehicles present

Permanent Building

East Exit
Two machine-pistols, less well-guarded

South Side
One machine-pistol located at building corner

Figure 12.2.   Presidential palace plans. Credit: Author creation.

Longements northwest side of palace. From these two points they executed a crossfire of automatic weapons and rockets on the presidential palace.

According to the intelligence Denard used to plan the operation, Kérékou spent most of the time at the presidential palace. On weekdays he would arrive at the palace by car with a heavily armed military escort driving a "Peugeot van armed with two mounted AA52 machine guns manned by six soldiers. This van remained on the Palace's ground at all times."[19] On Wednesdays, the number of soldiers in the security detail increased due to regular meetings of the Council of Ministers, which took place at 10:30 a.m. During the planning stages of the operation, a Wednesday attack was excluded for this reason; the covert operation would have been too risky given the daylight and early morning traffic, complicating the Omega's advance toward their targets and compromising the critical element of surprise needed for a successful clandestine operation.

Opening mortar fire on the presidential palace, the attackers did not realize that President Kérékou was not there. Various explanations arose for Kérékou's absence. The Beninese official account suggested that Kérékou, after receiving a message from the airport control tower alerting him to the landing of foreign soldiers, left the palace for Camp Guézo, located a few blocks north, in order to direct resistance. Sources less favorable to Kérékou claim that the president had been warned by his *marabout* (i.e., spiritual guide)[20] of imminent danger the day before and therefore spent this night elsewhere. Other explanations for his absence note that although the presidential palace was suited for residential purposes, Kérékou did not spend nights there. As to the palace's surroundings, Denard's information was that no traffic was allowed from west to east from 9:00 p.m. to 6:00 a.m. and east to west from 6:00 a.m. to 9:00 p.m.[21]

The action of shelling the part of the presidential palace dedicated to private use of President Kérékou turned out to be an effect of a lack of correct intelligence information because apparently the building, including the presidential quarters, was empty since it was used by the president only for ceremonial occasions. Even President Omar Bongo, trying to disassociate from Opération Crevette in an interview with *Jeune Afrique*, stated, "everybody knows that Kérékou doesn't live at the palace."[22] Only years later did Denard recognize the intelligence he was relying on to be "less than reliable," as, in fact, "Kérékou did not spend night at his residence."[23]

Recently, there has been yet another explanation offered. Beninese historian Sylvain Akindès claims that Mathieu Kérékou had been informed of the mercenary operation was coming and had made necessary arrangements. "It is now certain"—maintains Sylvian Akindès—"that Mathieu Kérékou was informed of the invasion and the date when it was to take place." It was Karim da Silva, a Beninese political actor who had passed the information to Eustache Prudencio, the Benin's ambassador to Lagos at the time. "According to the testimonies of certain advisers to the Presidency at the time of the events, the latter had been asked not to appear at the Palace of the Republic during the day of January 16, 1977."[24] Since Mathieu Kérékou did not leave us with any known memoires, it is impossible to recognize conclusively any of the above versions as a true version of events explaining his absence from the presidential palace during mercenary assault on it.

Attacked with a mortar fire, a small security detachment of the Presidential Guard responded with machine-gun fire. The exchange of fire lasted at least an hour and a half. During that time, the Omegas never tried to approach the building, and besides causing damage to the building, they failed to obtain the primary goal of the operation: to seize Mathieu Kérékou.

According to contemporary accounts, the presidency had three or four bazooka hits. The presidency also received several mortar shells, two of which had gone through the roof and subsequently the ceiling of the president's bedroom. There were also traces of bullet impacts on the wall of the adjoining bathroom. Foreign diplomats were later invited to visit the palace to observe the damage to its in and exterior. Many holes on inside walls and windows had been caused by fire coming from the defending the building palace guard and reinforcements dispatched from Camp Guézo.[25]

Later examination of damages showed that mortar shells damaged the roof, walls and windows, and decorative interior of the building, "whose reception rooms resembled the film set for Cleopatra."[26] Shelling also caused damage of multi color mosaic staircases, marble flooring, and gold covered balconies, and so on,[27] as well as the empty bedroom. The head of the Organization of

African Unity's inquiry mission to Benin, Assistant Secretary General Peter Onu, reported that the worst damage was at the presidential palace and, within the palace, especially the bedroom, which indicates that "neutralization" of President Kérékou meant to kill him. "The bedroom of the President, who apparently does not live in the palace, was in ruins"—Peter Onu reported.[28] "I saw three missiles shells among the rubble in the room . . . and I was told by military experts that these were shells fired from 81 mm mortars," the same weapons abandoned by the Omegas at the end of the operation.

However, the nearby Ministry of the Interior, which controls all-powerful state police, and which is right across the street from the presidency, did not take a single hit, not even a rifle shot.

KÉRÉKOU'S RESIDENCE

It is not clear from the plan of Opération Crevette whether an attack on Kérékou's private residence was meant to be an attack on the residence located on the ground of the presidential palace complex or at a different location. According to the plan, Kérékou's home was to be attacked within first thirty to sixty minutes of the ground operation. During this time, Kérékou was "to be neutralized."[29] This information seems to indicate that the assaults on the presidential palace and president's private residence would be directed against two different locations. It seems that the planners of Crevette were unsure whether the president would in fact be spending the night at the presidential palace or, rather, at its residential compound, therefore targeting both. However, the timeline of the first phase of the operation shows evident discrepancy in this matter.

Denard optimistically planned the Omegas would need "about five minutes to reach gates of the presidential palace and *then about two minutes at best to reach the house of K* [Kérékou]."[30] The presidential private residence, *Les filaos*, at which he lived since 1965, already for more than twelve years to the time of Opération Crevette, was located on Boulevard de la Marina about thirty minutes' walking distance east from the presidential palace.

It is not clear from Denard's operation plan whether when he observed that Kérékou's residence would be "constantly guarded with three machine-pistols and perhaps others inside. Shutters always closed"; did he refer to the private residence on Boulevard de la Marina or part of the presidential palace building mistakenly considered to be Mathieu Kérékou's private residence?

No available records or accounts of Opération Crevette describe any attack on Kérékou's private residence, and that building have not been listed among the nineteen buildings damaged during the assault on Cotonou.[31]

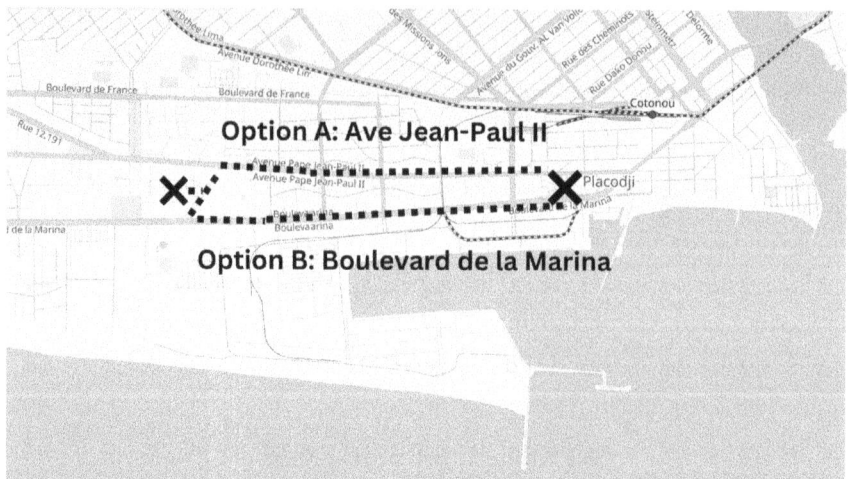

Figure 12.3.   Routes—Presidential palace to Kerekou's residence. Credit: Author creation based on Open Source Maps.

AZONHIHO RESIDENCE

There is also no information about the Omega's assault against the home of Kérékou's closest advisor, Colonel Martin Dohou Azonhiho. The plan of the operation, unlike in the case of the private residence of the president, does not show any information related to Azonhiho's residence location or security arrangements around it. Instead, there is only a question mark suggesting that the exact address of that residence might have been unknown to the coup organizers, which would be justified considering his position in Kérékou's government.

Colonel Martin Dohou Azonhiho, a political hardliner, was the Minister of Interior, Head of the Gendarmerie, Minister of Information, National Orientation leading ideologue, and the *éminence grise* of Kérékou's regime and was known for his harsh treatment of political oppositionists. According to Azonhiho "the counter-revolution is those who think badly of the revolution. We have to reconvert them. . . . But if we do not succeed, if they continue, we must actually liquidate them on the ground. . . . Our revolution does not want to be bloody uselessly. But in purity one can kill for a noble cause. It is the instinct of preservation. If you do not kill your enemy, he will kill you."[32]

Unlike the "elimination" planned for President Kérékou, the plan only provided for "the seizure of AZ [Azonhiho]." However, it does not appear that the Omega commanders even knew Azonhiho's address. Punctuated with question marks, the plans only note that Azonhiho resided somewhere in the center of Cotonou.[33] Without the apprehension of Colonel Azonhiho, a coup against the president had no chance of being successful.

CAMP GUÉZO

The Yellow Group's primary objective was to neutralize the third target: the military base of Camp Guézo,[34] a thirty-minute walking distance of about 2.5 miles from the airport via Route de L'Aéroport and Rue 900 IA.[35] Located at an almost equal distance of about 492–656 feet north of Quarante Logement and south of the presidential palace, Camp Guézo was positioned at the corner Rue 900 IA, an extension of Rue 395 and Avenue Yekpe. The Yellow Group moved from the airport through the Haie-Vive and Cadjehoun districts following Route de Lomé (intercity highway RNIE 1). Like the other two groups, the Yellow Group "indiscriminately" fired "here and there" at any public and private buildings they encountered.

Passing the Social Security Administration (*L'Office Béninois de Sécurité Sociale*) building on the right side of Rue 395, the Omegas opened fire injuring, among others, international personnel members who were observing the ongoing attack from their windows. At least two experts of the United Nations Development Program, a Vietnamese and a Canadian, had been severely wounded and were immediately evacuated from Benin.

When the group reached the vicinity of Camp Guézo, it turned on Rue 610. From the corner of Rue 900 IA and Rue 610, its members opened machine gun fire toward the camp from a distance of about 4,224 feet (0.8 miles). Their action was supported by bazooka, and mortar fire by two Browning .50-caliber heavy machine guns and two eighty-one-millimeter mortars provided by the group remaining at the airport.

The fire was directed not at the front of the base, but a west side of the camp complex. They were also firing at Polyclinique de Cotonou located between their position and the presidential palace. The shelling lasted about half an hour, between 7:30 a.m. and 8:00 a.m.

According to the eyewitness account, President Kérékou was inside Camp Guézo where he was broadcasting his call to arms and counterattack against the invading mercenaries. Denard probably did not know this, and instead of concentrating the Omega's assault onto Camp Guézo, they were split across three different aforementioned target locations. The shelling of the Camp Guézo by the Red Group from the airport area and by the Yellow Group from the streets in close vicinity to the camp was, however, effective because, as the same eyewitness says, "shells fell inside the Camp compound."[36]

The groups of Omegas moving through Cotonou along three separate routes failed to keep contact with each other on their agreed-upon radio frequencies. Each team was only able to communicate directly with the command post at the airport. The main reason for communication failure was, according to the critical account of one European mercenary, that the military French radiotelephone TR PP13 "seemed to be insufficient" for purposes of this operation. This resulted in a lack of coordination between the three Omega teams, lack of orientation in an unknown terrain, and confusion as to the location of and actions taken by two other groups. In one instance, this almost resulted in friendly bazooka fire against an armored vehicle tank that was jacked from Beninese soldiers by members an Omega team. Bloodshed caused by friendly fire was only avoided due to the lack of Energa anti-tank rifle grenades and the guns required to launch them when the vehicle in question suddenly appeared in front the group.

TIME TO WITHDRAW

With the Beninese soldiers from Camp Guézo supported by the North Korean unit taking joint action against the Omegas, Denard concluded that his commando would not be able to fight against them successfully to achieve the aim of the operation and called for a retreat.

Around 9:30 a.m., the Omegas commenced a quick withdrawal, moving in a single file line toward the airport. Denard, hampered by leg injury from the Congo, fled via a commandeered jeep. Three wounded mercenaries were also transported in commandeered vehicles. Initially, Benin's official reports mistakenly described one Belgian mercenary, Michel Lourdais, a veteran of mercenary activities in the Congo, as shot and deceased after separating from the rest of his group. This mistake was later corrected when, for purposes of investigation, Marc Colot was identified as the only deceased European member of the Force Omega.[37] Colot's name also appears on the website *Orbs Patria Nostra* presenting biographic notes of Denard's deceased associates. Michel Lourdais's name later appeared on a list of mercenaries convicted by trial before the Beninese National Revolutionary Tribunal.

The relatively safe withdrawal of the Omegas was possible because the Beninese soldiers remained at their positions, continueing defensive fire rather than pursueing the retreating mercenaries. Similarly behaved were the civilian volunteers who, responding to Kérékou's call to action, joined the defense against their attackers. However, to Denard's surprise, the civilian population not only failed to show "any active sympathy" for the Omegas but many civilians informed Beninese soldiers as to the Omega's positions.[38]

When the Omegas arrived at the airport, Gratien Pognon and his secretary were waiting onboard the DC-7(F), prepared for a quick escape. According to one account, a visibly terrified Pognon insisted that the DC-7(F) pilot take off immediately. Aggravated by the operation's failure, the pilot—Malloch—allegedly slapped his face and sent him to the back of the plane.

Even in this rush to safety, the aircraft could not take off immediately. Upon landing, as per Denard's orders, the plane's wheels were blocked with a jeep ensuring that, in case of failure, the plane could not depart before the Omegas returned to the airport. Evidently, based on his bad experiences from the Congo, Denard did not even trust his closest associates. The DC-7(F) finally taxied round and moved slowly up the airstrip while the Omegas were running alongside until one by one, they were dragged aboard. A mere three hours after arriving in Cotonou, at 10:00 a.m., DC-7(F) began to take off with an open hatch and under fire from Beninese soldiers who tried to hit its tires. "Sitting in the back of the plane Denard could see the Beninese soldiers below jumping up and down and brandishing their rifles in the air."[39] It looked like the Omegas' escape from Cotonou was successful, although an unplanned part of the Opération Crevette.

The DC-7(F) flew back to Libreville where the plane landed in a decommissioned section of the airport. To maintain secrecy surrounding the Omegas' return, they were flown inland to Franceville (Gabon) where they spent ten days at the ranches owned by President Bongo's ardent supporters ensuring their safety. Some other accounts say that they spent those ten days "at an abandoned base without running water or sanitary facilities."[40]

After obtaining consent from Moroccan authorities, the Omegas moved to the south part of that country from where, after a month-long stay, its members returned in small groups back to France.

The Beninese authorities later summarized the failed operation as "whistling, crackling and rumbling noises were the work of drug-maddened mercenaries armed with the most modern and sophisticated weapons for the cynical purpose of physically liquidating the responsible figures of our Party and revolutionary state."[41]

THE UNDELIVERED PROCLAMATION

The blueprint of Opération Crevette provided that upon seizing the ORTB radio station, the putschists would broadcast a communiqué announcing the coup d'état and deliver Gratien Pognon's proclamation to the nation. This proclamation would call upon Beninese to support the FLERD organized coup and the new authorities established in its outcome.

Phrased in the typical French revolutionary and paternalistic jargon used by Kérékou in addressing the Beninese, the FLRED Proclamation called on "Children of Dahomey" to rise, as "the tyrant is no more."[42] Assuming success of the coup, the authors of the proclamation planned to announce:

Dahomeyan patriots from inside and outside the country, unified under the banner of the Front for Liberation and Rehabilitation, have today launched a vast and totally successful offensive against all bastions of dictatorship and fascism. At the present hour, the forces of the Front for the Liberation and Rehabilitation of Dahomey have destroyed or taken control of the large arsenal of violence and death, which Kérékou, his accomplices, and their foreign masters had built up at various points of the national territory. It is true, in particular—intended to announce Pognon—at Cotonou, in the case of the Palace of the Republic, of Camp Guézo and of the fortified residences in which the tyrant and his chief lieutenants had entrenched themselves.[43]

Pognon further envisioned that "[t]aken by surprise and put to flight, Kérékou and his chief officers, civilian cadres and henchmen at all levels, who shared with him an unspeakable fury against the security and liberty, the dignity and well-being of Dahomeyans, have now been neutralized once and for all." And, after justified criticism of Kérékou's socialist regime and promising return to political and economic normalcy, Pognon was ready to announce that the putschists were ready "to consolidate that effective and definitive control held by the Front for the Liberation and Rehabilitation of Dahomey over the entire national territory."[44]

Eager to deliver his proclamation, Pognon anxiously waited for news about the operation on the ground floor of the airport passenger hall. "At one time"—related an eyewitness Omega from the group that remained at the airport—"he came up to the roof to ask us, 'What about the operation? Where are they? Is there anything that you have to mention?'" But there was no news coming from the attacking groups, and thus, Pognon was blissfully unaware that the Omegas failed to take over the ORTB radio station building before it broadcasted the government's calls to the public for resistance to an armed aggression at Cadjehoun Airport. Neglected taking of control of the radio station *La Voix de la Révolution* turned out to be a huge blunder allowing the Beninese authorities access to the flow of information on the attempted coup and to organize resistance against it.

NOTES

1. "African Land, No Stranger to Coups, Repulses an Attack by 'Mercenaries,'" *New York Times*, January 17, 1977, 1.

2. Ibid.

3. Benin, "Letter Dated 77/04/04 from the Charge d'Affaires a.i. of Benin to the United Nations Addressed to the President of the Security Council: Addendum" (New York: United Nations, April 5, 1977), https://digitallibrary.un.org/record/564452, see

19—white men were dressed in khaki uniforms, with one yellow and one green ribbon on the epaulets.

4. "Who Raided Benin and Why Still Mystery," *International Herald Tribune*, February 8, 1977.

5. UN, Special Mission of the Security Council Established under Resolution 404 (1977), "Report of the Security Council Special Mission to the People's Republic of Benin Established under Resolution 404 (1977): Addendum" (New York: United Nations, March 8, 1977), https://digitallibrary.un.org/record/564391.

6. Ibid., see Annex VI, 14.

7. Benin, "Letter Dated 77/04/04," 18.

8. "Report of the Security Council Special Mission to the People's Republic of Benin Estabilshed under Resolution 404 (1977)," see 25, para. 88.

9. [CSL STYLE ERROR: reference with no printed form.]. Ibid., see Annex VI, 10.

10. Between 1972 and 1990 radio station was named *La Voix de la Révolution*.

11. ORTB TV broadcasted its first program on December 31, 1978.

12. Place de Martyrs, located at confluence of Route de L'Aéroport and Rue 390 (6.353835, 2.404497).

13. Close to the roundabout where Route de L'Aéroport and Rue 230 meet.

14. Aziz Badarou, "Agression du 16 janvier 1977: Sanni Mouftaou, un survivant, retrace l'histoire," *Matin Libre* (blog), February 1, 2019, https://matinlibre.com/2019/01/31/agression-du-16-janvier-1977-sanni-mouftaou-un-survivant-retrace-lhistoire/.

15. Ibid.

16. Ibid.

17. Decalo, 297.

18. "Report of the Security Council Special Mission to the People's Republic of Benin Established under Resolution 404 (1977)," see Annex VI, 9, plan of Opération Crevette.

19. Ibid., Annex VI, 95.

20. Muslim monk, spiritual guide.

21. S/12294/Add. 1, Annex VI, 93.

22. *Jeune Afrique*, April 29, 1977, 28, Interview of Omar Bongo: "Chacun sait que Kérékou n'habite pas le palais."

23. Bob Denard and George Fleury, *Corsaire de la République* (Paris: Robert Laffont, 1998), 292.

24. Sylvian Adékpédjou Akindès, *Essai d'histoire du temps présent au Bénin postcolonial: Problématique d'un engagement politique* (Cotonou, Bénin: Star Editions, 2017), 224.

25. "Report of the Security Council Special Mission to the People's Republic of Benin Established under Resolution 404 (1977)," S/12294/Rev. 1, Special Supplement 3, 26.

26. Kaye Whiteman, "Hubert Maga," *The Guardian*, July 24, 2000, sec. News.

27. Decalo, 297.

28. *Africa Confidential* 18, no. 6 (March 18, 1977): 7.

29. "Report of the Security Council Special Mission to the People's Republic of Benin Established under Resolution 404 (1977)," S/12294/Add. 1, Annex VI, 63.

30. Ibid., Annex VI, 13; emphasis added.

31. "Revised Report on the Evaluation of Damages and Losses of Various Kinds Occasioned to the People's Republic of Benin During the Imperialist Aggression of Sunday, 16 January 1977." "Letter Dated 13 October 1977 from the Permanent Representative of Benin to the United Nations Addressed to the President of the Security Council," S/12415, 4.

32. *Daho-Express*, no. 1598, February 7, 1975.

33. Listed as "Azonhiho's address CII?"

34. In use is also term Ghézo or Gezo. The name is a name of the nineteenth-century Dahomeyan king Ghezo.

35. In August 2019, Camp Guézo building in Cotonou had been decommissioned and its buildings turned to rental property. Military installation of Camp Guézo had been moved inland to town of Allada located about thirty-one miles (50 km) from Cotonou.

36. "Le Massacre a Été Évité de Justesse à l'armée Béninoise Le 16 Janvier 1977," *Agence Benin Presse*, accessed November 18, 2021, http://www.agencebeninpresse .info/web/message.

37. "Report of the Security Council Special Mission to the People's Republic of Benin Established under Resolution 404 (1977): Addendum," see Annex IV, 109.

38. Pierre Lunel, *Bob Denard: Le roi de fortune* (Edition^0 1, 1991), 461–62. Initial reports claimed that one of the civilians named Comlan was grabbed by escaping mercenaries as a hostage and taken with them to the airport. See for example Veronique Vucher-Bondet.

39. Job Bradshaw, "The Man Who Would Be King," *Esquire*, March 27, 1977, 65.

40. Veronique Vucher-Bondet, "Bénin, le cuisant échec d'un raid audacieux," *Historia*, no. 406, 1980, 102.

41. Benin, "Letter Dated 13 June 1979 from the Permanent Representative of Benin to the United Nations Addressed to the Secretary-General" (New York: United Nations, June 19, 1979), Imperialist Armed Aggression of Sunday, 16 January 1977. Decisions of the Session of the National Revolutionary Council sitting as a National Revolutionary Tribunal to Deal with the Facts of the Aggression (Special communiqué issued by the Revolutionary Military Government), S/13402, Annex, 1.

42. *La Marseillaise* begins with phrase: "Let's go children of the fatherland, the day of glory has arrived! Against us tyranny's Bloody flag is raised!"

43. "Report of the Security Council Mission," see Annex VI, 158–60.

44. Ibid.

Chapter 13

The Aftermath

SEARCHES, ARRESTS, RESTRICTIONS

The first news shared about the situation developing in Cotonou on Sunday morning was repeatedly broadcasted by government-controlled radio station *La Voix de la Révolution* from 8:30 a.m. to 9:00 a.m. It briefly stated: "Ce matin un DC-8 est atterri à l'Aéroport de Cotonou. Ses passagers ont été signalés en train de tirer" (This morning a DC-8 landed at Cotonou Airport. Its passengers were reported shooting). At 10:30, *La Voix de la Révolution* announced a speech by the President Kérékou. It was a speech in which he solemnly summoned every citizen to face the armed attack on the country. "After the speech"—recalled an eyewitness—"the song 'Glory, Glory, Hallelujah!' was repeatedly played." She wondered, why they had chosen this song, the "Battle Hymn of the Republic," the song of the American Civil War?[1] The official version of the events of that day published by the Beninese political authorities state that the president's appeal was broadcasted by *La Voix de la Révolution* "a little before 9:00 a.m."[2] If the time of broadcast of the president's appeal to citizens to join the army's efforts to thwart the mercenary assault given by the French eyewitness of the events is correct, it would mean that an appeal was published at the time when the Omegas had already been withdrawing to the airport. In such a case, the stories describing the massive participation of Cotonou's residents in repelling the mercenary attack seem to be government propaganda rather than fact.

The immediate reaction of the government after the failed Omagas' operation was, as has been done in similar situations, the imposition of a police curfew; a two-month closure of border crossings with Togo (January 16 to March 18, 1977), and temporary closure of all country's local airports were also enacted.

The same eyewitness recalls that at 11:45 a.m., *La Voix de la Révolution* broadcasted an official message—an order addressed to foreigners living in Benin: "Today, all foreigners have to stay inside their houses. Searches of expatriate's houses were announced to take place at a later time."[3]

Indeed, at 5:20 p.m. the radio repeatedly broadcasted another message addressed, this time, to foreigners residing in two of Cotonou's districts bordering the international airport: "The mercenaries fled along the beach, and now all the houses of expatriates in the *Patte d'Oie* and the *Cocotiers* are subject to searching." Army troops and security forces conducted sweeping searches with troops in private homes and apartments looking for those mercenaries who might not have been able to escape from the country with the rest of the Force Omega. Soldiers even searched, in violation of the immunity of diplomatic premises, the residence of the American ambassador looking for weapons.

During the next few days, about three hundred out of two thousand Europeans living in Benin were shortly detained—most of them were in Camp Guézo. Soon after, all detainees were released except for two Germans, four French tourists, a Greek sailor, and an American Peace Corps volunteer.

The other consequence of the failed Opération Crevette was the issuing of a decree introducing by the Council of Ministers imposing tight restrictions on the movement of foreigners. The law stipulates that foreign visitors must notify their presence to the local authorities. Foreign visitors could only stay in hotels or buildings designated by the government. Under no circumstances could a foreign visitor stay at a private home without a special permit issued by local authorities.[4]

The second decree imposed on foreign residents, except for diplomats, to obtain before leaving the place of towns they registered their residence requirement of obtaining prior permission from local offices.[5]

DEAD AND WOUNDED

The seven Beninese soldiers who were killed repelling the mercenary attack were buried during a solemn state funeral. Their coffins, wrapped in national flags and decorated with flowers, were transported to downtown Cotonou where huge crowds of town residents bid them goodbye.[6] A monument to the victims of the coup attempt of January 16, 1977, was erected in 1979 halfway between the airport Cadjehoun International Airport and the presidential palace, at a site initially named *Place des Martyrs* for that purpose. It occupies the corner between 390 Street and Airport Road. The place is a venue of an annual military ceremony of placing a reef in memory of those six soldiers and one civilian killed by the mercenaries during Opération Crevette.

It remains unknown whether any North Korean instructors or soldiers lost their lives in the action against the mercenaries.

On the side of Denard's commando, two mercenaries were killed in action. They were, according to information issued by the International Commission of Inquiry into the Imperialistic Aggression of January 16, 1977: Belgian Marc Colot, using the alias Lieutenant Cemaer, and Benin national Alimiyahou Salifou-Bogu. The International Commission did not provide any specific information about the cause of death but only stated it identified "white and black mercenaries killed during armed imperialist aggression."[7]

The death of Colot is also confirmed on the website of *Orbs Patria Nostra* with a brief entry: "Marc Colot—Belgique—Benin—*Mort en operation le 16 janvier 1977 au Benin.*"[8]—(Marc Colot—Belgian—Cotonou—Died in operation on January 16, 1977 in Benin.) The only publicly available detail of his death is that after he received an injury to a thigh, he allegedly committed suicide to avoid being apprehended by Beninese or North Korean soldiers and be forced to reveal, possibly under torture, details of Opération Crevette. This version of Colot's death is based on a 2012 interview with the former European mercenary identified as "JP D., known as Jean-Philippe."[9]

Much less is known about the Omegas who were wounded during action on the streets of Cotonou. Unverifiable information comes from a Beninese eyewitness, Sergent Major Favi, who, with a few other Beninese, was taken hostage by the mercenaries after they disembarked the aircraft. According to his recollection, as early as 8:15 a.m., wounded mercenaries were being brought to the airplane. He estimated their number, without specifying their race, as about forty men,[10] which, considering that attacking mercenaries for about an hour was acting in small groups and practically unopposed, seems exaggerated.

From the same source comes information that lives of the Beninese hostages kept by Omegas at the airport were saved by no other but Bob Denard. According to testimony of Innocent Favi, when Denard's commando was in a panic boarding the aircraft, "He and other hostages were asked to join the plane," but following their command orders, they refused to do so. "Later"— testified Favi—"a white man alighted and wanted to shoot them [hostages] but someone whom he [Favi] thought was a Colonel prevented him from doing so."[11] There was only one man among Omegas who was addressed "Colonel" and it was Bob Denard.

However, another unforeseen impact by Beninese patrons of the failed Opération Crevette was toughening the political regime of Kérékou's government and strengthening his and his entourage's dictatorial role in the country's political life—a regime that survived for the next twelve years.

MATERIAL DAMAGES

The exchange of fire between the Force Omega mercenaries, repelling the Beninese, and accompanying North Korean soldiers resulted in various material damage to several Cotonou buildings. Much of such damages had been caused by initial chaotic fire by the groups of mercenaries advancing toward the assigned objects of attack.

The Security Council in its Resolution No. 419 (1977)[12] appealed "to all States and all appropriate international organizations, including the United Nations and its specialized agencies, to assist Benin to repair the damage caused by the act of aggression" and called on the secretary general "to provide Benin with all necessary assistance" in implementation of that goal.

In fulfillment of the recommendation of Security Council Resolution No. 405 (1977), two chosen by the secretary general and approved by Benin expert consultants visited Cotonou between June 27 and July 26, 1977, to help Beninese experts of the National Evaluation Commission to assess the various kinds of damages occasioned by the mercenary assault. They accepted the following list of the buildings damaged during Opération Crevette:[13]

Public Buildings

The palace of the president of the Republic

The Congress Hall

The hotel "Croix du Sud"

The houses of the Conseil de l'Entente

The building of the Ministry of the Interior

The radio building

The television building

The building of the Benin Social Security Office

The Central Treasury

The SONAGRI building

The building of the Ministry of Foreign Affairs

The buildings of Cotonou Airport

The BCEAO villas

The ASSANI Polyclinic

The "Quarante Logements" building

The Cadjehoun Tax Collection building

The Embassy of Nigeria

The Embassy of Zaire

The residence of the ambassador of the United States.

According to Benin's government assessment, the damages to the listed buildings resulted in the collapse of the walls, the shattering of the glass of doors and Windows, the demolition of stone floors, railings, and so on, and various installations.

Private Buildings

Thirteen private buildings situated in neighborhoods near the airport (Iiaie-Vive and Cadjehoun) that were subjected to mortar fire and automatic weapons bullets also showed some damages. The initially assessed the value of the damages to both public and private buildings at 273,456,000 CFA[14] francs[15] was subsequently revised to 225,544,625 CFA francs.[16]

Material Losses Suffered by People's Armed Forces

The damages occasioned to military structures and equipment were estimate at 596,045,000 CFA francs. They included considerable losses to:

One command aircraft disabled;

Two DC-3/C-47 aircraft damaged;

Several pieces of military equipment seriously damaged or destroyed;

Ground installations of National Escadrille;

Expenditure and loss of munitions of various kinds; and

Consumption of essential materials.

Thus, the value of total material losses suffered by Benin was estimated at 821,589,625 CFA francs, an equivalent of about $3,295,586 at the exchange rate of March 1977.[17]

These were losses relatively easy—easily measurable, and easy to assess. The problem, however, was who exactly was responsible for them to happen and, thus, who should be liable for covering them. As we have seen above, although the United Nations (UN) Security Council condemned the mercenary assault on Cotonou, it avoided naming any country or countries as directly or indirectly involved in the organization or support of Opération Crevette. Therefore, the UN Security Council Special Mission to Benin was established as an inquiry (fact-finding) rather than an investigative body.

Unable or unwilling to designate any concrete party liable for the losses suffered by Benin, the Security Council addressed, in Resolution No. 419 its appeal for assistance to Benin to "all States and all appropriate international organizations, including the United Nations and its specialized agencies." The same formula applied the then Organization of African Unity in the Council of Ministers Resolution CM/Res. 639 (XXXI) adopted on July 8, 1978. Although it "strongly condemned" the armed aggression and "all those who conceived, organized, financed, and executed it," the council recommended that "immediate financial assistance" to Benin be given from the Organization of African Unity (OAU) Special Fund.

There are also the other losses, less reliable to account for without special investigation (due to their nature), enumerated in the UN report such as personal injury, loss of life, economic present and future losses, losses in agriculture production, electrical outages, and so on. Some of them would require extensive economic and statistical analysis, and other complex projections of Benin's economy's social or economic development. Although listed in the experts' report, they could hardly result from the three-hour mercenary operation conducted in the heart of Cotonou. Nevertheless, the UN experts concluded that total "direct and indirect losses" incurred due to Opération Crevette equal 6,994,688,870 CFA francs—that is, $28 million US.[18]

Since no specific country or countries were named in either case of the UN or OAU resolutions or report, the covering of Benin's expenses caused by Opération Crevette had been spread between the members of the international community, including those who was not involved with the operation itself.

Expulsion of Beninese Citizens from Gabon

Accusations by President Mathieu Kérékou of Gabon at the fifteenth OAU summit in Khartoum in July 1978 for their involvement in Opération Crevette resulted in the massive expulsion of Beninese citizens temporarily residing in Gabon. The decision on expulsion preceded anti-Beninese violent riots by the Gabonese population that began on July 28, 1978. When a few days later, president of Gabon, Omar Bongo, returned to Libreville, he delivered a speech at the airport in which he condemned the "excesses" but also declared himself "in solidarity with his people"; at the same time, he announced the expulsion of all Beninese residents of Gabon, except those who were already Gabonese citizens or political refugees. Bongo's speech was an encouragement to continue reprisals against the Beninese. On Monday, July 31, 1978, the Beninese were gathered by the police in front of the mosque and transferred to the High School of the Estuary, near the airport. There began for them a long wait, in conditions that undermine their dignity as human began, lasting until August 23, 1978, when the last Beninese departed from Gabon. The number of expulsed Beninese was estimated to be between ten and twelve thousand individuals.

NOTES

1. Marjolijn Aalders Grool, *A Journey to Gods and Comrades: Recording Voodoo Stories in Benin (1975–1977, 2014, 2015)*, Series: Topics in Interdisciplinary African Studies, vol. 45 (Köln, Germany: Rüdiger Köppe Verlag· Köln, 2017), 169.

2. S/12319/Add. 1. Report on the imperialist armed aggression committed on Sunday, 16 January 1977, against the People's Republic of Benin, adopted by the Joint Special Session of the Central Committee of the Party of the People's Revolution of Benin, the National Council of the Revolution and the Revolutionary Military Government. Cotonou, March 1977. "Letter Dated 4 April 1977 from the Charge d'Affaires a.i. of Benin to the United Nations Addressed to the President of the Security Council: Addendum," People's Republic of Benin. Office of the President of the Republic, 12.

3. Grool, *A Journey to Gods and Comrades*, 169.

4. "Décret No. 1977–54 du 04 mars 1977 portant règlementation de l'hébergement des étrangers en République Populaire du Bénin": https://sgg.gouv.bj/doc/decret-1977-54/.

5. "Décret No. 1977–55 du 04 mars 1977 portant règlementation de la circulation des étrangers résidant en République Populaire du Bénin": https://sgg.gouv.bj/doc/decret-1977-55/.

6. John Darnton, "Benin Raid an African Mystery," *New York Times*, February 4, 1977, 37.

7. "Report of the Security Council Special Mission to the People's Republic of Benin Established under Resolution 404 (2977). Security Council Official Records. Thirty-Second Year. Special Supplement No. 3 (New York: United Nations, 1977), Annex IV, 108.

8. "Marc Colot—Belgium—Benin—Died in action on January 16, 1977, in Benin." In Memoriam, *Orbs Patria Nostra*, https://www.orbspatrianostra.com/in -memoriam.html.

9. Interview with JP D., known as Jean-Philippe conducted in Aix-en-Provence, October 20, 2012, by Walter Bruyère-Ostells [in:] Walter Bruyère-Ostells, "Treatment of the Bodies of Those Killed in French Mercenary Operations between 1960 and 1989," *Human Remains and Violence* 5, no. 2 (2019): 10–11; https://missingpersons .icrc.org/library/treatment-bodies-those-killed-french-mercenary-operations-between -1960-and-1989.

10. "Report of the Administrative Secretary—General on Events of January 16, 1977," in Cotonou, Republic of Benin, 1977–2. Organization of African Unity/ African Union, CM/805(XXVIII), 5: https://archives.au.int.handle/123456789/9824.

11. Ibid.

12. S/Res. No. 419 (1977)/ adopted by the Security Council at its 2049th meeting, on November 24, 1977, para. 5: https://digitallibrary.un.org/record/66647?ln=en.

13. "Revised Report on the Evaluation of Damages and Losses of Various Kinds Occasioned to the People's Republic of Benin During the Imperialist Aggression of Sunday, 16 January 1977." "Letter Dated 13 October 1977, from the Permanent representative of Benin to the United Nations Addressed to the President of the Security Council" (S/12415, 13 October 1977), 4–5: https://digitallibrary.un.org/record/36398 ?ln=en.

14. CFA franc stands for *Communauté Financière Africaine* (African Financial Community). The CFA franc zone is an economic and monetary area bringing together France and fifteen countries in sub-Saharan Africa. The CFA franc zone. Banque de France, November 2015: https://abc-economie.banque-france.fr/sites/ default/files/medias/documents/816153_fiche_zone-franc.pdf.

15. "Letter dated 4 April 1977 from the *Chargé d'affaires a.i.* of Benin to the United Nations addressed to the President of the Security Council: Addendum: Report on the evaluation of damages and losses of various kinds occasioned to the People's Republic of Benin during the imperialist aggression of 16 January 1977," S/12318/ Add. 1, 5.

16. Revised Report on the Evaluation of Damages and Losses of Various Kinds Occasioned to the People's Republic of Benin During the Imperialist Aggression of Sunday, 16 January 1977. Letter Dated 13 October 1977 from The Permanent representative of Benin to the United Nations Addressed to the President of the Security Council. (S/12415, 13 October 1977), 5: https://digitallibrary.un.org/record/36398?ln =en.

17. At the time of Opération Crevette CFA 249.30 = $1.00. *Treasury Reporting Rates of Exchange of March 31, 1977*. Department of the Treasury, Fiscal Service Bureau of Government Financial Operations: https://www.govinfo.gov/content/pkg /GOVPUB-T63_100-45728fcb131fefb32e2376c70c60690a/pdf/GOVPUB-T63_100 -45728fcb131fefb32e2376c70c60690a.pdf.

18. Revised Report on The Evaluation of Damages and Losses of Various Kinds Occasioned to the People's Republic of Benin During the Imperialist Aggression of Sunday, 16 January 1977. Letter Dated 13 October 1977 from The Permanent

representative of Benin to the United Nations Addressed to the President of the Security Council. (S/12415, 13 October 1977), 11: https://digitallibrary.un.org/record /36398?ln=en.

Chapter 14

Whose Victory?

It seems quite natural that since the Omegas' assault on Cotonou had been repelled, and the invaders forced to abandon the execution of the operation, the Beninese authorities claimed victory. But whose victory was this, really?

NORTH KOREA'S INVOLVEMENT

Immediately after the attack in January 1970, and until the changes in political system in Benin two decades later, in the 1990s, the official opinion in Benin's media and historiography was that it had been due to the immediate and effective counter action of the Beninese armed forces on the ground that Opération Crevette had been thwarted. For all that time, Benin's authorities had maintained it was the members of the Beninese army, *Forces armées populaires* (FAP), alongside local volunteers, members of various state sponsored civil and paramilitary organizations, who successfully repelled the Omega's assault. Thirty-six years after Opération Crevette, some military and civilian witnesses were asked "to reconstruct the facts" relating to the mercenary invasion; they maintained the story of a strong military response to the mercenary attack by "the battalions of the Presidential Guard and the units of the National Gendarmerie and the Army."[1]

In a message to then–Libyan leader Colonel Muammar Khadafi, Kérékou stated that the mercenaries were thwarted by the Beninese army and the forces of the popular resistance without mentioning any role of the North Koreans. The "popular resistance" phrase was also used by Beninese authorities to describe the response by the political activists and residents of Cotonou to Kérékou's call to join the military forces in stopping the mercenary units from destroying more governmental buildings and utility installations and causing more damage within the city. According to official version of events, local residents erected barricades on the main streets of Cotonou that contributed to the containment of Omegas who were moving toward the city center.

However, information that there were "three hours of fighting using machetes and clubs against cannon fire"[2] seems to be seriously exaggerated and does not find support in any contemporary descriptions of the course of events on January 16, 1977, provided by their participants. Notably, this version of Opération Crevette's events had no place for the role of foreign military in the Beninese thwarting the coup d'état.

The government of the Democratic People's Republic of North Korea (DPRNK, i.e., North Korea) was one of the closest political and military allies of revolutionary Benin at the time of the coup, and it demonstrated its support by publicly disclaiming any role its soldiers may have played in leading or participating in repelling the Omegas' assault on Cotonou. The *charge d'affaires* of the North Korean embassy in Cotonou maintained that he was an eyewitness of the fighting from the balcony of his residence, located between the airport and the presidential palace, because he was concerned about the safety of the DPRNK dignitaries visiting Cotonou at that time. However, not once in his personal accounts of the events of January 16 did he mention that any members of the DPRNK's delegation security detail, or the North Korean military instructors attached to the Beninese army, took any part in repelling the Omegas' attack. This would mean that the DPRNK detail staying at the same location as the delegation did not take any protective action despite the fact that mercenaries temporarily occupied the ground floor of the Conseil d'Entente—the building in which the ministerial delegation from Pyongyang was staying at the time. Clearly unaware of the high North Korean delegation and its security detail's presence in the building, the Omegas had unpacked packages of anti-tank rockets and prepared munitions for action in this same building. The North Korean diplomat on record had remained at that location during this time and, in telephone contact with the delegation, stated he was "safe and sound" during the attack; this account had no reference of action by the North Korean security detail.[3]

Also interesting is that none of the foreign diplomats or representatives of the various international organizations accredited in Cotonou, or any other eyewitnesses who submitted to the United Nations (UN) Special Mission their accounts of events of January 16, 1977, mentioned any role played by the North Korean military instructors or members of the security detail in thwarting of the Omegas' attack.

However, in light of statements of some former Beninese officers—participants of events of January 16, 1977—made only after political changes in Benin in 1989, one could have serious doubts as to effectiveness of counterattack conducted by Beninese armed forces.

In an interview given forty-two years after Opération Crevette, Officer El Hadj Sanni Mouftaou still glorified the military leadership of Kérékou and revealed that about a hundred of newly conscripted young soldiers stationed at Camp Guézo were unprepared to join the armed action against advancing armed mercenaries. They were unfamiliar with use of the main weapon that was to be the armament of the Beninese forces. Alarmed, President Kérékou "came to the camp and started to take out the AKM from the crates and he was teaching us for the first time to use AKM. We didn't know what we called AKM weapons, we were trained with Max 36 weapons."[4] Sanni Mouftaou stated also that although the young recruits heard about AKMs, they "never used them," and that "Kérékou taught us how to use an AKM weapon for the first time [that] day [i.e., January 16, 1977]."[5]

A similar opinion about the readiness of the Beninese—this time referencing the gendarmerie—to fight the invading Benin mercenaries was given by the officer of the gendarmerie, Christophe Sogla Blèochi. In an interview with *Agence Bénin Presse*, he recalled that on the day the Opération Crevette, January 16, 1977, "Under the pressure of the aggressors, the military officers delivered a hundred soldiers not trained in the handling of weapons, to the front to fight the mercenaries."[6] They spent only a week at Camp Guézo prior to the described events. The officers asked them to "put [them]selves in groups of ten to go and take up arms."[7] Allegedly, it was only thanks to the personal intervention of President Kérékou these young gendarmes have not "served as cannon fodder [i.e., soldiers regarded or treated as expendable in battle[8]]."[9]

A high-ranking Beninese officer and former commander of the military camp in Ouidah, Lieutenant Colonel Philippe Akpo, accused the military staff of Camp Guézo of a "lack of initiative and courage" in taking up an effective pursuit of the mercenaries withdrawing to the airport. "In reality"—writes Akpo—"with the exception of the elements of the presidential guard, the officers, non-commissioned officers and commanders in Cotonou had lacked initiative and courage to pick up rocket launchers and, even on foot passing the neighborhoods located behind the Aupiais College could have moved to the north side of the airstrip" and, from the houses of the street parallel to the runway on which Omegas DC-7 was parked, "could have blown the cursed plane."[10] To the contrary—concludes Akpo—"each wanted to save his skin" by designating someone else to do it.[11] The motorized parachutist unit under Akpo's command drove to Cotonou, twenty-five miles from its headquarters in Ouidah. But when it reached the airport, the DC-7 aircraft had already taken off and, thus, avoided being hit and immobilized by the machine-gun fire from AML Panhard.[12]

The other former high-ranking Beninese officer of the gendarmerie, and former head of the national security agency Sûrete National, General François Kouyami, when asked the question, "Who repelled Bob Denard? Were they Korean instructors?" stated that: "Bob Denard's mercenaries were repulsed by the Koreans who were in Benin for a very specific mission, the protection of their Foreign Minister."[13]

As to the active response by the FAP against the assault, only very general information has been made available. One such information included in UN document reads that Adjutant Atèmènu Jean Kouton "led the first unit of the Beninese People's Armed Forces involved in the counter-attack on the landing field."[14] Although he was considered to be "one of the closest eyewitnesses" by Beninese authorities, unlike in the case of other official Beninese eyewitnesses, none of his testimony about the course of the action his unit took was produced to the public.

Questions about the extent of Beninese military actions in repelling the Omega's assault on Cotonou can be found in the brief "testimony" of Alain Chevalerias using the alias "Alain Marc."[15] In his statement, he mentions two groups whose moved through the streets of Cotonou from the airport toward designated areas of assault, but soon found themselves at risk of encirclement by the counter-attacking units: one North Korean and the other likely Beninese FRAP. Chevalerias, however, refers to these units only as "enemies," without identifying them either as local or foreign troops. According to his statement, his group had been forced to withdraw from the ongoing assault due to heavy fire from Beninese army: "Automatic weapons *claqements* [i.e., 'clicks'] coming from the position of the other unit of assault reach us. We stop our progress in order not to separate ourselves and especially not be left behind. The exchange of fire continues for a while, and I hear the thud of mortar shells hitting. The enemy seems to be moving and the intensity fire continues for a moment. We are afraid of being surrounded. It is with relief that I received the order to withdraw."[16]

It was Bob Denard, when trying to bleach the failure of his operation publicly in 1998 in his book *Corsaire de la Republique*, who claimed that it was the members of the North Korean military who had in fact played an important role in the military failure of Opération Crevette. Denard complained that instead of expected support of the Omegas from Beninese gendarmes and parachutists, along with Cotonou population, the Omegas had "come up against the unforeseen resistance of North Korean soldiers, who accompanied dignitaries of Pyongyang participating in a congress."[17] Interestingly, in the hagiographic biography of Bob Denard published by Pierre Lunel in 1991, the is no mention of a North Korean participation in counter-attack against the Omegas. Lunel writes that Denard recognized only an hour after debarkation that the success of the operation would be impossible because "the enemy [was] on alert [and] reacted fast and strong."[18] Also, the only memoire regarding Opération Crevette published on the webpage of *Orbs Patria Nostra* as an alleged eyewitness account does not contain in its publicly available version any reference to the North Korean participation in forcing the Omegas to withdraw to the Cotonou Airport.[19] However, in an unpublished criminal court record contained in Denard's private archive, there is the testimony of the mercenary quoted by Walter Bruyère-Ostells, that a group of the Omegas moving toward presidential palace "unexpectedly" encountered in front of the palace North Korean soldiers with "three machine gun nests in front of the Presidency" had "forced the group to turn back."[20] It is, however, questionable that it was a North Korean unit protecting Kérékou's presidential palace. The palace was regularly protected by the Presidential Guard detachment equipped with a Peugeot van armed with two mounted French-made machine guns (AA52A) and manned by six soldiers.[21] The Guard had been established by Kérékou in the mid-1970s, comprised of individuals descended overwhelmingly from the Fulani (northern tribe). It soon became the military bastion of the regime against mutiny from other parts of the military. Trained and equipped by North Korean instructors, it was the most competent unit in the country[22] and it is doubtful whether President Kérékou would entrust his personal security to any foreign units.

The role of North Korean soldiers and advisors became generally accepted in Beninese and other African media only after the Beninese political changes in the early 1990s, and became even more prevalent in Benin's media after Mathieu Kérékou's death.[23] Omitting details as to a number of North Korean troops in Benin, and specifically in Cotonou, the media stated, for example, that "Soldiers of the North Korean army [had] come to Cotonou as part of the military cooperation between the two countries. This combination of forces resulted in an effective response to the attackers led by Bob Denard";[24] and that Kérékou "welcomed the arrival of North Korean military advisers who were useful to him in repelling Bob Denard's mercenaries";[25] that "Bob Denard's military expertise [was] rapidly facing not only the Beninese army but also the North Korean elements present in Cotonou under agreements of cooperation between socialist republics";[26] and "[s]upported by soldiers of the North Korean Army present in Cotonou in the framework of military cooperation between the two States, the FRAP had succeeded in defeating the mercenaries who left in disaster leaving some of theirs."[27]

What, however, still remains unclear is what role either the previously mentioned North Korean military instructors assigned to the Beninese FRAP or the security detachment of the North Korean delegation visiting Benin played in routing the mercenaries. Strict secrecy surrounding any political activities of North Korea has not changed since 1977 and contributes to various speculations regarding details of role of North Koreans in hindering the Omegas' attack on Cotonou.

Thus, many sources stress, however, that it was the elements of the North Korean military instructors and/or military guards who played an important role in "leading the first units to counter-attack"[28] what resulted in quick and effective repelling of the Omegas ground attack and forcing them to withdraw to the airport. Such opinion supports the now general Francois Kouyami, former head of Beninese gendarmerie and security services, and later a strong opponent and political prisoner of Kérékou. In his memoirs, published almost thirty years after the event, Kouyami claims that when faced with the weakness of the Beninese military it was the North Koreans who played a decisive role in thwarting the Omegas attack;[29] interestingly, this same opinion was later expressed in President's Kérékou obituary found in the magazine *Jeune Afrique*.[30] One African source went even so far as to state with the grain of exaggeration that "[t]heir [North Koreans] heavy response to the attackers' fire completely changed the situation."[31]

KÉRÉKOU'S TRAP EXPLANATION

For others who rejected the notion of any foreign intervention in Benin, the operation's failure was accredited to a trap set up by President Kérékou. Although the course of events at the airport seems to negate that Beninese authorities were ever aware of the plane's landing, some accounts claim that Kérékou had sent his military to lay-in-wait in order to thwart the operation at its very beginning. Thus, for example, President Omar Bongo, rebuffing accusations that Gabon participated in the preparation of Opération Crevette and stubbornly claiming that it was Benin who organized the attack on Cotonou to turn attention away from its economic problems,[32] was "convinced that a most pathetic charade has been cleverly staged to discredit Gabon with a view to undermining the plans to hold the next Organization of African Unity (OAU) Conference at Libreville."[33] He further added that this particular OAU meeting was expected to "salvage" Africa from splitting up the OAU due to ideological differences between member states due to armed intervention between them or by outside actors. Since, according to the OAU rules, Bongo would be elected for a coming year as Chairman of the organization, it was extremely important for him that his support for Opération Crevette is not publicly revealed at that time. What was, however, more important was that the African heads of states were supposed to adopt during this conference, as aforementioned, an important regional treaty on elimination of use of mercenaries on African continent.

A government monument donated by North Korea to Benin also supported the story of Kérékou's trap, given that it was dedicated to the victory of the FAP soldiers who died repelling the Omegas. The only reference on the monument to North Korea was, and still is, a plaque on the back about its Korean creators.

Looking for any excuse to justify his military failure, Denard claimed that when Pognon was initially informed about organized resistance against the Omegas, he asked Denard "to call back" his men and "to give as quickly as possible the order to depart."[34] It seems rather unlikely, however, that a professional mercenary, such as Denard, would take military orders from a civilian politician lacking any military training or experience, sitting in location away from the action, and unable to make firsthand evaluations of the situation in the field. This was rather yet another excuse justifying operation's failure and his order to cease the operation, saving himself and his associates from decimation or apprehension. Only six months earlier, thirteen mercenaries had been sentenced to death by the local revolutionary tribunal during the Luanda Trials for participation in Angola's civil war: four met deaths by firing squad, and the remaining received long jail terms. Thus, Denard followed the rule "better safe, than sorry" in deciding to escape rather than be caught in action and risk criminal prosecution by a revolutionary tribunal. The European mercenaries, at least, had to be aware of fate of those mercenaries caught in Angola and the German famous mercenary, Rolf Steiner, who spent three years in Sudanese jail (1971 to 1974), during which was supposedly tortured and finally was sentenced to death. He saved his head only because of the hard pressure by the German authorities on government in Khartoum (the capital of Sudan). Both cases, of the Luanda trial and Steiner's fate in Sudan, were at that time highly publicized in European mass media. Echos of these events could be found in a story of one of the European participants.

As he relayed many years later, retreating to the Cotonou Airport:

> They had left behind two dead, a European and a prisoner (Guinean). The white mercenary had been wounded in the thigh during the retreat to the airport. The recollection of previous operations and the fate that he could expect led him to immediately shoot himself in the head: the man preferred to kill himself rather than fall prey to the Beninese alive. This decision was perhaps also influenced by the fear of being tortured in order to reveal information about his comrades in arms and their mission commanders.[35]

The only European mercenary who died during Opération Crevette was identified by Beninese authorities as Marc Colot (a.k.a. Lieutenant Cemaer). Since a death certificate in his case was not issued, there is no formal cause of his death reported.[36]

NOTES

1. "Agression du Bénin par les mercenaires: Ce qui reste du 16 janvier 1977," *Le Matinal* (Cotonou), January 16, 2013: http ://egbade.over-blog.com/article-agression-du-benin-par-les-mercenaires-ce-qui-reste-du-16-janvier-1977-114431051.html.

2. Yao Vie, "Bénin: Attaque du 16 janvier 1977, L'Opération Crevette, 16 janvier," https://ici1fo.com/benin--attaque-du-16-janvier-1977-l-operation-crevette-article-1845.html.

3. UN, Special Mission of the Security Council Established under Resolution 404 (1977), "Report of the Security Council Special Mission to the People's Republic of Benin Established under Resolution 404 (1977)" (New York: United Nations, 1977), https://digitallibrary.un.org/record/564622. (See Statement by Mr. Tchoe Hyeun IL, Charge d'affairs a.i. of the Democratic People's Republic of Korea, 52.)

4. The AKM is an assault rifle—the Kalashnikov's Automatic Rifle Modernized. The Beninese army probably received Type 68 also known as Type 68 NK, a North Korean version of the AKM, adopted in 1968 to replace the Type 58. Reference to Max 36 is probably a misspelled reference to the MAS Modèle 36 (also known as the Fusil à répétition 7 mm 5 M. 36). The MAS-36 was extensively used by French army and colonial defense forces during France's postwar counter-insurgency operations. MAS-36 was used later by many former French colonies, among them Benin: MAS-36 rifles.

5. Aziz Badarou, "Agression du 16 janvier 1977: Sanni Mouftaou, un survivant, retrace l'histoire," *Matin Libre* (blog), February 1, 2019, https://matinlibre.com/2019/01/31/agression-du-16-janvier-1977-sanni-mouftaou-un-survivant-retrace-lhistoire/.

6. "Le Massacre a Été Évité de Justesse à l'armée Béninoise le 16 janvier 1977," *Agence Benin Presse*.

7. Ibid.

8. "Cannon Fodder," *Merriam-Webster*, accessed November 28, 2021, https://www.merriam-webster.com/dictionary/cannon+fodder.

9. "Le massacre a été évité de justesse à l'armée Béninoise le 16 janvier 1977."

10. Philippe Akpo, *Role et implications des forces armees beninoises dans la vie politique nationale: Temoignage, ma part de vérité sur les faits et les non-dits* (Cotonou, Bénin: Editions du Flamboyant, 2005), see 217.

11. "Le Massacre a Été Évité de Justesse à l'armée Béninoise le 16 janvier 1977."

12. Ibid.

13. François Kouyami, *Affaires d'état au Bénin: Le général François Kouyami parle: Livre-interview, Les grandes interviews* (L'Hay-les-Roses, France: Les Editions IBIDUN, 2011), 90.

14. Benin, "Letter Dated 77/04/04 from the Charge d'Affaires a.i. of Benin to the United Nations Addressed to the President of the Security Council: Addendum" (New York: United Nations, April 5, 1977), https://digitallibrary.un.org/record/564452, see 17.

15. Walter Bruyère-Ostells, *Dans l'ombre de Bob Denard: Les mercenaires français de 1960 à 1989* (Paris: Nouveau monde, 2014), 182. Bruyère-Ostells maintains

that Chevalerias not only is not the author of that text but also did not participate in Opération Crevette.

16. "OPS Bénin," *Orbs Patria Nostra*, accessed November 18, 2021, https://www .orbspatrianostra.com/ops/ops-benin/temoignage-alain-marc.html.

17. Bob Denard and George Fleury, *Corsaire de la République* (Paris: Robert Laffont, 1998), 292.

18. Pierre Lunel, *Bob Denard: Le roi de fortune* (Edition⁰ 1, 1991), 461.

19. "OPS Bénin."

20. "OPS Bénin."

21. UN, Special Mission of the Security Council Established under Resolution 404 (1977), "Report of the Security Council Special Mission to the People's Republic of Benin Estabilshed under Resolution 404 (1977): Addendum" (New York: United Nations, March 8, 1977), https://digitallibrary.un.org/record/564391, see Annex VI, 95. AA-52 (designation in French: *Arme Automatique Transformable Modèle 1952*, "Transformable automatic weapon model 1952").

22. "Benin Army (l'Armee de Terre)," *Global Security*, accessed November 18, 2021, https://www.globalsecurity.org/military/world/africa/bn-army.htm.

23. See, for example, Léonce Adjevi, "40e anniversaire de l'agression du 16 janvier 1977 au Bénin: Don de sang et dépôt de gerbe au programme," *Le Matinal*, January 16, 2017: seances-de-don-de-sang-et-depot-de-gerbe-au-programme; Charly Hessoun, "Bénin: Il y a 38 ans, l'historique agression du 16 janvier 1977 (vidéo)," *La Nouvelle Tribune* (blog), January 16, 2015, https://lanouvelletribune.info/2015/01/ benin-il-y-a-38-ans-l-historique-agression-du-16-janvier-1977-video/.

24. Le souvenir du 16 janvier 1977: http://newsyoung.fr/benin-le-souvenir-du-16 -janvier-1977.

25. Christophe Boisbouvier, "Bénin: Mathieu Kérékou, une histoire africaine," *Jeune Afrique*, no. 2858, October 21, 2015, 12.

26. Matthieu Kairouz, "Ce jour-là: le 16 janvier 1977, Bob Denard lance l'"Opération crevette' contre Kérékou au Bénin," *Jeune Afrique*, January 16, 2017, https://www.jeuneafrique.com/360952/politique/jour-16-janvier-1977-bob-denard -lance-l-operation-crevette-contre-kerekou-benin/.

27. Hessoun, "Bénin."

28. Jean Establet, *Mathieu Kerekou: L'inamovible président du Bénin* (Paris: Editions L'Harmattan, 1997).Original quote: "Les instructeurs nord coreens font merville et encadrent les premieres unites de contre-attaque"; Hessoun, "Bénin."

29. François Kouyami, "Affaires d'État au Bénin: le général François Kouyami parle, livre-interview." *Les grandes interviews*, 90.

30. Boisbouvier, "Bénin."

31. Pierre Cherruau and Marcus Boni Teiga, "Les 10 coups d'Etat les plus foireux en Afrique," *7sur7.cd*, August 12, 2015, https://7sur7.cd/les-10-coups-detat-les-plus -foireux-en-afrique.

32. "Le lresident de La Republique du Gabon: 'Tout Est Faux,'" *Jeune Afrique*, April 1977. Jean Louis Buchet interview with Omar Bongo.

33. UN, Secretary General and Gabon. President, "Letter Dated 77/04/04 from the Secretary-General Addressed to the President of the Security Council" (New York: United Nations, April 4, 1977), https://digitallibrary.un.org/record/564428.

34. Ibid.

35. Walter Bruyeré-Ostells, "Treatment of the Bodies of Those Killed in French Mercenary Operations between 1960 and 1989," *Human Remains and Violence* 5, no. 2 (October 2019): 3–16, https://doi.org/10.7227/HRV.5.2.2.

36. "Report of the Security Council Special Mission to the People's Republic of Benin Established under Resolution 404 (1977)," see Annex III, 3.

Chapter 15

Pandora's Boxes

The seemingly successful emergency escape of the Omegas from Cotonou turned out to be just as flawed as the operation itself. "Shortly after takeoff, Bosco[1] tells me that the Beninese sergeant who served the machine gun placed on the roof of the aerodrome had not embarked. He fell asleep of fatigue," recalled Denard.[2] It was Bâ Alpha Oumarou, a Guinean assigned to Red Group under the command of a European mercenary,[3] who was to maintain control of the airport and shell the presidential palace and Camp Guézo from the airport's rooftop. Despite the energizing pill provided to the Omegas prior to landing in Cotonou, and amid the shooting around him, Bâ Alpha Oumarou had fallen asleep from exhaustion and failed to board the aircraft in time for departure.

Hurried at the time of departure, Denard's commando left behind on the airport tarmac some weapons and still packed boxes with ammunition. This equipment included mortars, anti-tank weapons, heavy and light machine guns, sub machine guns, automatic rifles, pistols, and grenades, various ammunition, radio communication equipment, and some other items of both military and non-military nature. President Kérékou showed all these items three days later to members of the diplomatic corps accredited in Benin who had been invited for the occasion to the Hall of the People, a stately, columned edifice next to the presidential palace.

Among the weapons left on the tarmac were Belgian FN automatic assault rifles, a 7.62-millimeter-caliber light machine gun, a French-manufactured eighty-one-millimeter mortar, an eighty-nine-millimeter anti-tank rocket launcher, a nine-millimeter-caliber automatic pistol, a cardboard tube that might have held a mortar accelerator charge and had Cyrillic printing on side, two fifty-caliber machine guns, and one eighty-millimeter mortar tube (these last three being of apparent US origin).[4]

No less impressive was the amount and the diversity of the ammunition abandoned by the mercenaries on the airport's tarmac. Strikingly, there was a large volume of various explosives and variety of hand grenades.

145

There were 1,256 nine-millimeter cartridges with regular bullets, PA-PM, Lot No. 23–4-SFM75, of French origin; 405 NATO-type nine- millimeter cartridges with regular bullets, of Belgian origin; 33,668 NATO-type 7.62-millimeter cartridges with regular bullets, of Belgian origin; 10,230 NATO-type 7.62-millimeter cartridges on detachable magna-metal belts (one tracer and four regular bullets) of Belgian origin; three thousand 7.62-millimeter cartridges on detachable magno-metal belts (one tracer and nine regular bullets) with Arabic markings; 1,875 12.7-millimeter cartridges on detachable magno-metal belts (one tracer and four regular bullets), of Belgian origin; six offensive hand grenades, D-37, Lot No. SPA 38–60, of French origin; five fuses for offensive explosive hand grenades, Lot No. 42 RYN 60; seven explosive hand grenades, D-37, Lot No. 4-EB-59, of French origin; four explosive hand grenades, D-37, Lot No. 6-TYN-58, of French origin; one explosive hand grenade, D-37, Lot No. 4-TNP-60, of French origin; five fuses for hand grenades, D-37, Lot No. 5-EB-59, of French origin; four fuses for explosive hand grenades, D-37, Lot No. 114 RYN-58, of French origin; fifty-three forty-millimeter explosive rifle grenades, APAV, Lot No. 2-MPA-77, four of which were destroyed, of Belgian origin; ten offensive-defensive hand grenades, M2, with fuses, M-204 AI, Lot No. I MI-6–71, of American origin; eighteen explosive shells, eighty-one millimeter, FA-32 5 BT 36, Lot No. 32, of French origin; twenty propellant cartridges for eighty-one-millimeter shells, Lot No. 44CF-51, of French origin; twenty fuses, DP 24/31 RYG 18, for eighty-one-millimeter shells, Lot NO. 9 ATS-62, 1 of which was destroyed, of French origin; sixty-four relays for eighty-one millimeter shells, Lot No. 122, CF-51, of French origin; eleven eighty-one-millimeter smoke shells, complete, with fuses, Lot No. 211–71 (fuse, Lot No. 441.76), of British or American origin; five explosive eighty-one-millimeter shells, complete, with fuses, Lot No. 211–71 (fuse, Lot No. 441–76), of British or American origin; four sixty-five-millimeter AC explosive rifle grenades, with Arabic markings, two of which were destroyed; thirty-two sixty-six-millimeter AC explosive rockets, M-72-A-2, Lot No. LS 220-R-8–74, twenty-six of which were destroyed, of American origin; twelve eighty-nine-millimeter AC explosive rockets, BM-66, Lot No. 1-73, one of which was destroyed, of Spanish origin.[5]

However, the diplomats had not been presented with all the items found upon the Omegas escape; this turned out to be a serious tactical error on part of the Beninese. Among the effects left behind on the tarmac was a crate with an identifying inscription: "Colonel Maurin. 10 Smoke Grenades, CB 16-w 550-a, 81mm Mortars, 55 kg Volume: 0,077m 3." One can imagine the surprise of the Beninese soldiers who discovered the contents of the crate were not weapons, as inscribed, but rather typed and hand-written notes, memoranda, diagrams, charts, and sketches that, by their nature, appeared directly related to the events of January 16 in Cotonou; this included airline tickets with the Omegas' real names and bank records listing payments for the participants in the operation. Also found within were *laissez-passes*,[6] health certificates, identity cards, photographs, driver licenses, checkbooks, payment slips, private correspondence with an indication of names, addresses, and other information concerning the bearers of those documents. Except for several documents in Arabic, all documents were in French. The airline tickets had been placed in a black briefcase bearing the inscription "A. B-B."[7] As it turned out, this abandoned crate contained the complete documentation of the operation and turned out to be the "Pandora's box" of Opération Crevette. This crate was allegedly never shown to the diplomats invited for the presentation of items left behind by escaping Omegas. All the documents found in the crate, plus the extended testimony of Bâ Alpha Oumarou, became critical evidence providing detailed information used in investigations of Opération Crevette.

In the days after Opération Crevette, Guinean and Beninese media published photographs of nine Europeans whom they described as mercenaries caught in the aftermath.[8] None of them, however, were ever presented to the foreign media or interviewed by any of many international commissions making inquiries as to events of January 16, 1977. The reason was simple: the published photographs showed European mercenaries apprehended not during the attempted coup in Benin, but during a similar failed mercenary operation that in fact took place seven years earlier (1970) fighting revolutionary leadership in Guinea. Under these circumstances, the convenient finding of the crate with Denard's personal documents and those others relevant to participants of Opération Crevette raised natural doubts as to their authenticity. If the photographs presented were from previous operations, maybe no documents had actually been found? Or maybe those found were forged?

The only picture showing the authentic participant of Opération Crevette seems to photograph of the Guinean mercenary, Bâ Alpha Oumarou, published in *Ehuzu* two months later in connection with the report of results of Beninese investigation of events of January 16.[9]

Gabon's president, Omar Bongo, immediately questioned the authenticity of documents released by the Beninese. Because Benin had waited two months to publish their findings, President Bongo claimed they had plenty of time to prepare falsified documents. President Bongo went on to deny ever knowing a Gilbert Bourgeaud (or Bob Denard), or ever signing any document pertaining to his person. He claimed that the Beninese who worked at that time at Gabonese banks participated in the falsification of bank records left at the airport by the Omegas.[10]

The United Nations Special Mission to Cotonou could not confirm the authenticity of the documents found at the airport, as it had no mandate to conduct forensic investigations. The chief of the UN Special Mission, however, observed at that time, "It's hard to say that all had been fabricated. It would require a genius to do all of this." Referring to the volume of personal documents found on a tarmac, it was concluded, "they must be sure of the success of a coup and because of that they took with themselves such a huge number of the documents."[11] A Madagascan representative of the Security Council posed a similar question: "Who can prove that the government of Benin forged a single false document among the many documents contained in the file, raised a similar argument? One would have to prove false only one document to demolish the whole lot."[12]

Responding to allegations that the documents recovered were fabricated, the representative of Benin responded that one "would have to be naive or really ill-intentioned to believe that the People's Republic of Benin had forged the national identity card of Lieutenant-Colonel Gilbert Bourgeaud or that of Sy Sawane. One would have to be intellectually dishonest to believe that the People's Republic of Benin had invented the bank account numbers, the airline tickets, the names, and addresses of those hired killers who are the mercenaries that invaded Cotonou on Sunday, 16 January 1977."[13]

The representative of Gabon, however, questioned not only the authenticity of President Bongo's signature on a document appointing Gilbert Bourgeaud (Bob Denard) as his advisor but even the authenticity of navigational maps found among other documents.[14] In a desperate attempt to prove that at least one document found in the Denard's crate was not authentic, Gabon's ambassador claimed that the name of the institution allegedly issuing Denard's nomination was at the time of its alleged issuance different from the one listed on a document.

As expected, Paris also rejected Benin's accusations that were based "exclusively on documents which [were] alleged to have been abandoned at the airport and on the testimony of a single witness."[15] One can only assume that either due to deep secrecy surrounding the clandestine operation, or acting on deceptive instructions received from Quay d'Orsay, the French ambassador was unwilling to admit that Opération Crevette was a "colonialist," "destabilization" operation organized with the full knowledge and even support of French special services.[16] Thus, during a debate in the Security Council that took place three months after the failed operation, the ambassador of France resorted to total denial: "My delegation was indeed surprised—I might even say stupefied—when we heard certain passage of the statement of the representative of Benin. He suggested that the whole of the operation originated in France, that it was mounted in France and carried out by Frenchmen. . . . I do not see what France would have had to gain by encouraging such a shocking operation."[17] As it turned out, the ambassador's statements classically illustrated the conduct of a diplomat—"an honest gentleman sent to lie abroad for the good of his country."

As to the authenticity of the documents, Denard would later not only fail to deny the documents had been left by his commando on the tarmac or question their authenticity, but would admit in his book published a decade after the operation that they belonged to him.[18] Similar claims were made in an earlier account given by Denard to Pierre Lunel.[19] He attempted to minimize his irresponsibility, saying that they were "foolishly abandoned."[20] He maintained that because three Omegas were wounded during the operation, he ordered that they be brought on board, and the crate with ammunition be left of a tarmac:

I have the heavy equipment[21] under the plane whose propellers are already rotating. Some men return with prisoners whom I immediately release. One of them, a civilian in charge of Legrand's bag, managed to get into the plane where Gratien Pognon and his secretary were already standing. Once my groups meet at the airfield, I worry about our losses. I put on board my three, light wounded, and then ordered to abandon most cases of ammunition.[22]

Although Denard's actions are presented as those of a pure humanitarianism, one might wonder why the single most significant crate was not loaded onto the departing DC-7(F), given its load capacity was a flight crew of three, ninety-nine passengers, a total cargo weight of 34,600 pounds (15,700 kilograms), and a takeoff weight up to 143,000 pounds (64,864 kilograms).

In a separate instance, Denard claimed that after noticing Bâ Alpha Oumarou had been left at the airport: "To crown it all, Bruni[23] does not find the box of ammunitions which contained papers concerning the operation, and which I had not wanted to leave in Gabon. As I get impatient, he quickly makes search the plane. Apparently, one of the civilians forced by the Omegas to unload the material lowered it with the other boxes of ammunitions. Thus, our documents remained on the tarmac of Cotonou."[24]

Thus, Denard confirmed the authenticity of the documents found at the airport and later referred specifically to the identification papers specifying, "my driver license, my identification card in the name of Gilbert Bourgeaud, and also my accreditation card for service for the Republic of Gabon, were among seized documents."[25] Denard's statement was the long overdue answer to the question posed by a representative of Benin during a Security Council debate: "What were the personal papers of Bourgeaud doing at Cotonou Airport on 16 January 1977?" "Perhaps," the Beninese diplomat continued sarcastically, "he came to Cotonou as a tourist on that day and just lost his papers. In that case, why did he not make the proper declaration as he did, in fact, at Abidjan, when he lost his driving license, which had been issued in Morocco?"[26]

A few days prior to the mercenary action in Cotonou, on January 11, 1977, the French minister of foreign affairs, Louis de Guiringaud, had a private audience with the Moroccan king, Hassan II, who himself had paid an official visit to Paris only two months earlier. At the time of Guiringaud's visit, the Omegas had already been trained at the Ben Guerir Air Base for Opération Crevette. It was therefore conceivable that the upcoming operation was the topic of conversations between Hassan II and his French guest. Interestingly, it was Louis de Guiringaud who in a 1979 interview with French magazine *L'Express* articulated the opinion that Africa was the continent "in our grasp and within our means," and France "with five hundred men, [could] change the course of history."[27]

Either by pure coincidence or by design, a second visit took place on January 17. King Hassan II received Gabon's president, Omar Bongo, in Rabat. These two were more than close friends. It was under king Hassan's II influence that President Bongo converted in 1973 from Christianity to Islam and took name El Hadj Omar Bongo Ondimba (born Albert-Bernard Bongo). Further, they were related through family ties. It would be rather naive not to assume that the international consequences of Opération Crevette for both Morocco and Gabon were the subject of their meeting.

Always protective and appreciative of Denard's activities in Africa, his powerful protector, Jacques Foccart, tried to save Denard's reputation by blaming the actions of his subordinates back in Paris, commenting, "the trained puppets who form the bulk of the mercenaries' troops are not selected, as far as I know, on intellectual criteria. The only possible explanation is that this trunk was near the boxes of arms and ammunition and that it was loaded into the plane by mistake."[28] The box was never supposed to have been on that plane.

The content of this single crate would become the basis of numerous international inquiries into the events of January 16, 1977, which would result in prison sentences and enlighten the world as to France's intervention in the politics of its former colonies.

NOTES

1. Bosco was a soldier known to Denard from previous mercenary operations in Congo.

2. Bob Denard and George Fleury, *Corsaire de la République* (Paris: Robert Laffont, 1998), 293. Denard mistakenly calls him "Beninese sergeant" while in fact it was a Guinean national living in exile in Senegal.

3. The European mercenary was named Garnier. No surname is available.

4. UN, Special Mission of the Security Council Established under Resolution 404 (1977), "Report of the Security Council Special Mission to the People's Republic of Benin Established under Resolution 404 (1977)" (New York: United Nations, March 8, 1977), Special Supplement No. 3, s/12294/Rev. 1, Annex V, Inventory of Armaments, Ammunition and Supplies Left Behind by the Attacking Force in Cotonou on 16 January 1977, 111–12.

5. S/PV. 1986, Security Council Official Records 1986 Meeting 7 February 1977, para. 1.

6. A *laissez-passer* (English: to let pass) is a travel document issued by a national government.

7. UN, "Report of the Security Council Special Mission to the People's Republic of Benin Established under Resolution 404 (1977)," see paras. 121–24. No reference to what this may have stood for.

8. *Ehuzu*, January 16, 1977, 2; *Ehuzu,* January 17, 1977, 2–3.

9. *Ehuzu*, March 18, 1977, 8.

10. "Le president de la Republique du Gabon: 'Tout est faux,'" *Jeune Afrique*, April 29, 1977, 28–29.

11. "Un rapport qui ne dissipe pas les equivoques," *Jeune Afrique*, March 25, 1977, 32.

12. "Security Council Official Records, 32nd Year: 2002nd Meeting, 12 April 1977, New York" (New York: United Nations, 1977), https://digitallibrary.un.org/record/224234, para. 110.

13. "Security Council Official Records, 32nd Year: 2000th Meeting, 6 April 1977, New York." (New York: United Nations, 1977), https://digitallibrary.un.org/record/224232, para. 60.

14. Ibid.

15. "Security Council Official Records, 32nd Year:2001st Meeting, 7 April 1977, New York" (New York: United Nations, 1977), https://digitallibrary.un.org/record/224233, para. 61.

16. R. C. Vinen, "Foccart parle, vol. 2, entretiens avec Philippe Gaillard," *English Historical Review* 114, no. 455 (1999): 259.

17. "Security Council Official Records, 32nd Year," 1977.

18. Denard and Fleury, *Corsaire de la République*, 293.

19. Journalist who spoke with Denard firsthand and published the book Pierre Lunel, *Bob Denard: Le roi de fortune* (Edition[0] 1, 1991), 461

20. Denard and Fleury, *Corsaire de la République*, 293.

21. Most likely, he refers here not only to the heavy weapons but also to a jeep that was placed, on his orders, in front of the aircraft's wheels to block its potential, unexpected departure without the commando if the operation failed.

22. Denard and Fleury, *Corsaire de la République*, 293.

23. Roger Bruni was a French paratrooper known to Denard from earlier operations in the Congo.

24. Denard and Fleury, *Corsaire de la République*, 293.

25. Ibid.

26. "Security Council Official Records, 32nd Year: 2003rd Meeting, 13 April 1977, New York" (New York: United Nations, 1977), https://digitallibrary.un.org/record/224235.

27. Philippe Moreau Defarges, "Samy Cohen et Marie-Claude Smouts (dir.): La politique extérieure de Valéry Giscard d'Estaing," *Politique étrangère* 51, no. 1 (1986): 310–12; Daniel Bach and Valery Giscard d'Estaing, *La France en Afrique subsaharienne: Contraintes historiques et nouveaux espaces economiques* (Paris: Ass. fr. de sci. po., 1983), 284.

28. Vinen, "Foccart parle, vol. 2, entretiens avec Philippe Gaillard," 264.

Chapter 16

No End to Troubles

THE UNITED NATIONS AND ORGANIZATION
OF AFRICAN UNITY INQUIRIES

Ten days after the fiasco of Opération Crevette, Benin, which at the time was a rotating non-permanent member at the UN Security Council from 1976 to 1977, began extensive diplomatic action in the forum of various international organizations. This was importantly carried out at the United Nations and the Organization of African Unity (OAU), Benin asking for international inquiries into the Omegas' failed assault on Cotonou. Thus, on January 26, 1977, the government of Benin referred the matter of the mercenary attack on their nation to the UN Security Council and requested that, in accordance with Article 35 of the UN Charter, the council discuss the "cowardly and barbarous aggression committed by the imperialists and their mercenaries against the People's Republic of Benin."[1] To Benin's benefit acted the council's membership that included, as a non-permanent rotating member, not only Benin itself but also several countries politically sympathetic to its case: Czechoslovakia, Libya, Panama, and Romania. Later the council also invited the representatives of Algeria, Cuba, Guinea, Madagascar, Mali, Rwanda, Senegal, Somalia, and Togo to participate in the discussions, however, without vote. Although some, including permanent, members of the council, were initially against accepting Benin's complaint and suggested, instead, its referral to the OAU as a regional African issue, the council, under heavy pressure from many so-called Third World UN-member countries, decided to take it up for consideration.

Taking the floor during the UN Security Council's initial meeting on February 7, 1977, a representative of Benin to the UN did not name any particular country suspected of supporting Opération Crevette.[2] After a two-day debate, the Security Council adopted Resolution 404 (1977),[3] by which it

153

recommended sending a three-member fact-finding special mission to Benin to investigate the circumstances of the attack and submit a report to the council. On the same day, the Security Council recommended establishing a commission of inquiry composed of representatives from India, Libya, and Panama in an effort to investigate the events of January 16, 1977, at Cotonou.[4] Two days later, on February 10, the president of the Security Council issued a note in which he stated that an agreement had been reached through consultations between the members; the Special Mission of the Security Council to the People's Republic of Benin (UN Special Mission) would be composed of the following three members of the Security Council: India, represented by Ramesh N. Mully; Libya, represented by Mansur Rahid Kikhia; and Panama, represented by Jorge Enrique Illueca, who chaired the Mission.[5]

A similar request submitted on February 1, 1977, by Benin with the OAU also resulted in the set-up, this time by the OAU, of a seven-member commission of inquiry (Libya, Nigeria, Niger, Angola, Guinea, Mozambique, and Zambia) to investigate the attack on Cotonou independently from the UN inquiry. Later, the administrative secretary general of the OAU also sent his deputy, Peter Onu, on a separate mission to Benin.

In early communications after the escape of the Omegas from Cotonou, Beninese radio station *Voix de la Revolution* immediately pointed to France as the principal supporter and co-conspirator of Opération Crevette. Along with France, however, the Beninese also identified various African countries, among them Gabon, the Ivory Coast, and Senegal, all closely related politically, economically, and militarily with Paris. Even more aggressive in accusing France and her African allies for organizing a thwarted attack on Cotonou was the president and the media of Guinea; Guinea was the other African socialist-oriented country that seven years earlier had successfully repelled a mercenary raid aiming for a regime change under President Sékou Touré. It was also in a forum of the UN Security Council that the Guinean delegation led, in 1970, the charge against the "imperialists" and their African "lackeys" who were responsible for organizing assistance for mercenary action in Guinea.

UNITED NATIONS SECURITY COUNCIL INQUIRY

The UN Special Mission met from February 16 to 25, 1977, in Cotonou to interview foreign and Beninese eyewitnesses, along with the staff of the diplomatic and international missions located close to the sites of the Omega's activity. A lengthy and extensive interview was also conducted with the only mercenary left behind at the Cotonou Airport, Guinean Bâ Alpha Oumarou. During this time, the Special Mission also examined material evidence, including documentation of Opération Crevette belonging to Denard that had been left on the tarmac by a participant of the operation fleeing in a panic.

Oumarou's testimony and the voluminous documentation supporting it found in Denard's file turned out to be damning for some African members of the United Nations, who were involved in the organization or execution of Opération Crevette in different ways. The governments of the African states named in the report of the Special Mission as supporters of the operation—Gabon, Morocco, Senegal, and Togo—immediately publicly questioned the report that implied their involvement. It was especially important for Togo and Gabon to avoid any accusations of involvement in the failed coup d'état in another African country due to two upcoming conferences: the Organization of African Unity and the Council of Ministers, the first of which would take place in February 1977 in Togo's capital Lomé and, second, in June/July 1977 in Libreville, Gabon, both preceding the annual fourteenth OAU's Assembly of Heads of State and Governments conference in July 1977, also in Libreville.

In a report submitted in April 1977 to the UN Security Council, the Beninese government summarized the results of the UN Special Mission, the OAU Special Commission of Inquiry, and the results of a three-member International Commission of Inquiries (namely those of Benin, Guinea, and Nigeria), as well as its own investigation regarding January 16, 1977, attack.[6] In its statement, Benin specifically accused the Ivory Coast of allowing the recruitment of thirteen Beninese citizens on its territory to serve in Denard's mercenary commando. Benin also complained that, on the day of the attack, two Ivory Coast–registered aircrafts flew over its territory without obtaining required permission from Beninese authorities, thus suggesting that those aircrafts were possibly collecting intelligence related to Opération Crevette. This was a strange allegation as only two months earlier, Benin's minister of foreign affairs announced during a press conference on February 14, 1977, that he had been convinced that neither the Ivory Coast nor Senegal was involved in the failed Opération Crevette.[7] At that time, Benin accepted as reasonable the Ivorian president's explanation that two airplanes, a Fokker 28 and a Grumm Gulfstream, that flew over Benin without earlier permission from Cotonou were carrying the president himself and his entourage for a world festival of Negro-African art taking place in Lagos, the capital of Benin's neighbor, Nigeria.

As a result of its visit to Cotonou, the UN Mission submitted an extensive three-hundred-page report describing the results of its inquiry to the Security Council.[8] Since the mission's mandate provided only for fact-finding and not for an investigation of the circumstances surrounding the assault on Cotonou, its report had not presented any conclusions as to who personally, or which country, should be held responsible for the attack. Because the UN

Mission had no mandate to verify the veracity of statements of witnesses who appeared before it, or to authenticate any material evidence received from the Beninese authorities, its final report, therefore, was limited to a description of events in chronological order, statements from interviewed eyewitnesses, lists of weapons and ammunition, and the documents left by Omegas escaping the airport.

After accepting the report, the UN Security Council adopted, without a vote, Resolution 405 (1977) by which it "strongly condemns an act of armed aggression perpetrated against People's Republic of Benin on January 16, 1977."[9] This resolution, however, like earlier Resolution 404 (1977) did not name any particular state or non-state actor committing the aggression. Instead, the council referred only to an "invasion force." Most of the resolution's text dealt with the general condemnation of mercenary activity and contained an appeal to all states to take necessary steps to terminate the use of mercenaries. Although a mere ten days earlier the representative of Benin had named Gabon, France, Morocco, and the Ivory Coast as Opération Crevette organizers, this time, taking the floor, he only referred to "reactionary neocolonial circles" in France and their African collaborators.

ON THE DEFENSIVE

Gabon

Gabon commenced its defensive action in the forum of the Security Council as early as March 7, 1977. The Report of the Special Mission was presented to the council. In a telegram addressed by the president of the Gabonese Republic in connection with the report of the Security Council Special Mission to Benin, the president of Gabon expressed "astonishment at the conclusions contained in the report and at the cursory manner in which the mission's inquiry had been conducted. President Bongo invited the members of the mission to Gabon "to supplement their information" and assured the Security Council members that his "country was at no time involved, either directly or indirectly, in the alleged aggression." During the debate, Gabon's delegate, Leon N'Dong, assured the UN Security Council that there was no basis for implicating his country in the attack. He claimed that any effort to do so was an insidious effort to promote friction between fraternal African countries by the "enemies of Africa and of Gabon in particular" and "strongly protested against these unfounded and unverified allusions and the long-standing resolutions of the Gabonese government, which have no other purpose than to tarnish the situation in Gabon." Ambassador N'Dong also ridiculed the fact that despite the claim by Benin's authorities that the attack on Cotonou was undertaken by a commando of foreign mercenaries, Benin was only able to produce one African member of that commando to the Special Commission. In support of his criticism of the report, N'Dong quoted the earlier statement of President Bongo in which he wondered what happened to all other participants of the operation when he jokingly concluded: "All the white mercenaries have disappeared and been transformed into a single black" and invoked an old Latin adage: *testis unus, testis nullus*, meaning "one witness, is no witness."

Commenting on the fact that the Beninese found such a huge volume of documents very specific to the operation on the airport tarmac, the representative of Gabon, not without a good reason, wondered how the professional mercenaries "should have embarked on the attack of a country taking with them such compromising personal articles as identity cards, cheque-books, family photos, credit slips and even pay slips and bank statements." Expressing his government's doubt as to whether any mercenary attack against Benin even took place, Gabonese ambassador concluded his statement by saying, "we in Gabon are firmly convinced that this was a rather clumsily staged scenario, hastily pieced together, and we would even go so far as to say that it is a joke in very bad taste."

In an interview with monthly magazine *Jeune Afrique*, President Bongo maintained not only that all the documentation used by the OAU Special Mission for the preparation of the Report was falsified but also that he first learned about the mercenary attack in Cotonou while on a flight between Lagos and Nouakchott (the capital of Mauritania), to which he was to pay a state visit.[ix] President Bongo also denied that he ever personally knew or met Bob Denard, who under the name of Gilbert Bourgeaud (the same as listed on the ID document found on the Cotonou Airport), served in his Presidential Guard as an advisor. Bongo's denial of knowing Denard was particularly unbelievable since it was well known, as stated by Pierre Pean—a renowned French investigative journalist, former employee of various governmental institutions in Gabon, and author of many books concerned with political scandals—that "between 1975 and 1978, Gabon was a main hub for the mercenaries, in particular the most famous among them, Bob Denard."

Even two years later, when most of the facts relating to Opération Crevette became well-documented public knowledge, Gabon's authorities claimed, in a letter addressed to UN Secretary General, that "the Gabonese delegation wishes to repeat here that the DC-7 aircraft which allegedly transported mercenaries to Benin did not take off from Gabon." The basis for their repeated denial was that "this can be confirmed by reference to the statements made by the Gabonese delegation during the various Security Council debates on this matter." These statements were clearly unsubstantiated and self-serving, as Leon N'Dong cited himself, the signatory of the quoted by him a denial letter to the secretary general. Twenty years later, the chief African policy advisor to France, Jacques Foccart, responded to an inquiry regarding the role of Gabon in Opération Crevette and outright confirmed Gabon's involvement. He attributed the country's involvement to the personal ambitions of President Bongo who "was only waiting for an opportunity that could give him a continental role," thus suggesting that Bongo became involved without Paris's request or encouragement, helping the Hexagon get rid of Benin's troublemaker on his own accord. President Bongo's deliberate personal involvement in Opération Crevette seems to be best described by the following statement: "He covered up French President Valérie Giscard d'Estaing's failed attempt at overthrowing Benin's nationalist leader, Mathieu Kérékou. This decision was significant: Bongo might have helped his Gaullist allies like Jacques Chirac, who were political opponents of Giscard d'Estaing, by revealing the affair. However, on such matters, Bongo deferred to overall French strategic interests."

Asked about the role of Gabon in Opération Crevette, Maurice Robert—Bob Denard's case officer and a man with intimate knowledge of the internal situation of *Françafrique*, and particularly of the politics of Gabon—answered that, in his opinion, Gabon joined Morocco, Togo, and the Ivory Coast as a gesture of solidarity among Francophone African countries. He further stated that Gabon "was not directly involved in the operation" serving only as a transit base for the Omegas.

The confirmation of Gabon's active support of Opération Crevette also appeared in the memoires of Guy Penne published in 1999, who from 1981 to 1986 had served as an advisor of African affairs to the French president, François Mitterrand. According to him, Gabon "facilitated the equipping" of Denard's commando and allow them to use its airport for purposes of the operation, which confirms findings of the UN Special Mission report on Opération Crevette.

France

The plan of Opération Crevette was not only known to French president Giscard d'Estaing's advisor on African affairs, René Journiac, who had been informed, allegedly, in its regard by Denard himself, but also to various other leaders of French intelligence. Maurice Robert, chief of the African section of SDECE, described Journiac's involvement in Opération Crevette claiming, "Journiac had been informed of Denard's project by Jeannou Lacaze, Director of Intelligence . . . Lacaze was favorable to an orange [yellow] light, the one we have already spoken about, which is reflected in an absence of opposition but also of formal acquiescence, which means: 'I do not want to know anything, I . . . do not forbid you to do so, but if you do, it is under your responsibility.' Journiac told me that he had agreed to this position."

"I knew," claimed Denard, "that President Giscard d'Estaing was very interested in it." According to chief adviser to the French government on African policy, Jacques Foccart, Journiac was interested in "replacing" Kérékou with "someone closer to French point of view." Although Journiac never denied that he was, in fact, aware of preparation for Opération Crevette, he always maintained that he had not actively supported this operation because he considered it to be badly planned.

However, during the United Nations Security Council debate, Paris pursued the tactic of not denying, much like Gabon, that Opération Crevette in fact took place but, rather, undermining the authenticity of the documents presented to the Security Council. Thus, during the April 7, 1977, council meeting, the French delegate stated that his government reacted with surprise upon hearing the allegations that a French colonel named Gilbert Bourgeaud led the operation. The investigations conducted by French authorities "showed there was no such officer in the French Army, either on active service, in the reserves, or serving under special arrangements." And assured council that "no French service took either close or a remote part, or was in any way associated, with the raid of January 16 against Cotonou."

This statement shed light on relevant biographical information of Denard's alleged military service in the French army under his birth name, Gilbert Bourgeaud. No such record has ever existed because, contrary to popular belief, he had never served in a French military and thus, had never achieved any military grade in French armed forces. This confusion may be accredited to his service in the 1960s with different factions of internal conflict in the Congo, where he was awarded the rank of colonel by then–Congolese general Mobutu. This fact is often overlooked in descriptions of his colorful life in English language media. However, the French mainstream newspapers usually refer to Denard using quotation marks for the word "colonel," or referring to him as Bob Denard known as "colonel" (*colonel*).

The French delegation—said the ambassador—was "surprised" or even "stupefied" when the representative of Benin suggested in his statement that "the whole operation originated in France, that it was mounted in France and carried out by Frenchmen." As an argument why France would not be involved in Opération Crevette, ambassador Jacques Leprett described it as "shocking" and "infantile." Thus, argued Leprett, France cannot allow any accusations regarding events in which "we were not involved in anyway."

Six months after the initial debate, in November 1977, the UN Security Council concluded that the attack on Cotonou had been, in fact, committed by commando of mercenaries and requested all member states "to collect more information about the mercenaries who operated against the People's

Republic of Benin on 16 January 1977." The council further accepted "the desire of the Government of Benin to have the mercenaries who participated in the attacking forces against the People's Republic of Benin on 16 January 1977 subjected to due process of law." Ambassador Leprette immediately assured the council that his government was acting "on its own initiative and according with its laws" in investigating all individuals named in Benin's complaint as French citizens. However, "The investigation produced nothing." Justifying obvious French unwillingness or ineptitude identifying French nationals involved in Opération Crevette, Leprette tried again to cast doubt on the authenticity of documents left behind by Denard, expressing, "It is true that the mysterious circumstances-surprising for an operation of that nature in that the perpetrators of the raid left 'documentary evidence' on the spot—cast doubts on the value of the documents appended to the report of the mission of inquiry."

French archivist, Jean-Pierre Bat, however, has no doubts about France's involvement in Opération Crevette. Basing his research upon documents contained in Foccart's archives, he states that "the French authorities (Journiac, Lacaze, SDECE, and Delanuey in Libeville) were closely linked to organization of the operation." In a 1999 interview with *Le Figaro* magazine, Denard confirmed that after the departure of Colonel Maurice Robert—chief of the SDECE's Africa section—from the SDECE in 1973, Colonel Jeannou Lacaze, a deputy director of French intelligence SDECE (1971–1976) was his handler (*officier traite*) on behalf of French intelligence services. He stressed that although he "worked" for the agency, he was never the SDECE agent but only kind of an independent contractor. Year later, both Maurice and Lacaze testified at Denard's criminal trial in Paris that he had never conducted any mercenary operation without tacit approval of French intelligence services. Finally, Paris recalled, upon Beninese request, its ambassador to Cotonou and reduced its economic aid to Benin by two-thirds.

Morocco

Morocco's representative to the United Nations did not take part in the debate during the meetings of the Security Council dedicated to Omega's raid on Cotonou, held prior to publication of the Special Mission's report. It seems that Morocco's diplomatic tactic was to wait for the Report of the Special Mission to be released in order to then learn, after its publication, of its contents, and specifically the extent of information it contains about Rabat's involvement in the Opération Crevette attack. This was a tactic similar to the one pursued by Gabon: ridicule Benin's complaint and criticize the Special Mission's report as hastily prepared and unsubstantiated; further question whether mercenary's raid on Cotonou really even happened.

The Moroccan government must have already been aware of the findings included in the OAU report prepared by OAU's assistant secretary general, Peter Onu, regarding Morocco's involvement in Opération Crevette. Peter Onu visited Cotonou on February 16, 1977, and his report was to be discussed at the OAU's Council of Ministers meeting in Lomé, Togo, scheduled for February 21 to 28, 1977. However, due to the unauthorized distribution of his report to the delegates by an OAU secretariat's employee, its content became known to the Moroccan delegation prior to the similar, but more detailed, report of the UN Special Mission.

Four days before the publication of the Special Mission Report, on March 3, 1977, King Hassan II of Morocco addressed Benin's allegations in a speech from his throne declaring "his categorical rejection of charges so baseless, so impertinent (insolent), and revolting." His highness could not foresee that Bob Denard would later admit that the Omegas not only conducted military training in the Ben Guerir base but also that he allegedly met the monarch twice to discuss the forthcoming operation. The king further ignored the fact that Colonel Dlimi, chief of his personal security detail, personally visited the Omegas at the conclusion of their training at Ben Guerir. It seems hard to believe that a security advisor so close to Hassan II would have not appraised, advised, or informed Hassan II about the presence of ninety foreign mercenaries on the Moroccan military base undergoing training for an operation against leftist troublemaker Kérékou, who had actively supported the Western Sahara liberation movement (POLISARIO) against the territorial claims of Morocco to Western Saharan territory.

Moroccan denials of any knowledge of Bob Denard or of the Opération Crevette were rather hard to accept, particularly given the contacts between Denard and the Moroccan monarch stretching back to the early 1970s when King Hassan II hired Denard to conduct an operation against Colonel Muammar Gaddafi—the then–ruler of Libya whom King Hassan II accused of inciting internal disturbances leading in July 1971 to bloody coup attempt on the monarch's life. Some units of the Moroccan army troops attacked the summer palace of King Hassan II at Skhirat outside Rabat, but loyalist troops thwarted the uprising quickly and the king remained in control. Although the coup was an internal matter of kingdom, Hassan II decided to take against not only against military men involved in an attempt but also charged Libya's socialist regime of Colonel Gaddafi as inciting the failed uprising. In revenge, Hassan II came up with a plan to overthrow Colonel Gaddafi. It was at this point that Denard met both Hassan II and Colonel Ahmed Dlimi, the king's close advisor and country's security chief, in person. Both were later named as involved in the organization of Opération Crevette.

During the Security Council meeting on April 7, 1977, the delegate of Morocco sharply criticized the "slanderous" report (in reference to the Report of Security Council Special Mission to Benin) prepared by the government of Benin that was circulated among the Council's members and submitted on March 8, 1977. The report was described by ambassador Ali Bengelloun as containing "fallacious" with "slanderous accusations" and "speculations that proceed from a morbid imagination." Commenting on the UN Special Mission Report, a Moroccan representative first praised the mission members for carrying out "an extremally difficult task in so short time," only to conclude that it includes "accusations against sovereign States Members . . . unsupported by any proof." The Moroccan ambassador also disqualified Bâ Alpha Oumarou as a witness as a person who has been "manipulated [to recite] a lesson learned by heart" or perhaps who is even "an agent provocateur very aware of the role he is to play." Therefore, he rejected all falsified testimony and documents and declared that the King Hassan II "cannot be implicated either directly or indirectly in the tragic events of which the people of Benin were the victims on 16 January 1977." Finally, Moroccan ambassador Bengelloun declared on behalf of his government "condemnation of the use mercenaries" and declared its willingness to collaborate in all UN undertakings to establish an international mechanism to prevent mercenary operations in order to protect more effectively the sovereignty and integrity of small countries.

Since at that time there was no other proof of Moroccan involvement in the coup, and both reports—UN Special Mission Report to Benin and the OAU Special Mission to Benin, both of which were disputed by Gabon and Morocco—were based mainly on the testimony of one witness, neither the UN nor OAU named, not to mention condemned, the involvement of Gabon or Morocco in their resolutions regarding Opération Crevette. Only two decades later, first Pierre Lunel in Denard's biography, *Le roi de fortune*, and then Maurice Robert in his media interviews confirmed Morocco's active involvement in the operation.

In a 1993 interview, Maurice Robert revealed that the inspiration for Opération Crevette came from King Hassan II who, in response to Benin's recognition of POLISARIO, wanted to remove Mathieu Kérékou from power, even discussing his "physical elimination." A year later, Maurice Robert revealed that on the French side, it was Rene Journiac who organized Opération Crevette at the request of the Ivory Coast's president, Felix Houphouet Boigny, Gabon's president, Bongo, Togo's president, Eyadema, and Morocco's king, Hassan II, with the assistance of Bob Denard. Commenting on the same issue, Jacques Foccart excluded President Senghor's (then president of Senegal) involvement in the operation and expressed an opinion that "the king of Morocco played a more important role than Journiac." Noticeably, neither of the two French officials mentioned any involvement by Dr. Zinsou or FLERD in initiating or organizing of Opération Crevette.

THE OAU INQUIRIES

Africa's reaction to the raid on Cotonou illustrated deep political divisions between members of the Organization of African Unity (OAU, present-day African Union) resulting from the Cold War atmosphere of animosity among Western and, then, so-called socialist countries.

The first of the two OAU's missions to Benin was a mission of the special envoy sent by OAU's administrative secretary general, William Eteki Mboumoua. It was sent in response to the invitation of President Mathieu Kérékou "to investigate the atrocities perpetrated by the mercenaries who invaded Cotonou on January 16, 1977."[10] The mission was led by Eteki's deputy, Peter Onu, who arrived in Cotonou at night from February 15 to 16, 1977,[11] and stayed until February 20. His stay in Cotonou coincided with the visit of the fact-finding UN Security Council Special Mission but preceded the OAU's Council of Minister's Special Mission visit only by a few days. The decision to send the OAU Special Mission was taken during the council ordinary session held in Lomé, Togo, between February 21 and 28, 1977. On February 22, the council designated a seven-person mission composed of foreign ministers of Angola, Guinea, Libya, Mozambique, Niger, Nigeria, and a representative of the OAU of the general secretariat of the OAU chaired by Libyan delegate Ali Terek. The mission was immediately dispatched to Benin and met next day, February 23, with President Mathieu Kérékou and other members of the political bureau of PRPB.[12] After a brief inquiry with Beninese authorities, the delegation returned to Lomé to its observation at the plenary meeting of Council of Ministers. It did not conduct interviews with witnesses nor conduct any independent investigation. The next day, the council heard both reports, one of Peter Onu and the other submitted by the Special Mission and the delegates from Benin, Gabon, and Morocco.

Without mentioning any state or non-state actors involved in the attack, the council stated that it "strongly condemns the act of armed aggression against the People's Republic of Benin."[13]

Peter Onu's report that had been based on information from the local eyewitnesses, documents left by the Omegas, and visiting locations in Cotonou damaged during the mercenaries' assault[14] was immediately harshly criticized by delegations of Gabon and Morocco. Rabat not only denied any allegations of its involvement in the Opération Crevette but also withdrew from further discussion at the council and suspended its further participation in activities of other OAU organs.[15] Moroccan delegates described the distribution of the Peter Onu's report as a "flagrant violation" of the OAU Charter and in particular of the sovereignty of states and their territorial integrity." Morocco denounced report on the events in Cotonou as "grossly defamatory."[16] In defense of his report, Peter Onu maintained, however, that elements contained in the report circulated by him, which caused Morocco to withdraw, "coincided perfectly" with the first unpublished information gathered by the OAU Commission of Inquiry in Cotonou.

Gabon, as a host of the forthcoming summit of the leaders of the member states of the OAU scheduled for July 1977, preferred not to suspend its membership but defended itself against Benin's accusation, claiming that they were aimed at "discrediting" Gabon as a venue of the OAU annual summit. As a result of Benin's public accusations of countries involved in the planning or support of Opération Crevette, political and economic relations with those two countries understandably deteriorated. When Benin continued its allegations of Bongo's support for Opération Crevette during the OAU summit in Khartoum, President Bongo retaliated by ordering the expulsion of thousand Beninese nationals temporarily employed in Gabon from its territory.

On its part, Benin requested during the June/July session of the Council of Ministers, scheduled for July 1977, OAU Summit of Heads of States and Governments be cancelled because that state, for example, Gabon, which "arms and supports" mercenaries, should not be hosting the organization's summit conference.[17] When its request was ignored, Benin refused to participate in the summit.

Cotonou also demanded from Gabon, France, and Morocco reparations of $28 million for damages resulting from the January attack. Since none of these countries showed any intent to pay requested damages to Benin, the OAU Council of Ministers, on its July 1978 session in Khartoum, recommended that immediate financial assistance be given to Benin from the OAU Special Fund.[18]

DIPLOMATIC SOLUTION

Despite Benin's request for the cancellation, the OAU's annual summit took place in Libreville. After five months of boycotting work of the organization, Morocco sent its delegate, Prime Minister Ahmed Osman, to the summit. This time it was Mathieu Kérékou who boycotted the summit, but in his submission to the conference members described the African heads of state who, in his eyes, were involved in this abortive raid led by Colonel Bourgeaud, alias Morin, as "criminals"; he further spoke of "high treason" by the heads of states involved in support of Opération Crevette. The Libreville summit was mainly concerned with internal and border problems of OAU members and questions of decolonization of countries like Southern Rhodesia or Western Sahara. Thus, the issue of mercenary aggression against Benin or Sao Tome was only a subject of marginal but heated exchange of speeches between delegations of Gabon and Morroco on one side and delegation of Benin on other. The delegates adopted only two resolutions and neither of them related directly to the aggression against Benin. One of them addressed this issue in a very diplomatic language that was also applicable to other conflicts, including the ones with foreign intervention, for example, Angola. Thus, in the "Resolution on the Interference of the Internal Affairs of African States," the Assembly of Heads of State and Government called "all extra-African powers, particularly the big ones, to refrain from interfering in the internal affairs of African States," and as for OAU members, they called "Member States to prohibit the use of their territories as base for political subversive activities against another African State." Also, to the OAU members referenced, was a call "to refrain from harboring, financing and using nationals of neighboring countries against their Countries of Origin."[19] Since there was no separate resolution adopted that referred to the issue of mercenary assault on Cotonou, and no country was named in that resolution, it could be, as its drafters intended, used in case of any coup d'état, rebellion, or secession in any African country in which there was foreign intervention or the use of mercenaries.

Despite the political divisions among the OAU members, the Assembly of Heads of States and Governments was able to reach an agreement on approval of the draft of the convention for the elimination of mercenaryism in Africa,[20] which entered into effect only on April 22, 1985,[21] after its ratification by required number of OAU member states. Benin became a party to this convention in 1982,[22] Gabon, in 2007, and Morocco has yet not accessed to the Convention. Article 3 of the convention provides that "Mercenaries shall not enjoy the status of combatant and shall not be entitled to the prisoner of war status."[23] Such provision removes, from individuals recognized as mercenaries, an international humanitarian law protection that usually covers combatants taking part in armed international and non-international conflicts. Although the convention entered into force in 1985 it could still be applicable in legal actions taken by Benin much earlier, in 1979.

NOTES

1. Benin, "Letter Dated 26 January 1977 from the Chargé d'affaires, a.i., of the Permanent Mission of Benin to the United Nations Addressed to the President of the Security Council," 1977, S/12278; https://digitallibrary.un.org/record/224331. See

also Walter Bruyére-Ostells, *Dans l'ombre de Bob Denard: Les mercenaires français de 1960 à 1989* (Paris: Nouveau Monde Èditions, 2014), 282–85.

2. Security Council Official Records, Thirty-Second Year, 1986th Meeting: 7 February 1977, para. 10–441. (S/PV 1986): https://digitallibrary.un.org/record/224218 ?ln=en. See also "Benin Asks UN Study of Attack on Cotonou," *New York Times*, February 8, 1977, 2, sec. Archives, https://www.nytimes.com/1977/02/08/archives/ benin-asks-un-study-of-attack-on-cotonou.html.

3. Resolution 407 (1977) adopted by the Security Council at its 1987th meeting, on February 8, 1977, https://digitallibrary.un.org/record/66645?ln=en#record-files -collapse-header.

4. SC. Res. 404 (1977), UN Doc. S/Res./404 (1977).

5. Note by the President of the Security Council, February 10, 1977 (S/12286) https://digitallibrary.un.org/record/224337?ln=en.

6. Benin, "Letter Dated 4 April 1977 from the *Charge d'Affaires a.i.* of Benin to the United Nations Addressed to the President of the Security Council" (New York: United Nations, April 5, 1977) (S/12319. Add. 1), https://digitallibrary.un.org/ record/564452.

7. "Cotonou ne compte plus ses agresseurs," *Jeune Afrique*, no. 847, April 1, 1977, 72.

8. UN, Special Mission of the Security Council Established under Resolution 404 (1977), "Report of the Security Council Special Mission to the People's Republic of Benin Established under Resolution 404 (1977)" (S/12294/Rev. 1) (New York: United Nations, 1977), https://digitallibrary.un.org/record/564622.

9. UN, Security Council (32nd year: 1977), "Resolution 405 (1977) / Adopted by the Security Council at Its 2005th Meeting, on 14 April 1977" (New York: United Nations, April 14, 1977), https://digitallibrary.un.org/record/66646, see para. 2.

10. CM/805 (XXVIII). "Report of the Administrative Secretary-General on the Events of January 16, 1977," in Cotonou, Republic of Benin, 1, Organization of African Unity/African Union: https://archives.au.int/handle/123456789/9824.

11. "La frère Peter Onu envoyé spécial de l'OUA est arrivé à Cotonou," *Ehuzu*, February 18, 1977.

12. "Un délégation du Conseil des ministres de l'OUA en mission d'enquête à Cotonu," *Ehuzu*, February 24, 1977, 1 and 6.

13. CM/Res. 527 (XXVIII). "Resolution on Armed Aggression Against the People's Republic of Benin," Council of Ministers, "Resolutions of the Twenty-Eighth Ordinary Session of the Council of Ministers" (Lome, Togo: Council of Ministers, February 21–28, 1977), https://au.int/sites/default/files/decisions/9590-council_en _21_28_february_1977_council_ministers_twenty_eighth_ordinary_session.pdf.

14. "Report of the Administrative Secretary-General on the Events of January 16, 1977," in Cotonou, Republic of Benin, Organization of African Unity/African Union, 1977-02, https://archives.au.int/handle/123456789/9824.

15. "Morocco Quits O.A.U. in a Rift," *New York Times*, February 26, 1977, 4. Archives, https://www.nytimes.com/1977/02/26/archives/morocco-quits-oau-in-a -rift.html.

16. "Le Maroc justifie son retrait par une 'violation flagrante' de la Charte," *Le Monde*, March 1, 1977, https://www.lemonde.fr/archives/article/1977/03/01/le-maroc -justifie-son-retrait-par-une-violation-flagrante-de-la-charte_2862891_1819218.html.

17. "Le Bénin poursuit ses efforts pour faire annuler le 'sommet' de l'O.U.A.," *Le Monde*, June 24, 1977, https ://www.lemonde.fr/archives/article/1977/06/24/le-benin -poursuit-ses-efforts-pour-faire-annuler-le-sommet-de-l-o-u-a_2866869_1819218 .html.

18. Resolution on Aggression and Invasion Attempts by Mercenaries Against the People's Republic of Benin, the Democratic Republic of Sao Tome and Principe. Council of Ministers, Thirty-First Ordinary Session, Khartoum, Sudan, July 7–18, 1978, CM/Res. 639 (XXXI); https://au.int/sites/default/files/decisions/9584 -council_en_7_18_july_1978_council_ministers_thirtieth_first_ordinary_session .pdf.

19. AHG/Res. 85 (XIV). "Resolution on the Interference of the Internal Affairs of African States."

20. OAU Convention for the Elimination of Mercenarism in Africa, CM/817 (XXIX) Annex II Rev.1; https://au.int/sites/default/files/treaties/37287-treaty-0009 _-_oau_convention_for_the_elimination_of_mercenarism_in_africa_e.pdf.

21. Organization of African Unity Convention for the Elimination of Mercenarism in Africa. Concluded at Libreville, Gabon, on July 3, 1977, entered into force April 22, 1985, 1490 UNTS 25573.

22. Benin ratified Convention in 1979. See Ordonnance No. 79–4 du 17 janvier 1979 portant ratification de la convention de l'O.U.A. sur l'élimination du Mercenariat en Afrique; https://sgg.gouv.bj/doc/ordonnance-1979-4/.

23. Art. 3 of the Convention is patterned on Art. 1 of Protocol Additional to the Geneva Conventions of 12 August 1949 and relating to the Protection of Victims of International Armed Conflicts (Protocol I), 8 June 1977, related to mercenaries which also provides in "A mercenary shall not have the right to be a combatant or a prisoner of war," Part III, Section II, Art. 47(1): https://www.un.org/en/genocideprevention/documents/atrocity-crimes/Doc.34_AP-I-EN.pdf. Adopted in 1989 General International Convention Against the Recruitment, Use, Financing and Training of Mercenaries. New York, 4 December 1989, entered into force 20 October 2001, 2163 UNTS 37789 leaves a decision as to what punishment should be meted to mercenaries apprehended on its territory to applicable provisions of its national law.

Chapter 17

Justice Delayed

After a successful 1975 mercenary operation in the Comoros whereby Denard helped Ali Soilih remove then-president Ahmed Abdallah from power, and later was accused of allowing for the assassination of the same Ali Soilih in order to allow return of Ahmed Abdallah to power, Denard and his subordinates got off scot-free. There was no investigations or trial, either in the Comoros or in France, of Denard himself or any of his associate regarding criminal responsibility for Ali Soilih's death. But the times had changed due, among other things, to change of the French policy toward African states, including those with leftist or socialist governments. And Benin was no exception.

This time, Denard and some of his underlings were to face legal consequences for their participation in Opération Crevette. There were already precedent trials against foreign mercenaries for participating in thwarted operations in Conakry, Guinea, in 1970; in Khartoum, Sudan, against Rolf Steiner in 1971 for his support for anti-government rebels *Anya-Anya*;[1] and in 1976, there was a mercenary trial in Luanda, Angola.

In case of Opération Crevette, a "mega" trial was conducted in 1979 before the Revolutionary Tribunal in Cotonou against all ninety members of the Force Omega as well as some of the Beninese citizens accused of being involved in organization of Opération Crevette. Later on, not one, but two criminal proceedings against Denard and some of his close associates were opened in France resulting in the trials held in Parisian courts: one *in absentia* in 1991, and a second in 1993 in which Denard appeared before the Fourteenth Criminal Chamber of Tribunal in Paris (*Quatorzième Chambre Correctionnelle du Tribunal de Paris*).

Cotonou Trial (1979)

In preparation for the trial of the individuals involved in Opération Crevette, after establishing, based upon the documentation left by the Force Omega on tarmac of Cotonou Airport (see chapter 15. "Pandora Boxes"), the names and nationalities of the African and European Omegas, Benin requested their extradition from France and was promised some form of legal cooperation by French authorities. But for the next two years, Paris did not take any legal action against the mercenaries listed on the documents pertaining to Opération Crevette. Besides any possible political reasons for France's non-cooperation in response to Benin's request laid fact that on principle, France refuses to extradite its own citizens for prosecution by foreign authorities to be judged by foreign courts. Article 696-2 of the Code of Criminal Procedure stipulates that France may extradite "any person who *does not have* French nationality."[2] Moreover, although at the time of Benin's request France had the law[3] allowing, under certain conditions, for extradition from her territory of foreigners sought for crimes committed abroad, Benin's request pertained to the mercenaries who were, with the exception of a few Belgians, mostly French citizens.

Although between Benin and France existed the agreement regarding mutual assistance in legal matters,[4] it was also not applicable to Benin's request because, first, it contained a customary (for such agreements) provision that "[c]ontracting States shall not extradite their respective nationals" (Aricle 54) and, second, specific offense for which extradition is requested had to punishable in both countries (Article 55[1]). However, these laws were somewhat irrelevant because neither Benin nor France had on the books any laws defining a crime of "mercenaryism" nor did they provide for the criminal prosecution of individuals defined as "mercenaries." Also the argument that individuals sought by Benin committed criminal and not a political offenses could not result in extradition; although the Article 56 stated that "[f]or the purposes of this Agreement, the assault on the life of a Head of State or a member of his family shall not be considered a political offence," and one of the aims of Opération Crevette was to "liquidate" President Mathieu Kérékou, the request for extradition could not apply—it did not apply to French mercenaries present on French territory nor to African participants of the operation (mostly Guinean citizens) presumably given that they did not reside within French jurisdiction.

Nonetheless, President Kérékou complained to Robert Galley the French minister of cooperation visiting Benin a few weeks before the upcoming trial of the Omegas held in Cotonou. He stated, "all the official representations by the Beninese Government vis-a-vis the French Government aimed at arranging for the extradition of the French mercenaries so that they may be judged by the competent Beninese courts have thus far elicited no favorable reaction."[5] So, unable to obtain evidence directly from testimonies of extradited mercenaries, simultaneously with its efforts on forums of the United Nations (UN) and the Organization of African Unity (OAU), the Beninese

government took internal and regional steps to establish investigative bodies—national and international commissions of inquiry.

On the day of the mercenary assault, President Mathieu Kérékou appointed
a "Commission of Inquiry into Events occurred in Cotonou on 16th January
1977."[6] For some reason, it was disbanded twelve days later and did not
publish any publicly available report.[7] Its work was to be continued by a new
commission of inquiry created by the presidential ordinance on February
18, 1977.[8] This commission was empowered to search for and discover any
"internal ramifications" regarding internal network of mercenaries and "traitors of Beninese cause." To do so, the commission was supposed to interro-
gate officers, soldiers, and personnel of the Forces armées populaires (FAP)
and all commanders of the FAP units were obliged to cooperate with the commission's requests. Since no report has been published by the commission,
its detailed findings remain unknown. Interestingly, however, the members
of this commission were designated to yet another investigative body, created on December 3, 1977: "Special National Commission of Inquiry into the
Ahoussinou's Theodore Network and its consorts." The assignment of this
commission was to investigate "him and all accomplices" of his "subversive
and contra-revolutionary" network against leaders of the Beninese revolution. Since, again, no findings of work of that commission were ever made
public it is unclear whether the investigated network had any ties to Opération
Crevette or whether it was just looking into a plan of yet another coup d'état
unrelated to this operation.

The two international commissions of inquiry created by Beninese authorities were: the Military Commission composed of representatives of Benin,
Guinea, and Nigeria, and the International Commission, with the same composition.[9] This commission was soon replaced by the new commission that
was to continue her predecessor's works and also submit its findings directly
to Mathieu Kérékou. None of such reports ever became available to the public. However, the Beninese government published in the official newspaper
Ehuzu a series of articles presenting information about Opération Crevette
obtained from the statements of Bâ Alpha Oumarou and the documents left
on the tarmac of Cadjehoun Airport by Denard's commando.[10]

Benin also took legislative measures to make mercenary activity on its
territory a crime. Until it did so, its penal law had not provided a definition
of the crime of serving as a mercenary. Therefore, mercenary activity on its
territory could not be legally punished as a separate crime.

Thus, on October 19, 1978, President Mathieu Kérékou issued an ordinance that defined activities recognized as committed by mercenaries as
punishable by death.[11]

When the French courts failed, for over two years, to respond to Benin's
request for the extradition of mercenaries participating in Opération Crevette,

Cotonou decided to prosecute *in absentia* the organizers and participants of Opération Crevette before a Beninese court. On April 9, 1979, in accordance with the then–Beninese law, the seventy-three-member National Council of Revolution sitting as the National Revolutionary Tribunal examined the criminal case against alleged organizers and planners, and participants of Opération Crevette.[12] The material evidence available to the tribunal constituted documents and weaponry left by the Omegas at the Cotonou airport. Nothing in the tribunal's decision indicated that such evidence was actually used in the proceedings. Because of the generally accepted rule of prohibition of retroactivity in criminal law, criminal penalties may not be applied to acts that took place before the relevant rule entered into force. The National Revolutionary Tribunal, therefore, could not invoke in its proceedings provisions of the Ordonnance No. 78–34. Because of this, the tribunal based its decision on the findings of the inquiry commissions, which were very similar to each other. Besides the results of the national commissions of inquiry, the tribunal also had available the reports of the international commissions: the UN Special Mission (India, Libya, and Panama), the Special Missions of the OAU and the OAU's Secretariat headed by Peter Onu, and the Military Commission (Benin, Guinea, and Nigeria). However, the tribunal relied in the proceedings and, subsequently, its decision was only based on the findings of the above-mentioned report of the National Commission of Inquiry to the events of January 16, 1977.[13]

Thus, on April 9, 1979, after hearing the National Commission of Inquiry report and "after extensive discussion," the National Revolutionary Tribunal ruled case by case and pronounced . . . by simple majority in a secret ballot" more than one hundred death sentences *in absentia* against seventy-one European and twenty-seven African participants of Opération Crevette, among them Bâ Alpha Oumarou and eleven "Beninese traitors" including Denard and Dr. Émile Zinsou.[14] Referring to the convicted individuals, the tribunal—in colorful, revolutionary language—described them as "drug-maddened mercenaries armed with the most modern and sophisticated weapons for the cynical purpose of physically liquidating the responsible figures of our Party and our revolutionary State."[15]

Surprisingly, court proceedings based only on facts but without any legal grounds (no applicable law was cited by the tribunal) ending with one hundred death sentences did not provoke any international protest. Even Amnesty International in its 1980 report, while demanding from Beninese authorities release of thirteen arrested students, limited itself to brief information about the Cotonou trial. "In May 1979," reads AI report, "it was reported that the 73-member National Council of the Revolution, sitting as a Revolutionary Tribunal, had passed 100 death sentences *in absentia* for participation in the January 1977 attack on the capital, Cotonou, by an airborne mercenary force. Of those sentenced to death, 89 were said to be African and European mercenaries and 11 were described as 'Beninese traitors.'"[16] The note does not even mention that "judgments" of the Revolutionary Tribunal under then–Beninese law were issued in cases of "such acts and events as it declares to political infractions and attempts against State security," basically politically motivated acts and that its "judgments" could not be appealed.

The rest of the accused received the jail terms, and some had even been acquitted. The wife of Colonel Marc Soglo received a ten-year sentence, two others received five-year jail terms, and four have been acquitted. Also acquitted were Theodore Ahoussinou and seven other members of the alleged subversive, anti-revolutionary network which were a subject of investigation by mentioned earlier special commission.

The tribunal's sentences of death were solely symbolic; most of the coup's direct participants and suspected organizers were safely living abroad and, thus, out of reach of the Beninese jurisdiction. Also, although a death penalty was at that time still on the books, and Benin was not a party to international agreements regarding elimination of death penalty,[17] Benin authorities did not typically execute political prisoners.

Paris Trial (1991)

With Francois Mitterrand's victory in the French presidential elections (May 1981), Paris's relations with her former colonies that had chosen a socialist political and economic model after independence, such as Guinea or Benin, changed. Socialist president Mitterrand named former socialist senator Guy Penne as his African affairs advisor (1981–1986). Guy Penne, called the "Foccart of the Left," decided to revive relations with leftist African governments. Invitations to Paris and the exchange of high-level visits followed with many heads of African states that were held at arm's length (if not conspired against), under Giscard d'Estaing's presidency. One of the African leaders invited to Paris was Benin's Kérékou. To improve France's relationship with Benin, and prior to President Kérékou's September 1981 visit, France issued, on June 23, 1981, a warrant for the arrest of Denard for his participation in Opération Crevette. Thus, the opening of formal criminal proceedings against Denard evidently resulted from the French government's intent to improve Paris's economic and political relationship with radical African leaders, including Mathieu Kérékou.

With Benin unwilling, even under pressure from prospective foreign donors such as France, to grant amnesty to the organizers or participants of Opération Crevette, France slowly instituted criminal proceedings against Denard and one of his associates. On September 18, 1991, fourteen years after the failed operation, a French prosecutor filed charges against two commando members, Denard and his associate, Philipp Boyer (one of the Omegas), in the 14th Chamber of the Paris Criminal Court. They were accused of acting in "criminal association" to conduct the coup d'état in Benin and, more seriously, were accused of causing the deaths of at least three Beninese individuals killed during the failed operation. The latter charge was dropped because the prosecution was unable (or unwilling) to pin it on Denard.

However, despite the fact that Franco–Beninese relations had gradually improved, the warrant against Denard remained unexecuted for the next twelve years during which Denard remained out of France's jurisdiction, staying on the Comoros Islands. In early November 1989, Denard even claimed his intent to return to France from the Comoros to answer the criminal charges brought against him in relation with his participation in Opération Crevette. But soon after, Comoros's president, Ahmed Abdallah, was killed in the middle of that November in Denard's presence, and Paris, acting in collusion with Pretoria, directed Denard to exile in South Africa instead of bringing him home. Thus, in 1989, France failed to execute the warrant despite the presence of French troops and intelligence personnel in the Comoros for Operation *Oside*, the operation specifically conducted for the removal of Denard and other French mercenaries from the archipelago. Instead of arresting Denard, commanders of French forces conducting the operation against the mercenaries even allowed Denard and his associates to leave the Comoros with military honors, despite pending criminal charges and arrest warrants against him.

Since the investigation conducted by the French authorities did not establish who caused the deaths of three out of the seven Beninese killed during the assault, the families of those three victims filed a civil lawsuit against Denard in Paris. However, at this time, Denard still resided in South Africa. Despite court proceedings against him pending in Paris, French authorities had refused to renew his French passport allowing or forcing him by such denial to remain out of the country and to continue avoiding prosecution.

Since there was no convention on mutual legal assistance in criminal matters or extradition treaty between France and South Africa, it was left to Denard whether he would voluntarily appear before French court. Denard's attorney claimed that because of his client's absence from the country, he couldn't effectively represent him, requesting that the case be postponed until Denard's return to France. On his part, Denard submitted a letter to the court challenging the complaint that he is hiding from justice and stating that the "whole world knows" that he was residing in South Africa. The judge, however, rejected Denard's plea to postpone his trial, stating that he should not pretend he does not have the same rights as others and decided to continue a trial without Denard's presence.[18]

Unlike Denard, his associate, Phillip Boyer, was present in court and testified in his own defense claiming that he was naive, answering the newspaper advertisement offering a job to security personnel in an African country. Only much later, during the flight from Libreville to Cotonou, did he learn from Denard that the real purpose of the advertisement was recruitment for a commando assignment.[19] Although, in light of the testimony of Bâ Alpha Oumarou before the UN Special Mission, this line of defense was supposed to allow Denard and Boyer to avoid the conviction of acting in "criminal association" with the other participants of Opération Crevette, as they allegedly lacked the knowledge required for the recognition of this criminal offense. A few years later, however, during another trial in Paris, Denard testified that he had briefed at least some members of Opération Crevette about details of the operation.[20] Such was also the understanding of the French investigative judge who charged Denard with participation in criminal enterprises in Benin. In his defense, Boyer claimed that he had not played a direct part in fighting with Beninese soldiers, but only helped to move the DC-8 load on the airport tarmac.[21] Boyer's defense raised an interesting legal argument: although French criminal law allows the punishment of French citizen for crimes committed abroad, it also requires that such act be also criminalized in a country in which it had been committed. At the time of Opération Crevette, neither Beninese nor Gabonese law had any provision regarding the crime of criminal association.[22]

On October 16, 1991, the judgment was rendered by the 14th Chamber of the Paris Criminal Court. Denard received, *in absentia*, a five-year jail sentence with suspension. In October 1991, the court also renewed international arrest warrants against Denard issued in 1981 since they had never been executed. Boyer was given a suspended three-year prison sentence.[23] Denard immediately criticized the court's ruling as "more political than legal" and declared an appeal of his sentence.[24] Later, Denard suggested that if he were to be accused of "criminal association," President Giscard d'Estaing and four "easily recognizably" heads of African states should also be considered his associates.[25] Noticeably, he did not mention the French special services as one of the "associates" in Opération Crevette, for which he, as per his own admission, "worked often and for long time."[26]

Denard would return to France two years later in order, as he announced, to "clear his name" from charges regarding the failed Opération Crevette.[27] By 1991, Denard was facing two warrants for his arrest; one, issued on July 16, 1991, on charges of murder and grand theft in connection with the assassination of Ahmed Abdallah (Comorian politician) in 1989, and the second, issued on October 16, 1991, on charges for "criminal association" in Opération Crevette against Mathieu Kérékou. His reasons for retuning to France, however, were more than just for the clearing of his name. While Denard sought refuge in South Africa, his entire family remained in France. "All my roots, all my family, all my children are in France."[28] "I could no longer stay away. I couldn't continue living like a pariah. I had to come home."[29] Denard added, "It's true that I wasn't a saint. You cannot be a saint in war. But I would not still be here if I had done truly reprehensible things."

Paris Trial (1993)

Openly ignoring the court verdict and both arrest warrants in his name, Denard asked the French embassy in Pretoria to guarantee his return home without facing arrest. Paris denied the request, but French lawyer Daniel Soulez Larivière continued to negotiate the conditions of his return, including a pre-arranged arrest. When it was agreed that upon arrival Denard would be arrested at the airport, he announced at the end of January 1993 that he would return to France in order "to clarify his legal situation."[30] A first-class Air France airline ticket for an overnight flight from Johannesburg to Paris Charles de Gaulle Airport was apparently paid by French newspaper *Le Figaro*.

Thus, on February 1, 1993, after twelve years of exile in South Africa, Bob Denard arrived at Charles de Gaulle Airport carrying a suitcase full of medication and surrendered to French Air and Border Police (*Police de l'air et des frontières*, PAF), he was served with an arrest warrant issued on October 16, 1991, in Paris following his conviction for "criminal association" *in absentia* for his role in Opération Crevette, as well as an international arrest warrant for "criminal association and aggravated robbery" issued on July 16, 1991, by Chantal Perdrix, investigating judge in Paris, this time about his role in the assassination of Comorian President Ahmed Abdallah, overthrown on November 26, 1989. He was handcuffed and promptly placed in the airport holding cell before he could even meet the relatives or the reporters waiting his return.

Directly from the airport he was transferred to cell 223 of the Third Department of the notorious La Santé prison in Paris.[31] He later appeared in a Parisian courthouse in handcuffs and was charged by the magistrate with complicity in the 1989 murder of President Ahmed Abdallah and with robbery in connection with the death of the Comorian leader. The 1991 five-year jail sentence rendered *in absentia* had been suspended until his return to France.

When on February 8, 1993, Denard's lawyer, Daniel Soulez Larivière, asked the court to order his release on bond from prison on the grounds of poor health (heart disease), judge Jean-Claude Antonetti denied the request, arguing that Denard was aware of the arrest warrant against him while in South Africa and decided to ignore it. Further, he stated, "the circumstances of a matter are extremely serious," because, as a result of his actions, "the public order as internal as well an international had been seriously affected."[32] But Saturday, April 3, just days before the upcoming hearing on merits, the Parisian investigating judge in charge of his case, Chantal Perdrix, released him from detention.

During the three-day hearing scheduled for early March 1993, before the 14th Chamber of the Paris Criminal Court, Denard was re-tried on the same charge of "criminal association" in Opération Crevette and tried based on a complaint filed in regard to the assassination of Ahmed Abdallah, president of Comoros, in his presence in November 1989, and aggravated theft (French: *vol aggrave*) of Comorian important state documents.[33]

Present in court, French journalists observed that Denard's trial was much different from the usual criminal court proceedings. The prosecution and the judge treated Denard like a celebrity. "Probably never has a hearing of a criminal court looked so little like a trial. In his cubicle, Bob Denard, glasses and blue blazer, explains what his life was. With him, the tribunal goes to Indochina, goes to Morocco, goes to the Congo, then from Biafra to Yemen, makes a stay in Angola and finally in the Comoros. The mercenary speaks little," observed the representative of *Le Monde*,[34] referring the first day of the trial on March 10, 1993.

The prosecution in this trial played a role much closer that of a defense lawyer than a prosecutor in criminal cases. The prosecutor had observed that the assault attempted on January 16, 1977, on Cotonou, which he called a "counter-coup," was a "strange affair" where the French secret service interfered, which, by definition, is "at the margins and outside the legality."[35] The term "counter-coup" was coined by Denard's defense in an attempt to justify his intent necessary for qualification of a criminal act and thus to alleviate in the eyes of the court the gravity of his action. Presenting the charges against Denard, the prosecutor also used a somewhat atypical prosecution argument that the events constituting grounds for prosecution happened long before the trial. While the "preparatory acts" for the operation—recruitment and purchase of weapons—are indeed constitutive of the crime of criminal association, "the passage of time," being what it was, and "world public order (having) changed considerably," raised the question of what point there was in attacking the secret service and diplomacy that sometimes "act on the margins and outside the law."[36] It meant the total disregard by the prosecution that it was both the French government's and Denard's decision to avoid his prosecution by eleven years by, first, not bringing any charges against him earlier and, second, by sending him to the Republic of South Africa and then allowing him or, in his view, even keeping him there out of the French jurisdiction. So, there was surprise when, on March 11, the prosecutor requested, once again, as it did in 1991, a "symbolic" penalty of three-to-five-year suspended jail sentence.[37]

During his testimony, Denard denied that using in his plan of Opération Crevette words to describe the aims of the operation, like "eliminations" or "destructions," did not have the usual meaning as substitutes for the word "killing" but that these were military terms: "It is not to be taken in the physical sense of the word. In the briefing organized before departure, I made it clear that we should not 'destroy' people." "The mercenary is formal. It was not about killing. It was only a question of ensuring the person of Mr. Mathieu Kérékou so that the new power would try him."[38] "For us," he claimed in defense, "it was a "counter-coup" like it would have any difference when compared with a coup d'état using armed mercenaries. Speaking about members of his Force Omega, Denard assured the court that "[t]hey were not hitmen as we seemed to say."[39]

In the 1993 trial, Denard used for the first time what became famous later, an "amber light" defense that was based on an admission during the hearings in an open court that his mercenary operation was, each time, more or less supported by the French intelligence service SDECE or, later, DSGE, or at least organized with its knowledge. Thus, at the 1993 hearing, he openly declared that he "informed the cell of the Elysée" and met "René Journiac several times; I asked him if he did not have any problems. He gave me the amber light. We never get the green light in those cases." Commenting on the line of Denard's defense, the journalist noticed: "To hear him, Bob Denard would not be a simple mercenary," because his actions would always be based, besides the approval by French intelligence, "on a kind of legitimacy" coming from the foreign actors ordering his services.

Not only did Denard's lawyer and the prosecutor ask the judge for leniency but there were also high-status political individuals whom the defense called upon to testify on Denard's behalf as character witnesses. All of them confirmed Denard's claim to "amber light" defense.

Maurice Robert, former ambassador of France who was, in 1977, a colonel in the SDECE, delivered in Denard's defense the tribute of the former "employer." "He first collaborated with us without knowing it," testified Robert. "Then," he continued, "our collaboration was loyal, honest, and without pay. Bob Denard has always served the free world."[40] As to Opération Crevette, Robert presented the court the reasons for which French officials had given Denard the "amber light" to accept this assignment: "Morocco was worried about Benin's rapprochement with the Polisario Sahrawis,[41] and Benin's radical orientations worried its neighbors. I was not surprised by this operation, which, in my mind, was a wake-up call to get Benin to collaborate with its neighbors."[42]

Similar testimony was offered by another witness, Maurice Delanuey—former ambassador to Gabon at the time—of Opération Crevette. Delanuey seemed to have an intimate knowledge of some events regarding the operation. Ambassador Delaunay told the court that the raid on Cotonou took place "with the tacit agreement of France," including persons like Jacques Foccart or former general Jeannou Lacaze, a gray eminence of the "services." He also assured the court that Denard "constantly served the interests of French politics in Africa."[43] Jacques Foccart, who did not appear personally in court, also submitted written affidavit asserting that Bob Denard is an "honest man, patriot who served his country." Two French generals, Jeannou Lacaze and Paul Aussaresses, both advised the judge that Denard "always served France."[44]

Quite a different opinion of Bob Denard was expressed by the French lawyer who represented the families of the victims of the Cotonou raid, who were civil parties in this case. Joe Nordman recalled that the accused was a "mercenary" who "kills for money," and "is not as he claims on the side of oppressed peoples, but rather that of extremely rich dictators, such as Mobutu in Zaire and Bongo in Gabon."[45]

On April 5, 1993, Judge Jean-Claude Antonetti gave Denard a five-year suspended prison sentence. "I am very surprised, surprised and delighted, that I am free," said Denard. "My lawyer's strategy was to paint me as France's corsair, but that depended on receiving back-up from important people within the establishment. I feel honoured and rehabilitated by their support," commented Denard on the court's decision in his interview for London's *The Independent*.[46]

NOTES

1. Later, in 1976, a number of mercenaries were put on trial in Angola. In 1981, there was a trial against Mike Hoare and his companions for a failed invasion in the Seychelles. In November 2004 and 2007, there were trials in Malabo against mercenaries involved in a failed coup d'état in Equatorial Guinea.

2. Emphasis added. Art. 696-2 "Le gouvernement français peut remettre, sur leur demande, aux gouvernements étrangers, toute personne n'ayant pas la nationalité française qui, étant l'objet d'une poursuite intentée au nom de l'État requérant ou d'une condamnation prononcée par ses tribunaux, est trouvée sur le territoire de la République." Code de procédure pénale: https://www.legifrance.gouv.fr/loda/article _lc/LEGIARTI000006577297/.

3. Loi du 10 mars 1927 relative à l'extradition des étrangers: https://sherloc.unodc .org/cl.

4. Accord de Cooperation en Matiere de Justice Entre le Gouvernement de la République Française et le Gouvernement de la République du Dahomey, du 12 septembre 1961: http://www.justice.gouv.fr/art_pix/eci_conv_benin.pdf.

5. Statement by President Kérékou to Mr. Robert Galley, the French Minister of Co-Operation, during his Official Visit to Benin. "Letter Dated 21 May 1979 from

The Permanent Representative of Benin to the United Nations Addressed to the Secretary-General," S/13365, May 30, 1979, 3.

6. Ordonnance No. 77–2 du 16 Janvier 1977 portant désignation des Membres de la Commission d'Enquête sur les évènements survenus à Cotonou le 17 Janvier 1977: https://sgg.gouv.bj/doc/ordonnance-1977-2/.

7. Ordonnace No. 77–4 du 28 Janvier 1977 abrogeant les dispositions de l'Ordonnance No. 77–2 du 16 Janvier 1977 portant désignation des Membres de la Commission d'Enquête sur les évènements survenus à Cotonou le 17 Janvier 1977: https://sgg.gouv.bj/doc/ordonnance-1977-4/.

8. Ordonnance No. 77–7 du 18 février 1977 portant designation des membres de la Commission Nationale d'Enquête chargée de poursuivre les travaux de la Commission Internationale d'Enquête créée par l'ordonnance No. 77–5 du 28 janvier 1977: https://sgg.gouv.bj/doc/ordonnance-1977-7/.

9. Odonnance No. 77–5 du 28 Janvier 1977 portant création de la Commission International d'Enquête sur l'aggression imperialiste perpetrée contre la République Populaire de Bénin le 17 janvier 1977: https://sgg.gouv.bj/doc/ordonnance-1977-4/.

10. See *Ehuzu*, March 18, 1977; *Ehuzu*, March 20, 1977; *Ehuzu*, March 21, 1977; *Ehuzu*, March 22, 1977; *Ehuzu*, March 23, 1977; *Ehuzu*, March 24, 1977; *Ehuzu*, March 25, 1977; *Ehuzu*, March 26, 1977.

11. Art. 2, Ordonnance No. 78–34 du 19 octobre 1978 portant incrimination et répression du mercenariat; https://sgg.gouv.bj/doc/ordonnance-1978-34/.

12. Ordonnance No. 79–15 du 9 avril 1979 Instituant un Tribunal Revolutionnaire National: https://sgg.gouv.bj/doc/ordonnance-1979-15/.

13. Decision of the Session of the National Revolutionary Council sitting as a National Revolutionary Tribunal to deal with the Facts of the Aggression. Special communiqué issued by the Revolutionary Military Government. (S/13402, Annex, p.1 – 2). Letter Dated 13 June 1979 from the Permanent Representative of Benin to the United Nations Addressed to the Secretary General: https://digitallibrary.un.org/record/2937/usage?ln=e.

14. "Letter Dated 13 June 1979 from the Permanent Representative of Benin to the United Nations Addressed to the Secretary-General" (New York: United Nations, June 19, 1979), [Imperialist Armed Aggression of Sunday, 16 January 1977. Decisions of the Session of the National Revolutionary Council sitting as a National Revolutionary Tribunal to Deal with the Facts of the Aggression (Special communiqué issued by the Revolutionary Military Government)] (S/l3402): https://digitallibrary.un.org/record/2937?ln=en.

15. Ibid.

16 XX Amnesty International Report 1980 (London 1980), 32.

17. Benin joined only in 2012, the Second Optional Protocol to the International Covenant on Civil and Political Rights of 1989, aiming at the abolition of the death penalty.

18. "Les suites judiciaires d'une tentative de coup d'etat au Bénin en 1977 L'embarrassant procès de Bob Denard," *Le Monde*, September 20, 1991, https://www.lemonde.fr/archives/article/1991/09/20/les-suites-judiciaires-d-une-tentative

-de-coup-d-etat-au-benin-en-1977-l-embarrassant-proces-de-bob-denard_4034196 _1819218.html.

19. Ibid.

20. "Au tribunal correctionnel de Paris Bob Denard, mercenaire ou corsaire?" *Le Monde*, March 12, 1993, https://www.lemonde.fr/archives/article/1993/03/12 /au-tribunal-correctionnel-de-paris-bob-denard-mercenaire-ou-corsaire_3918299 _1819218.html.

21. "I stayed at the airport to take care of the unloading, the logistics," said briefly Boyer.

22. "Les suites judiciaires d'une tentative de coup d'etat au Bénin en 1977 L'embarrassant procès de Bob Denard." *Le Monde*, September 20, 1991.

23. Ibid.

24. "Cinq ans de prison et un mandat d'arrêt pour Bob Denard," *Le Monde*, October 18, 1991, https://www.lemonde.fr/archives/article/1991/10/18/cinq-ans-de-prison-et -un-mandat-d-arret-pour-bob-denard_4035679_1819218.html.

25. "Mercenaire de la République," *Le Figaro*, July 4, 2009, https://www.lefigaro .fr/lefigaromagazine/2009/07/04/01006-20090704ARTFIG00098--mercenaire-de-la -republique-.php.

26. Ibid.

27. *Le Monde*, January 1, 1993.

28. "A French Soldier of Fortune Tries on the Mantle of Patriot and Finds It Fits," *The New York Times*, April 25, 1993, 18: https://www.nytimes.com/1993/04/25/ world/a-french-soldier-of-fortune-tries-on-the-mantle-of-patriot-and-finds-it-fits. html.

29. Ibidem.

30. "Sous le coup de deux mandats d'arrêt Le mercenaire Bob Denard souhaiterait rentrer en France," *Le Monde*, January 28, 1993, https://www.lemonde.fr/archives/ article/1993/01/28/sous-le-coup-de-deux-mandats-d-arret-le-mercenaire-bob-denard -souhaiterait-rentrer-en-france_3926711_1819218.html.

31. Bob Denard and George Fleury, *Corsaire de la République* (Paris: R. Laffont, 1998); Samantha Weinberg, *Last of the Pirates: The Search for Bob Denard* (New York: Pantheon, 1995); "Bob Denard et les 'services' au banc des accusés," *L'Humanité*, March 12, 1993, https://www.humanite.fr/bob-denard-et-les-services-au -banc-des-accuses-51832.

32. "Une décision du tribunal correctionnel de Paris le mercenaire Bob Denard reste en prison," *Le Monde*, February 10, 1993, https://www.lemonde.fr/archives /article/1993/02/10/une-decision-du-tribunal-correctionnel-de-paris-le-mercenaire -bob-denard-reste-en-prison_3914126_1819218.html.

33. "Sous le coup d'un mandat d'arrêt international. L'ancien mercenaire Bob Denard est rentré en France," *Le Monde*, February 2, 1993, https://www.lemonde.fr/ archives/article/1993/02/02/sous-le-coup-d-un-mandat-d-arret-international-l-ancien -mercenaire-bob-denard-est-rentre-en-france_3920693_1819218.html.

34. "Au tribunal correctionnel de Paris Bob Denard, mercenaire ou corsaire?"

35. "Proces Parisien Tres Favorable au Celebre Mercenaire Sursis et Liberte Pour Bob Denard," *Le Soir (be.)*, April 6, 1993: https://www.lesoir.be/art/%252Fproces -parisien-tres-favorable-au-celebre-mercenaire-su_t-19930406-Z06LHX.html.

36. Claude Kroes, "Bob Denard et les 'services' au banc des accusés," *L'Humanite.fr*, March 12, 1993: http://www.humanite.fr/node/51832.

37. "Bob Denard devant le tribunal correctionnel de Paris Le procès des merce-naires," *Le Monde*, March 13, 1993, https://www.lemonde.fr/archives/article/1993/03 /13/bob-denard-devant-le-tribunal-correctionnel-de-paris-le-proces-des-mercenaires _3918355_1819218.html.

38. Ibid.

39. Ibid.

40. Alain Leauthier, "Le baroudeur qui voulait être roi. Du Biafra aux Comores, Bob Denard est resté le 'corsaire de la République.'" *Liberation*, September 29, 1995: https://www.liberation.fr/planete/1995/09/29/le-baroudeur-qui-voulait-etre-roi _142843/.

41. POLISARIO is an national independence movement in Western Sahara.

42. "Au tribunal correctionnel de Paris Bob Denard, mercenaire ou corsaire?" *Le Monde*, March 12, 1993. https://www.lemonde.fr/archives/article/1993/03/12 /au-tribunal-correctionnel-de-paris-bob-denard-mercenaire-ou-corsaire_3918299 _1819218.html.

43. Denard and Fleury, *Corsaire de la République*, 421.

44. Ibid.

45. Claude Kroes, "Bob Denard et les 'services' au banc des accusés," *L'Humanite*, March 12, 1993, http://www.humanite.fr/node/51832.

46. Samantha Weinberg, "France Blesses Its 'Dog of War': In His First Interview Since Leaving Jail, Bob Denard Tells Samantha Weinberg in Paris of His Many French Connections," *The Independent*, April 7, 1993, https://www.independent .co.uk/news/world/europe/france-blesses-its-dog-of-war-in-his-first-interview-since -leaving-jail-bob-denard-tells-samantha-weinberg-in-paris-of-his-many-french -connections-1453994.html.

Chapter 18

The End of an Epoch

THE WIND OF CHANGE

"The wind of change is blowing through this continent," said Macmillan the address he had made during his visit to then–British colony the Gold Coast (today's Ghana). Macmillan's speech was an announcement of changes in British Conservative Party policy toward the independence expectations of the people of then–British African colonies. This term could be presently used in reference the political and economic changes in many African countries set in motion by such changes in Benin initiated in 1989 during the presidency of Mathieu Kérékou. Survivor of several attempted coup d'états and Opération Crevette, he is now recognized on the African continent as a leader who initiated the process of changes from leftist, socialist, or Communist's regimes to Western-oriented democratic governing systems. Whether the changes had been forced on him by the internal situation in Benin or by external pressure still remains a question of debate between historians and political scientists, and the answer often depends on one's old and new political affiliations. It seems, however, that the changes the sponsors of failed Opération Crevette intended to bring to Benin were dictated in some way by both of these factors.

LIGHT IN THE TUNNEL

In Benin, the regime crisis that led to the president's consent to introducing essential political and economic changes began with a failed coup attempt in March 1988. This event would not have been exceptional if it had not been for the involvement, or at least the accusations of involvement, of Kérékou's relatives, like the captain of the Presidential Guard, Pascal Houndtoundji, or two former companions from FAP, Colonels François Kouyami and Hilaire

Figure 18.1. Stamp issued in 1978 in honor of the 16 January 1977 coup d'état. Credit: Author collection.

Badjagoumé. In 1989, the government foiled two other attempts at overthrow Kérékou. One was led by Colonel Benoît Sinzoungan. The other involved trusted officers like Captain Abderamane Amadou, *aide-de-camp* of Kérékou, and Captain Gomina Fousseini, chief of intelligence and documentation.

On the other hand, Benin was reaching the stage of state bankruptcy and, in 1989–90, the country was swept by wave of protests, demonstrations, non-violent boycotts, grassroots rallies, opposition campaigns, and strikes against the government of Mathieu Kérékou, unpaid salaries, and new budget laws.

When it comes to external factors, Benin-born Francis Kpatindé, long-term editor in chief of *Jeune Afrique*, maintains that changes in Benin happened before the world events, such as those often connected in the public's opinion with Kérékou's decisions for internal changes in Benin: the fall of Berlin Wall and "above all with the speech by Francois Mitterrand in La Baule." If the first event is relatively well known, the La Baule speech may require a reminder that in that speech the French president told African leaders gathered in the French town of La Baule that they must move toward democracy if they want to continue to count on French financial and economic assistance. Kpatindé maintains that the decision to organize the National Conference was made in August and September 1989 before the Berlin Wall fell, and that the conference was held in February 1990, four months before La Baule's speech.[1] While he is right that the National Conference was opened in February 1990, the decision to abandon the socialist system in

Benin was, according to the Benin presidency website, made on December 6, 1989,[2] while the fall of Berlin Wall happened on November 9, 1989.

An insider, Robert Dossou,[3] one of Kérékou's advisers during this era, recalled his role in convincing President Kérékou to introduce the necessary changes: "I told him he must first install a multi-party system. Secondly, he must grant amnesty to all political prisoners in jail and allow all exiles living outside the country to return. Thirdly, stop the repression and negotiate with the protestors."[4] Asked what the reaction to such advice was, Robert Dossou recollected that Kérékou: "said that we must be free, that all proposals will be welcome, and that the most important thing is to make its contribution so that the country can move forward."[5]

Other, also Beninese, sources interpret the roots of Kérékou's decision by putting an accent on external pressure as his motivation to accept the need for change and even the temporary loss of the status of the president. Thus, states the website "Histoire de Bénin sur BéninWeb," around December 1989, the embassy of France sent a memo to Kérékou "advising him to organize a national conference and to change the constitution, Kérékou followed the advice and traded in his Marxist views to calling a national conference to revise the constitution."[6]

One is sure: faced with a dangerously worsening economic and political situation in Benin and a wave of political protests and disturbances around the country, Mathieu Kérékou became more susceptible to internal as well as foreign growing pressure from outside to end his eighteen-year dictatorial rein and introduced political and economic changes in his country. It must also be evident to him that as one of the longest-reigning presidents/dictators in Africa, he has to secure his future safety to avoid forcible removal from power, often ending in death or long-term incarceration in revenge for his long-term political activity, or ending in exile as did many African heads of states before him.

NATIONAL CONFERENCE

The decision was probably not easy since, in September 1989, there were reports that General Mathieu Kérékou was still questioning the need for a multiparty system in Benin. "Our country at the present time . . . can function democratically without needing multiple parties."[7] The country's experience with multiparty democracy was terrible, in that it had been based upon tribal allegiances and regionalism that contributed to Dahomey's/Benin's political instability and, ultimately, resulted in an unprecedented number of coups d'état in the 1960s and 1970s and earned the country's epithet as "a sick child of Africa."

Kérékou could have followed the advice of the hard-core Communists: to crush the rebellion. However, he followed Robert Dossou to organize the "national conference," which would assemble Beninois from all walks of life to discuss the national question.[8] On February 19, 1990, the National Conference of Active Forces of the Nation (National Conference) was held between February 19 and 28, 1990, in Cotonou. It was the first of its kind on the African continent. Participants included representatives of the ruling People's Revolutionary Party, trade unionists, civil servants, students, religious leaders, a few agricultural producers, elements of the military, former heads of state, as well as Beninese living and working abroad, members of the diplomatic corps, and officials from the international financial institutions. Altogether, there were 488 selected organizations and individuals.

President Mathieu Kérékou opened the conference with a call for political renewal, pledged to implement the International Monetary Fund's (IMF) structural adjustment program, renounced Marxism–Leninism as the political and economic system, publicly recognized his political errors, asked for forgiveness, and called for democratizing political life and a switch to a market economy.

Expressed by Mathieu Kérékou's self-criticism and critics of the political situation and economic conditions under his but also the previous presidencies of Dahomey found its reflection in the preamble to the 1990 Constitution of the Republic of Benin 1990: "The successive changes of political regimes and of governments have not blunted the determination of the Beninese people to search for, in their own spirit, the cultural, philosophical and spiritual values of civilization which sustain the forms of their patriotism."[9]

But even more severe criticism has been directed at the period of the seventeen-year reign of Mathieu Kérékou when, also in the preamble to the Constitution, its drafters included the statement by which they: "Reaffirm our fundamental opposition to any political regime founded on arbitrariness, dictatorship, injustice, corruption, misappropriation of public funds, regionalism, nepotism, confiscation of power, and personal power."

On December 8, 1989, *L'Office de Radiodiffusion et Télévision du Bénin* (ORTB) broadcasted a brief governmental communique saying, "From now on, Marxism–Leninism is no longer the official ideology of the state of Benin." Such a decision was made after a two-day joint meeting of the Central Committee of Party of the People's Revolution of Benin (PRBP), the Permanent Committee of the National Revolutionary Assembly, and the National Executive Council (the government). In a typical socialist planning style, the authorities announced to a Marxist-indoctrinated nation that "a healthy political climate" would be introduced in Benin beginning next year.[10] They also charged President Kérékou with convening a National Conference at the beginning of 1990.[11]

After securing himself immunity for his seventeen-year rule as a leftist dictator, Mathieu Kérékou agreed to release political prisoners, mainly to satisfy conditions for financial aid from the French government and the IMF. Earlier that year, he was under pressure from France and other international donors who conditioned normalization of the bilateral relations and renewing of providing financial aid for the release of political prisoners and amnesty for political prisoners.

Thus, on August 39, 1989, President Kérékou announced, on a state radio at 11:00 p.m., the decision to grant total amnesty to the Beninese previously convicted or suspected of involvement in coup attempts in 1975 and "perfidious armed aggression" on January 16, 1977. Altogether the amnesty covered more than one hundred Beninese, most of them listed as "activists and subversives" and members of the outlawed Communist Party, which was ironically the strongest internal opposition against the Marxist-oriented Kérékou regime. However, the amnesty did not cover the European mercenaries involved in Opération Crevette.

CHAMELEON OR PATRIOT

As mentioned before, Mathieu Kérékou was often called by his detractors by the nickname "Chameleon," which they used to describe his character in a pejorative way. Ironically, the term "Chameleon" comes from one of Kérékou's 1972 speeches when he used the proverb "the branch will not break in the arms of the chameleon" to articulate his power and ability as a new head of state. The term was, at that time, not used or understood to stress Kérékou's readiness or inclination to readily change his opinions. Nothing in his political views prior to 1989 would show any radical changes.

Kérékou, educated in the French educational system glorifying the French Revolution and laicization of society, as a young officer got involved in Dahomey's politics by circumstances created by Dahomey's political instability in the 1960s and the inability of politicians of older generations to resolve internal economic and political problems, tribal competition, and—what was unique for the Dahomey of 1950s and 1960s—no choice of other political statesmen besides three long-term civilian politicians—Justin Ahomadégbé, Migan Apity, and Hubert Maga—whose political terms were regularly interrupted by military coups d'état. Also, in many newly independent African countries in the 1960s, the experiment of trying to resolve economic, social, and political problems by applying different versions of Marxism, adopted to local conditions, was a very popular tendency. Politically inexperienced and under the influence of young radicals imbibed with Marxist ideology, *liguers*, educated in French, Soviet, Eastern German, or Chinese universities, and by his political, often French, advisors, Mathieu Kérékou decided to impose on Dahomey's traditional society a Marxist ideology in its local version—Marxism–*Beninisme*. Such choice was also dictated by the disappointment with the regrettable results of the colonial system of government that the newly independent countries experienced during the colonial period. Nothing indicates that as a political leader between 1972 and 1989, Mathieu Kérékou had changed his ideological or political views. Only after he thwarted Opération Crevette had he become more dictatorial in exercising his presidential powers.

The metamorphosis of his political views happened, as has been described above, only in the 1980s. It is unclear whether such change occurred under internal or external pressure, self-preservation instinct, patriotism, political realism, or a combination of each. Alternatively, it could have just been opportunism.

President Kérékou also quite easily adapted himself personally to new circumstances, converting from Catholicism to convinced atheist to Islam, finally to return to Christianity; and this former Marxist–Leninist even became an evangelical pastor. He also changed his publicly-worn-for-years Mao-styled shirts for evangelical pastor collared shirts and business jackets.

After, he received a guarantee of no impunity from the National Conference and was allowed to remain a head of state for one year and thirty-four days until the next presidential election. His political nemesis, Nicephore Soglo, under Western and, especially, French and IMF pressure was designated a prime minister and a year later, in the first free multiparty presidential elections in Benin, defeated Kérékou and was elected president of Benin for a five-year term from 1991 to 1996. This presidential election was the first successful power transfer from a dictatorship to a democracy on the African continent. Thus, the former "sick child of Africa" became a beacon of democratization in Africa, and Mathieu Kérékou himself became an example for other political dictators in Africa and a national hero in his country.

THE FINAL CHAPTER

As to the Beninese participants of Opération Crevette who were sentenced by the National Revolutionary Tribunal to death or long-term jail sentences in 1979, all of them received amnesty on August 30, 1989.[12] The amnesty applied to total of 192 individuals encompassing, among others, thirty organizers and participants of the thwarted coup attempts of January and October 1975 and failed Opération Crevette. Among the amnestied were Émile Derlin Zinsou and Gratien Pognon, and Marc Soglo.[13] Those who have been living in exile were allowed to return safely to Benin. All amnestied Beninese had their civil rights back, some of them even receiving compensation for material damages suffered because of the 1979 court sentences against them.

Kérékou's amnesty, however, did not apply to the European mercenaries convicted in 1979 by the Revolutionary Tribunal to death. Sadly, the only *Crevette* participant who had been left behind at the Cotonou airport by fleeing Denard commando, Guinean Alpha Bâ Oumarou, became a crown witness cooperating with Beninese authorities and the United Nations and the OAU's commissions of inquiry in regard to details of the Opération Crevette. By the 1989 amnesty, he had already spent twelve years in Benin's prison; he was not covered by the provision of the amnesty, as they were applicable only to Beninese citizens.[14]

After receiving amnesty with the change of political system in country, both Pognon and Zinsou returned to Benin and successfully re-engaged in the country's politics. Pognon was elected to parliament, and Zinsou, the former subject of three death penalty judgments for anti-Kérékou activity, became a political adviser to Mathieu Kérékou.

As for the families of seven Beninese soldiers who died repelling the Cotonou mercenary attack—they waited until 2005 to receive monetary compensation for their losses.

Much earlier, however, on the second anniversary of the attack (January 16, 1979), the government named the square located at the confluence of Rue de l'Aéroport and Rue 390, where the direct exchange of fire took place between Beninese soldiers and the mercenaries, Square of the Martyrs (*Place des Marthyrs*) in an effort to memorialize their deaths. That year (1979), in the middle of this square a monument was erected representing three soldiers raising over their heads a national Beninese flag. The monument was erected with help from North Korea. After the political changes of 1989, the square was renamed in 1990, not without much of a criticism, to Square of Remembrance (*Place du Souvenir*). The base of this monument originally housed an exposition of the weapons and equipment left by the fleeing mercenaries, but these were later moved to a cultural exhibition center named *Médiathèque des Diasporas*. Several buildings bear his name in Cotonou, such as the *Stade de l'Amitié* (Friendship Stadium) re-named *Stade Général Mathieu Kérékou*.

The lesson from the numerous successful and attempted coups d'état, and the 1977 mercenary invasion, had been reflected in the amendements to the Beninese Constitution in 1990. Article 66 provides that: "In case of a coup d'états, of a putsch, of aggression by mercenaries or of any action by force whatsoever, any member of a constitutional agency shall have the right and the duty to make an appeal by any means in order to re-establish the constitutional legitimacy, including recourse to existing agreements of military or defense cooperation."[15]

In these circumstances, "for any Beninese to disobey and organize himself to put a check to the illegitimate authority shall constitute the most sacred of rights and the most imperative of duties." The article therefore imposes on all Beninese nationals the requirement to reject support or active opposition of any "illegal rule" emerging as the result of the noted actions.

In attempting to democratize the political system of the country, Article 44 of the 1990 Constitution was adopted banning the application of any persons above the age of seventy for president. Obviously, this article was aimed at the "old staff" that alternately took power of the country, first by coups d'état and then by means of subsequent elections organized under their supervision. Both Pognon and Zinzou were in this group.

As for Mathieu Kérékou, after Opération Crevette, he hired, as a number of other African presidents had the habit of doing, his own marabout— Mohamed Cissé, a Malian Islamic "holy man" credited with supernatural powers. This "analphabet conjuror," as described by *Jeune Afrique*, wielded a strong influence over Kérékou, who considered him to be a "genius" regarding personal, financial, and political decisions, including the nomination of state ministers and directors of state agencies.

At the end of 1980s, when Kérékou felt forced to change the political course of the country, he launched an international arrest order accusing Mohamed Cissé, who had escaped to the Ivory Coast, of a huge financial malversation. Deported to Benin, Cissé was placed in prison in Porto Novo and subjected to continued criminal trials into the late 2000s.

In the first democratic and direct presidential election in March 1991, Prime Minister Nicéphore Soglo (since March 1990) won the second round of the presidential election by obtaining 67.73 percent of the votes cast, against 32.27 percent for the outgoing president, Mathieu Kérékou. The elections were overshadowed by ethnic violence between the north and the south, which left two dead and fifteen wounded: Mathieu Kérékou retained a large popularity in the north of the country where he was born, while the south supported Nicéphore Soglo.

On the 31st, the High Council of the Republic (HCR) granted President Kérékou immunity for all his years in power between 1972 and 1989.

The new administration of President Soglo tried to improve the country's economy, implementing fiscal policies imposed on Benin by international donors and financial organizations, and Benin started to make economic gains. However, the feeling among many Beninese was that economic progress came at too great a cost to the country—the disregard for democratization and the social well-being of its citizens—and Soglo's support slipped.

Thus, to no surprise, on a wave of political sentiment in the next presidential elections of 1996, incumbent Nicephore Soglo lost to Mathieu Kérékou who, as still the most popular Beninese politician, became the president for the next five years and was reelected for a subsequent term in 2001.

In 2005, he attempted, like presidents in many other African countries, to achieve the amendment of Article 44 of the Constitution from parliament allowing him, despite reaching the age of seventy-two, to be a candidate in the next presidential election. But his time was up in the eyes of both his opposition and French supporters. Under strong pressures, he was forced to not submit his candidacy in the 2006 election, philosophically concluding, "If you don't leave power, power will leave you."[16] However, likely following the view of Winston Churchill that one should not believe in elections results unless he himself cooked them up, Kérékou questioned the election's results.

Thus, after almost seventeen years as a military head of state, he became the first sub-Saharan African strongman who stepped-down and was subsequently twice democratically elected as a president and remained in office for next ten years and two days.

With the election of Thomas Yayi Boni, a solidly pro-Western politician, the thirty-year-long chapter of Kérékou's important, although not always positive, role in Benin's history ended.

As to Benin's relations with both countries supporting Opération Crevette, they became normalized within the coming decades. In 1991, Kérékou, upon the invitation of Hassan II, paid a visit to Morocco. Both countries signed a number of cooperation agreements in 1995 and re-established diplomatic relations in 1997 (March 21). In order to improve relations with Morocco and France, Cotonou suspended its earlier diplomatic recognition of the Sahrawi Arab Democratic Republic (SADR), the disputed-by-Rabat territory of a former Spanish colony bordering with Morocco. When in 2004 Moroccan king Mohamed VI visited Benin, Kérékou referred to both countries as "brothers and friends." Further, in recognition of his close of cooperation with France, Kérékou received from Jacques Chirac the order of *Grand Croix de la Legion d'honneur*.

On the thirty-eighth anniversary of the events that had taken place in January 1977, Kérékou ordered a Holy Mass to give thanks for the success of defeating the mercenaries' attack at the Catholic cathedral of Saint Peter and Paul in Parakou.

On October 14, 2015, Kérékou passed away at the age of eighty-two. He was eulogized in local and international media not as a failed Marxist and a long-term dictator but, rather, as a reformer who opened the door to a democratically political and economically liberal system of his country and as an example to follow in other countries on African continent. He ruled the country on and off for thirty years, after a twenty-year one-party reign and two democratically elected terms.

There was declared a seven-day mourning period after his death.

Figure 18.2. Place des Souvenirs / Place des Martyrs, Monument to the victims of the coup attempt of January 16, 1977.   Credit: Hemis / Alamy Stock Photo.

Nine months later, on July 29, 2016, at age of ninety-eight, Émile Derlin Zinsou passed away. To honor him, the president of Benin ordered a three-day mourning period and the lowering of national flags on all public edifices in Cotonou, except the twenty-two masts at the Square of Martyrs (today: Square of Remembrance), situated in the heart of Cotonou, approximately two hundred meters from the presidential complex and memorializing the Beninese military victims of the Opération Crevette. The memory of Zinsou's sponsored Opération Crevette remains alive in Benin. Each year, the day of January 16 is celebrated as a Day of Remembrance (*Journée de Souvenir*)[17] sometimes also called Day of Martyrs (*Jour des Martyrs*).

Prior to the political changes of 1989, the country also celebrated each October 26 as a Day of Armed Forces to memorialize Kérékou's October 1972 coup d'état but with the change of a political climate in Benin this day is no longer public holiday.

In 2020 the Beninese authorities decided to demolish *Les filaos*, the old house used by Mathieu Kérékou and his family for more than fifty years as his private residence. The remaining lot had been transformed into a public space: Les jardins de Mathieu—Mathieu Gardens.

With Kérékou's and Zinsou's death, a long, colorful, and often complicated chapter of Benin's history finally closed.

Bob Denard passed away at age seventy-eight on October 13, 2007. His death was noted by media all over the world. Denard's demise has ended the history of famous mercenaries as we knew it for most of the twentieth century. It was replaced by a new form of mercenary: private military security companies.

NOTES

1. Joel Donnet, "Mitterrand: African Nations Must Move Toward Democracy," *AP*, June 20, 1990, https://apnews.com/article/edfa5353874d34c97d3062d300bca767.

2. Histoire du Bénin, Présidence de la République du Benin: https://presidence.bj/home/le-benin/histoire/.

3. Robert Dossou, Dean of the Faculty of Law at the Université Nationale du Benin and an elected member of the Benin's legislature, Minister of Foreign Affairs from 1993–1995. *Historical Dictionary of Benin*, Mathurin C. Houngnikpo and Samuel Decalo, fourth edition (Lanham, MD: Scarecrow Press, 2013), 145.

4. Interview with Robert Dissou (accessed August 5, 2016): "Hopes on the Horizon - Benin Transcript," PBS, accessed November 16, 2021, http://www.pbs.org/hopes/benin/transcript.html.

5. Robert Dossou, *L'audace, La vérité et l'espérance. La Conférence Nationale: Ce que J'en ai dit en trente ans* (Cotonou, Benin: Editions Ruisseaux d'Afrique, 2020), 29.

6. "Histoire du Bénin sur BeninWeb," BeninWeb, accessed November 23, 2021, http://www.beninweb.org/benin/histoire/.

7. "Le president Kérékou rejette l'idée du multipartisme," *Fraternité Matin* (Abidjan), September 4, 1989.

8. Professor René Ahouansou and Robert Dossou met on July 28, 1989, with Mathieu Kérékou on behalf of concerned legislators and citizens to seek for solution to national crisis and convinced him to agree to organization National Conference in 1990. Dossou, *L'audace, la vérité et l'espérance*, 130–32.

9. La Constitution de la République du Bénin. Loi No. 90–32 du 11 décembre 1990 portant Constitution de la République du Bénin: https://assemblee-nationale .bj/wp-content/uploads/2017/10/Benin-La-Constitution-1990.pdf. English text of the Benin's Constitution is available at Benin's Constitution of 1990: https://www .constituteproject.org/constitution/Benin_1990.pdf?lang=en.

10. Dossou, *L'audace, la vérité et l'espérance*, 95–96; Reuters, "Upheaval in the East; Benin, Too, Gives Up Marxism for Reforms," *New York Times*, December 9, 1989, sec. World, 9, https://www.nytimes.com/1989/12/09/world/upheaval-in-the -east-benin-too-gives-up-marxism-for-reforms.html.

11. President Mathieu Kérékou issued the Decree No. 90–40 du 23 Février 1990 portant convocation de 1a Conférence Nationale et détermination de sa mission, https://sgg.gouv.bj/doc/decret-1990-40/. It describes in Article 3 the amies of the Conference as preparing the text of a new Constitution and elaboration of principles of a new liberal economic system of the country.

12. Loi 89–010. See also: "Exclusif: la liste complete des aministiés," *Jeune Afrique*, October 2, 1989, 39.

13. Francis Kpatindé, "Benin: Pardon pour les 'Impénitents,'" *Jeune Afrique*, no. 1500, October 2, 1989, 38.

14. Ibid.; "Mathieu Kérékou: 'Tous les Beninois peuvent renter,'" *Jeune Afrique*, December 4, 1989, 29–32.

15. "Constitution of the People's Republic of Benin," 1990, https://www.wipo.int/ edocs/lexdocs/laws/en/bj/bj001en.pdf.

16. Sam Roberts, "Mathieu Kérékou, Dictator Who Ushered in Democracy in Benin, Dies at 82," *New York Times*, October 16, 2015, sec. World, https://www .nytimes.com/2015/10/16/world/africa/mathieu-kerekou-dictator-who-ushered-in -democracy-in-benin-dies-at-82.html.

17. Art. 1, "Loi No. 90–019 du 27 Juillet 1990 fixant les Fêtes Légales en République du Bénin"; https://sgg.gouv.bj/doc/loi-90-019/.

Appendix A

PRESIDENTS AND HEADS OF STATE
OF BENIN FROM 1960 TO 2006

Name	Period of Power Start (mm/dd/yyyy)	Period of Power End (mm/dd/yyyy)	Duration(Excluding end date)
Hubert Maga	08/01/1960	10/27/1963	3 years, 2 months, 26 days
Christophe Soglo	10/28/1963	01/25/1964	89 days
Sourou-Migan Apithy	01/25/1964	11/27/1965	1 year, 10 months, 2 days
Justin Ahomadegbé	11/27/1965	11/29/1965	2 days
Tahirou Congacou	11/27/1965	12/22/1967	2 years, 25 days
Chistophe Soglo	12/22/1965	12/19/1967	1 year, 11 months, 27 days
Maurice Kouandété	12/20/1967	12/21/1967	1 day
Alphonse Amadou Alley	12/21/1967	07/17/1968	6 months, 26 days
Émile Derlin Zinsou	07/17/1968	12/10/1969	1 year, 4 months, 23 days
Maurice Kouandété	12/10/1969	12/13/1969	3 days
Paul-Émile de Souza	12/13/1969	05/07/1970	4 months, 24 days
Hubert Maga	05/07/1970	05/07/1972	2 years
Justin Ahomadegbé	05/07/1972	10/26/1972	5 months, 19 days
Mathieu Kérékou	10/26/1972	04/04/1991	18 years, 5 months, 9 days
Nicéphore Soglo	04/04/1991	04/04/1996	5 years
Mathieu Kérékou	04/06/1996	04/06/2001	5 years
Mathieu Kérékou	04/06/2001	04/06/2006	5 years

Appendix B

European mercenaries listed by Benin's authorities as involved in Opération Crevette (in alphabetical order):

- Marc Aubert
- Eric Berardengo
- Robert Bermont
- Siegried Birnbaum
- Dominique Boucher
- Daniel Bourre1
- Gervais Boutanquoi
- Philippe Boyer
- Roger Bracco
- Jacques Buteri
- Dominique Cabot
- Louis Capasso
- André Cau
- Benoît Charrier
- Jean-Michel Chesse
- Hugues de Chivre
- Jean Bernard Chretien
- Marc Colot
- Michel de la Contrie de Charette
- Olivier Danet
- Bernard Delrue
- Jean-Pierre Delstanches
- Bob Denard
- Christian Despres
- Philippe de Doyard
- Helmut Gruber
- Jacques Guillots
- Frantz Heimann
- Alfons Holzappel
- Yvon Jouguet
- Werner Kolibius
- Francis Leal
- Jean-Paul Lecorgne
- Guy Lefevre
- Gérard Lejon
- Jean-Yves Le Meur
- Michel Loiseau
- Patrice Loth
- Michel Lourdais
- Dominique Malacrino
- Jean-Pierre Malivert
- Gérard Michel
- Jean-Louis Milliote
- Dominique Musial
- Pierre Paillard
- Jacquy Perrin
- Gérard Peyre
- René de Says Resciniti
- Thierry Richelles
- Laurent de Sarnez
- Guy Scheeck
- Raymond Schenpf
- Denis Simon
- Didier Souppart

- Taddée Surma
- Jean-Pierre Sutter
- Raymond Thomann
- Gérard Thuret

- Guy Toumi
- Jean-Pierre van den Berghe
- Hugues Wagner
- Mercier et consorts

Source: S/13402 Annex, 5–6.

Appendix C

African mercenaries listed by Benin's authorities as involved in Opération Crevette:

- Marc Soglo (a.k.a. Montagne)
- Juste Parfait Rustico
- Cossi Paulin Tohoue
- Antoine Kohoun
- Mathias J. Adeochoun
- Roch Augustin Aissi
- Lucien Zogo (a.k.a. Scorpion)
- Issa Aliou Djato
- Ousman Boukari
- Mazou Idrissou
- Alpha Ba Oumarou
- Ibrahima Kaba
- Saliou Diallo
- Mohamed Dowgound
- Mamadou Ba
- Msmadou Diaïlo
- Ali Diawara
- Kalilcu Kone
- Mamadouna Sako
- A. Koholin
- A. Maman
- Barro Ba
- Bakary Zoumarou
- Lamine Kaba
- Oumar Sy Savaneh
- Ibrahima Diallo
- Abdourahmane Kaba

Source: S/13402 19 June 1979, Annex, 3–4.

Appendix D

RESOLUTION 404 (1977) OF 8 FEBRUARY 1977

The Security Council,

Taking note of the letter dated 26 January 1977 from the *Chargé d'Affaires, a.i.,* of the Permanent Mission of the People's Republic of Benin to the United Nations addressed to the President of the Security Council,

Having heard the statement of the Permanent Representative of the People's Republic of Benin,

Bearing in mind that all Member States must refrain in their international relations from the threat or use of force against the territorial integrity or political independence of any State, or in any other manner inconsistent with the purposes of the United Nations,

1. *Affirms* that the territorial integrity and political independence of the People's Republic of Benin must be respected;
2. *Decides* to send a Special Mission composed of three members of the Security Council to the People's Republic of Benin in order to investigate the events of 16 January 1977 at Cotonou and report not later than the end of February 1977;
3. *Decides* that the members of the Special Mission will be appointed after consultations between the President and the members of the Security Council;
4. *Requests* the Secretary-General to provide the Special Mission with the necessary assistance;
5. *Decides* to remain seized of the question.

Adopted at the 1987th meeting by consensus
Source: S/404 8 February 1977.

Appendix E

RESOLUTION 405 (1977) OF 14 APRIL 1977

The Security Council,

Having considered the report"' of the Security Council Special Mission to the People's Republic of Benin established under resolution 404 (1977) of 8 February 1977,

Gravely concerned at the violation of the territorial integrity, independence and sovereignty of the State of Benin,

Deeply grieved at the loss of life and substantial damage to property caused by the invading force during its attack on Cotonou on 16 January 1977,

1. *Takes note* of the report of the Special Mission and expresses its appreciation for the work accomplished;
2. *Strongly condemns* the act of armed aggression perpetrated against the People's Republic of Benin on 16 January 1977;
3. *Reaffirms* its resolution 239 (1967) of 10 July 1967, by which, *inter alia*, it condemns any State which persists in permitting or tolerating the recruitment of mercenaries and the provision of facilities to them, with the objective of overthrowing the Governments of Member States;
4. *Calls upon* all States to exercise the utmost vigilance against the danger posed by international mercenaries and to ensure that their territory and other territories under their control, as well as their nationals, are not used for the planning of subversion and recruitment, training and transit of mercenaries designed to overthrow the Government of any Member State;
5. *Further calls upon* all States to consider taking necessary measures to prohibit, under their respective domestic laws, the recruitment, training

and transit of mercenaries on their territory and other territories under their control;

6. *Condemns* all forms of external interference in the internal affairs of Member States, including the use of international mercenaries to destabilize States and/or to violate their territorial integrity, sovereignty and independence;

7. *Requests* the Secretary-General to provide ap- propriate technical assistance to help the Government of Benin in assessing and evaluating the damage resulting from the act of armed aggression committed at Cotonou on 16 January 1977;

8. *Appeals* to all States to provide material assistance to the People's Republic of Benin in order to enable it to repair the damage and lasses inflicted during the attack;

9. *Notes* that the Government of Benin has re- served its right with respect to any eventual claims for compensation which it may wish to assert;

10. *Calls upon* all States to provide the Security Council with any information they might have in connection with the events at Cotonou on 16 January 1977 likely to throw further light on those events;

11. *Requests* the Secretary-General to follow closely the implementation of the present resolution;

12. *Decides* to remain seized of this question.

Adopted at the 2005th meeting by consensus.

Source: S/RES/405(1977).

Appendix F

**UNITED NATIONS
SECURITY
COUNCIL**

Distr.
GENERAL
S/13402
19 June 1979
ENGLISH
ORIGINAL: FRENCH

LETTER DATED 13 JUNE 1979 FROM THE
PERMANENT REPRESENTATIVE
OF BEHTI\J TO THE UNITED NATIONS
ADDRESSED TO THE SECRETARY
GENERAL

On instructions from my Government, I have the honour to transmit to you herewith, for publication as a Security Council document in connexion with Benin's complaint which is still before the Security Council, a special communiqué issued by the Revolutionary Military Government on the sentencing of mercenaries and their associates involved in the imperialist armed aggression of Sunday, 16 January 1977.

(Signed) Thomas S. BOYA
Ambassador

S/13402

ANNEX

IMPERIALIST ARMED AGGRESSION OF SUNDAY, 16 JANUARY 1977
DECISIONS OF THE SESSION or THE NATIONAL REVOLUTIONARY
COUNCIL SITTING AS A NATIONAL REVOLUTIONARY
TRIBUNAL TO DEAL HITII THE FACTS OF THE AGGRESSION
(Special communique issued by the Revolutionary Military Government)

At the meeting of the Council of Ministers on Wednesday, 23 May 1979, the Head of State presented the decisions of the National Revolutionary Council following the conclusions of the investigations of two commissions of inquiry established after the imperialist armed aggression of Sunday, 16 January 1977: one to investigate the internal ramifications of the network of mercenaries and traitors to the Beninese cause, and the other to hear Theodore Ahoussinou, known cl.s "Radelec," and his accomplices concerning: the subversive network established by them with a view to carrying out attempts on the lives of the responsible figures of the Beninese revolution.

The National Revolutionary Council, having before it the two investigation files presented to it by the Head of State, the Chairman of the Central Committee of the Party of the People's Revolution of Benin, on the basis of ordinance No. 74–68 of 18 November 1974, which provides for the establishment, powers, composition, organization and functioning of the National Revolutionary Council and which stipulates in its article 7: "The National Revolutionary Council may sit as a National Revolutionary Tribunal to judge, without appeal, such acts and events as it declares to be political infractions and attempts against State security," sat as a National Revolutionary Tribunal on 9 April 1979 for the purpose of judging the perpetrators, accomplices and all persons involved in the events which were the subject of the above-mentioned two inquiries; this high authority of our revolution made public the record of its deliberations, the essence of which is as follows:

Everyone remembers the strange noises which on Sunday, 16 January 1977 awakened the working people of Cotonou, our economic capital.

Everyone also knows that those whistling, crackling and rumbling noises were the work of drug-maddened mercenaries armed with the most modern and sophisticated weapons for the cynical purpose of physically liquidating the responsible figures of our Party and our revolutionary State,

Everyone—except those who, entangled in their own contradictions, undermined by hatred and confusion, are struggling pitifully in an attempt to hide the truth—everyone, we say, knows that those mercenaries, vile stateless individuals, 'with no faith and no law, are the sadistic agents of international imperialism and its African henchmen.

Indeed, after the proclamation of the Programme Speech of 13 November 1972, after the choice of our socialist option for development on 30 November 1974, and especially after the birth on 30 November 1975 of our vanguard Party, the Party of the People's Revolution of Benin, a Party whose task it is to educate our people, organize it and harden it for war in its revolutionary struggle of national liberation, international imperialism decided to do everything in its power to succeed in its diabolical plan of colonial reconquest with a view to safeguarding its avaricious interests and keeping our people's cack forever bowed so that it could be enslaved and exploited.

Everyone is convinced that such efforts are possible only when the external network can count on the assistance and firm support of an internal network.

Everyone remembers also that after the joint session held from 7 to 12 March 1977, the Central Committee of the Party of the People's Revolution of Benin, the National Revolutionary Council and the Revolutionary Military Government, publishing the report of the special commission of inquiry, promised to deal with the matter of the internal network of that ignoble imperialist armed aggression of Sunday, 16 January 1977.

For that reason, and in conformity with that decision of the higher national authorities, there was established, by ordinance No. 77–7 of 18 February 1977 and ordinance No. 77–41 of 3 December 1977, a National Commission of Inquiry, which encircled, surrounded and dismantled this internal network of the aggression of 16 January 1977 and whose report has been submitted to the Central Committee of the Party of the People's Revolution of Benin.

Accordingly, at the close of its first regular session for the year 1979 and in application of the provisions of ordinance No. 74–68 of 18 November 1974, article 7, the national Revolutionary Council sat on 9 April 1979 as a National Revolutionary Tribunal to take note of the report of the National Commission of Inquiry and to pronounce sanctions against all the persons implicated in the internal network of the imperialist armed aggression of Sunday, 16 January 1977.

After hearing the said report and after extensive discussion, the National Revolutionary Tribunal ruled case by case and pronounced the following sanctions by simple majority in a secret ballot:

IMPERIALIST ARMED AGGRESSION OF SUNDAY, 16 JANUARY 1977:

Sentenced to death:

1. (1) Beninese traitors
   - Joseph A. Fadest
   - Nicolas Takin

- Achille Zogo
- Emile Derlin Zinsou, twice condemned to death
- Gratien Pognon
- Amadou Assouma, known as Tchinnin
- Amédée Adotevi, once condemned to death
- Paul Darboux
- Bertin Babliba Borna, once condemned to death
- Idelphonse Lenon, once condemned to death
- Adrien Houngbedji once condemned to death
2. (2) African mercenaries
   - Marc Soglo
   - Juste Parfait Rustico
   - Cossi Paulin Tohoue
   - Antoine Kohoun
   - Mathias J. Adeochoun
   - Roch Augustin Aissi
   - Lucien Zogo
   - Issa Aliou Djato
   - Ousman Boukari
   - Mazou Idrissou
   - Alpha Ba Oumarou
   - Ibrahima Kaba
   - Saliou Diallo
   - Mohamed Dowgound
   - Mamadou Ba
   - Mamadou Diallo
   - Alı Dıawara
   - Kalilou Kone
   - Mamadouna Salw
   - A. Koholin
   - A. Maman
   - Barro Ba
   - Bakary Zoumarou
   - Lamine Kaba
   - Oumar Sy Savaneh
   - Ibrahima Diallo
   - Abdourahmane Kaba
3. (3) European mercenaries
   - Bob Denard alias Colonel Maurin, alias Gilbert Bourgeaud
   - Marc Aubert
   - Eric Berardengo
   - Robert Bermont

- Siegried Birnbaum
- Dominique Boucher
- Daniel Bourrel
- Gervais Boutanquoi
- Philippe Boyer
- Roger Bracco
- Jacques Buteri
- Guy Lefevre
- Dominique Cabot
- Louis Capasso
- André Cau
- Michel de la Contrie de Charette
- Benoit Charrier
- Jean Michel Chesse
- Hugues de Chivre
- Jean Bernard Chretien
- Marc Colot
- Olivier Danet
- Bernard Delrue
- Jean Pierre Delstanches
- Christan Despres
- Philippe de Doyard
- Jacques Guillots
- Helmut Gruber
- Alfons Holzapfel
- Yvon Jouguet
- Werner Kolibius
- Francis Leal
- Jean Paul Lecorqne
- Taddée Surma
- Gérard Lejon
- Jean Yves Le Meur
- Michel Loiseau
- Patrice Loth
- Michel Lourdais
- Frantz Heimann
- Dominique Malacrino
- Hugues Wagner
- Thierry Richelles
- Jean Pierre Malivert
- Gérard Michel
- Jean Louis Milliote

- Dominique Musial
- Pierre Paillard
- Jacquy Perrin
- René de Says Resciniti
- Laurent de Sarnez
- Guy Scheeck
- Raymond Schenpf
- Denis Simon
- Didier Souppart
- Jean Pierre Sutter
- Raymond Thomann
- Gérard Thuret
- Guy Toumi
- Jean Pierre Van Den Berghe
- Gérard Peyre
- Mercier and associates

Sentenced to imprisonment for 10 years:

- Justine Caitano, wife of Marc Soglo

Sentenced to imprisonment for 5 years:

- Lucien Gnonhoue
- Keita Sanfa

Acquitted:

- Franck Lahami
- Rény Aizansi
- Odette Noudogbessi
- Codjo Paul Soglo. This person shall be subjected to a military sanction in accordance with the statute of the People's Armed Forces of Benin.

THE MATTER OF THEODORE AHOUSSINOU, KNOWN AS "RADELEC" AND HIS ASSOCIATES

The following persons were acquitted outright:
- Théodore Ahoussinou, known as "Radelec"
- Thomas Bodea
- Jean Kodoko Agbessi
- Désiré Adihou
- Maurice Guedegbe
- Martial Gohoungo

- Cathérine Ahouandjinou
- Paulin Zohoungbogbo

Death to the traitors! Death to the mercenaries! Ready for the Revolution! The struggle continues.

Cotonou, 24 May, 1979

Bibliography

"A Job with Little Future." *Time*, no. 25, December 19, 1969, 35.

"A Seasonal Coup." *Time*, no. 26, December 29, 1967, 24.

Africa Confidential 18, no. 6 (March 18, 1977).

Africa Info. "Bénin: Quelques repères historiques et différents présidents depuis 1960." *Africa News* (blog), December 26, 2015. http://infoafricanews.blogspot .com/2015/12/benin-quelques-reperes-historiques-et.html.

"African Land, No Stranger to Coups, Repulses an Attack by 'Mercenaries.'" *New York Times*, January 17, 1977. Sec. Archives. https://www.nytimes.com/1977/01 /17/archives/african-land-no-stranger-to-coups-repulses-an-attack-by-mercenaries .html.

Afrique-Asie, no. 129, February 21–March 6, 1977, 14–16.

Agbodji, Christophe D. "Coup d'état du 26 octobre 1972: Les troublantes révélations de Pascal Chabi Kao (Première Partie)." *Le Benin vu par un jeune* (blog), October 25, 2011. http://actudubenin.over-blog.com/article-coup-d-etat-du-26-octobre -1972-les-troublantes-revelations-de-pascal-chabi-kao-87267329.html.

Agence France Presse. "Décès de l'ancien mercenaire Bob Denard." *leparisien*, October 13, 2007. https://www.leparisien.fr/politique/deces-de-l-ancien-mercenaire -bob-denard-14-10-2007-3291315907.php.

Akindes, Adékpédjou Sylvain. *Essai d'histoire du temps présent au Bénin postcolonial*. Tome II; 1972–1990; L'équipée révolutionnaire (Problématique d'un engagement politique). Cotonou: Star Éditions, 2017.

Akpo, Philippe. *Role et implications des forces armees beninoises dans la vie politique nationale: Temoignage, ma part de vérité sur les faits et les non-dits*. Cotonou, Benin: Editions du Flamboyant, 2005.

Arnold, Guy. *Mercenaries: Scourge of the Developing World*. London: Palgrave Macmillan, 1999.

Association for Diplomatic Studies and Training. "The 1974 Coup in Benin (Dahomey)." Huffington Post, December 6, 2017. https://www.huffpost.com/entry /the-1974-coup-in-benin-da_b_8302874.

———. "Windshield Tour of a Military Coup in Benin." September 30. 2015. Accessed November 23, 2021. https://adst.org/2015/09/windshield-tour-of-a-military-coup -in-benin/.

"Au tribunal correctionnel de Paris Bob Denard, mercenaire ou corsaire?" *Le Monde*, March 12, 1993. https://www.lemonde.fr/archives/article/1993/03/12/au-tribunal -correctionnel-de-paris-bob-denard-mercenaire-ou-corsaire_3918299_1819218 .html.

Avèkes, Binason. "Pour l'histoire: Coup d'etat du 26 octobre 1972 et Affaire Covacs: Le Roman Crépusculaire de Pascal Chabi Kao." *Babilown*, February 12, 2012. https://babilown.com/2012/02/12/coup-detat-du-26-octobre-1972-et-affaire -covac-le-roman-crepusculaire-de-pascal-chabi-kao/.

Bach, Daniel, and Valery Giscard d'Estaing. *La France en Afrique subsahari- enne: Contraintes historiques et nouveaux espaces economiques*. Paris: Ass. fr. de sci. po., 1983.

Badarou, Aziz. "Agression du 16 janvier 1977: Sanni Mouftaou, un survivant, retrace l'histoire . . ." *Matin Libre* (blog), February 1, 2019. https://matinlibre.com/2019/01 /31/agression-du-16-janvier-1977-sanni-mouftaou-un-survivant-retrace-lhistoire/.

Banidje, K. Honoré, and Çağatay Benhür. "The Instrumentalisation of the History: The Benin's Aggression on 16th January 1977 and the Memory of the Victims." *The Pursuit of History International Periodical for History and Social Research* 19 (2018): 125–35.

Barnay, Martin. "Mémoire présenté à la Faculté des arts et sciences en vue de l'obtention du grade de maître ès arts en histoire." MA Thesis, Université de Montréal, 2014. https://papyrus.bib.umontreal.ca/xmlui/bitstream/handle/1866 /12478/Barnay_Martin_2014_memoire.pdf.

Benin. "Letter Dated 13 June 1979 from the Permanent Representative of Benin to the United Nations Addressed to the Secretary-General." New York: United Nations, June 19, 1979. https://digitallibrary.un.org/record/2937.

———. "Letter Dated 77/01/26 from the Chargé d'affaires, a.i., of the Permanent Mission of Benin to the United Nations Addressed to the President of the Security Council." New York: United Nations, 1977. https://digitallibrary.un.org/record /224331.

———. "Letter Dated 77/04/04 from the Charge d'Affaires a.i. of Benin to the United Nations Addressed to the President of the Security Council: Addendum." New York: United Nations, April 5, 1977. https://digitallibrary.un.org/record/564452.

———. "Letter Dated 77/10/13 from the Permanent Representative of Benin to the United Nations Addressed to the President of the Security Council." New York: United Nations, October 13, 1977. https://digitallibrary.un.org/record /565443.

"Benin Asks UN Study of Attack on Cotonou." *New York Times*, February 8, 1977. Sec. Archives. https://www.nytimes.com/1977/02/08/archives/benin-asks-un -study-of-attack-on-cotonou.html.

"Benin Coup Attempt: Look at the Goodies." Wikileaks Public Library of US Diplomacy. Benin Cotonou, January 20, 1977. https://wikileaks.org/plusd/cables /1977COTONO00143_c.html.

"Benin: L'affaire du 16 janvier selon l'ONU." *Jeune Afrique*, no. 850, April 1977.

Benin: La régime se structure. J. T., L'année politique africaine 1977, p. II – 73 – II 77.

"Benin: Ou est la verite?" *Jeune Afrique*, March 18, 1977.

"Bénin: Pour l'example." *Jeune Afrique*, no. 961, June 6, 1979, 23.

"Benin: Le complait nuis à nu." Mariam Sysle, *Afrique-Asie*, no. 132, April 4–17, 1977, 13–15.

Benin Web. "Histoire du Bénin sur BeninWeb." Accessed November 23, 2021. http://www.beninweb.org/benin/histoire/.

Bernichi, L. "A l'âge de 78 ans, Bob Denard, mercenaire français ayant." *Maghress*, October 19, 2007. https://www.maghress.com/fr/marochebdo/76312.

"Bob Denard devant le tribunal correctionnel de Paris le procès des mercenaires." *Le Monde*, March 13, 1993. https://www.lemonde.fr/archives/article/1993/03/13/bob-denard-devant-le-tribunal-correctionnel-de-paris-le-proces-des-mercenaires_3918355_1819218.html.

"Bob Denard et les 'services' au banc des accusés." *L'Humanité*, March 12, 1993. https://www.humanite.fr/bob-denard-et-les-services-au-banc-des-accuses-51832.

Boisbouvier, Christophe. "Bénin: Mathieu Kérékou, une histoire africaine." *Jeune Afrique*, October 21, 2015. https://www.jeuneafrique.com/mag/272530/politique/benin-mathieu-kerekou-une-histoire-africaine/.

Bourcier, Nicolas. "Bob Denard, mercenaire." *Le Monde*, October 17, 2007. https://www.lemonde.fr/disparitions/article/2007/10/17/bob-denard-mercenaire_967897_3382.html.

Bradshaw, Job. "The Man Who Would Be King." *Esquire*, March 27, 1977.

Bradshaw, Jon, and Benin. "Letter Dated 7 May 1979 from the Permanent Representative of Benin to the United Nations Addressed to the Secretary-General." New York: United Nations, May 8, 1979. https://digitallibrary.un.org/record/2894.

Bruyère-Ostells, Walter. "Mercenaires et/ou volontaires Engagements de combattants français de la Rhodésie à la Yougoslavie (1976–1995)." *Études Géostratégiques*, April 13 and 14, 2012, https://etudesgeostrategiques.com/files/ougoslavie-1976-1995_ghw7jonwovxwnh5biad7fb/#_ftn2.

———. *Dans l'ombre de Bob Denard: Les mercenaires français de 1960 à 1989*. Paris: Nouveau Monde, 2014.

———. "The 'Affreux': French Mercenaries, Types of Violence and Systems of Domination by Extra-African Forces (1960–1989)," 2014. https://hal.archives-ouvertes.fr/hal-01353545.

———. "Treatment of the Bodies of Those Killed in French Mercenary Operations between 1960 and 1989." *Human Remains and Violence* 5, no. 2 (October 2019): 3–16. https://doi.org/10.7227/HRV.5.2.2.

Bryden, Alan, and Boubacar N'Diaye. *Gouvernance du secteur de la sécurité en Afrique de l'Ouest francophone: Bilan et perspectives*. Wien: LIT, 2011.

Cheeseman, Nic, Eloïse Bertra, and Sa'eed Husaini. *A Dictionary of African Politics* (online). Oxford: Oxford University Press, 2019.

Cherruau, Pierre, and Marcus Boni Teiga. "Les 10 coups d'état les plus foireux en Afrique." *7sur7.cd*, August 12, 2015. https://7sur7.cd/les-10-coups-detat-les-plus-foireux-en-afrique.

Chevalerias, Alain. "OPS Oméga-raid sur Cotonou: Témoignage Alain Marc." *Orbs Patria Nostra*, April 1977. https://www.orbspatrianostra.com/ops/ops-benin /temoignage-alain-marc.html.

"Chronique de la vie d'un autocrate, Kérékou." Accessed November 23, 2021. https: //docplayer.fr/72524996-Chronique-de-la-vie-d-un-autocrate-kerekou.html.

"Cinq ans de prison et un mandat d'arrêt pour Bob Denard." *Le Monde*, October 18, 1991. https://www.lemonde.fr/archives/article/1991/10/18/cinq-ans-de-prison-et -un-mandat-d-arret-pour-bob-denard_4035679_1819218.html.

Clarke, Stephen John Gordon. *The Congo Mercenary: A History and Analysis.* Johannesburg South African Institute of International Affairs, 1968.

"The Colonel." *Orbs Patria Nostra*. Accessed November 15, 2021. https://www .orbspatrianostra.com/colonel.html.

Communism for Know-It-Alls. Minneapolis, MN: Filiquarian Publishing, 2008.

"Constitution of the People's Republic of Benin." 1990. https://www.wipo.int/edocs/ lexdocs/laws/en/bj/bj001en.pdf.

"Cotonou ne compte plus ses agresseurs." *Jeune Afrique*, no. 854, May 20, 1977.

Council of Ministers. "Resolutions of the Twenty-Eighth Ordinary Session of the Council of Ministers." Lome, Togo: Council of Ministers, February 21, 1977. https://au.int/sites/default/files/decisions/9590-council_en_21_28_february _1977_council_ministers_twenty_eighth_ordinary_session.pdf.

Daho-Express, December 1, 1974.

———. no. 1588, January 24, 1975.

———. no. 1598, February 7, 1975.

"Dahomey: Sounds in the Night." *Time* 19, no. 19, November 8, 1963.

Darnton, John. "Benin Raid an African Mystery." *New York Times*, February 4, 1977. Sec. Archives. https://www.nytimes.com/1977/02/04/archives/benin-raid-an -african-mystery-a-west-african-mystery-who-carried.html.

"Death Sentences given in Abortive Coup." March 29, 1975. Facts on File World News Digest. https://advance-lexis-com.ezproxy.lakeforestlibrary.org /document?crid=8b07d34d-6f23-49fc-80e6-63926d9b3177&pddocfullpath= %2Fshared%2Fdocument%2Fnews%2Furn%3AcontentItem%3A3SJ4-DF70 -000Y-N404-00000-00&pdsourcegroupingtype=&pdcontentcomponentid=7971 &pdmfid=1516831&pdisurlapi=true.

Debre, Michel, and Jean Foyer. "Projet de loi." Reunion de plein droit du Parlement en application de l'Article 16 de la Constitution, mai 1961. https://www.senat.fr/ leg/1960-1961/i1960_1961_0226.pdf.

Decalo, Samuel. "Full Circle in Dahomey." *African Studies Review* 13, no. 3 (December 1970): 447–57.

———. *Coups and Army Rule in Africa: Motivations and Constrains*. Second edition. New Haven, CT: Yale University Press, 1990.

"Une décision du tribunal correctionnel de Paris le mercenaire Bob Denard reste en prison." *Le Monde*, February 10, 1993. https://www.lemonde.fr/archives/article /1993/02/10/une-decision-du-tribunal-correctionnel-de-paris-le-mercenaire-bob -denard-reste-en-prison_3914126_1819218.html.

"Découverte d'un 'vaste complot ourdi par le Dr Zinsou.'" *Le Monde*, October 21, 1975. https://www.lemonde.fr/archives/article/1975/10/21/decouverte-d-un-vaste-complot-ourdi-par-le-dr-zinsou_2595642_1819218.html.

Decraene, Philippe. "Situation politique tendue au Dahomey." *Le Monde*, December 15, 1967.

Denard, Bob, and George Fleury. *Corsaire de la République*. Paris: Robert Laffont, 1998.

Dictionary.com. "Laissez-Passer." Accessed November 23, 2021. https://www.dictionary.com/browse/laissez-passer.

Dodenhoff, George H. "The Congo: A Case Study of Mercenary Employment." *Naval War College Review* 21, no. 8 (1969): 44–70.

Donnet, Joel. "Mitterrand: African Nations Must Move Toward Democracy." *AP*, June 20, 1990. https://apnews.com/article/edfa5353874d34c97d3062d300bca767.

Dossou, Robert. *L'audace, La vérité et l'espérance. La Conférence Nationale: Ce que j'en ai dit en trente ans*. Cotonou, Benin: Éditions Ruisseaux d'Afrique, 2020.

Droz, Benard. *Histoire de la décolonisation au xxe siècle* (Paris: Éditions du Seuil, 2006.

Emmanuel, Terray. "Les révolutions congolaise et dahoméenne de 1963: Essai d'interprétation." *Revue française de science politique* 14, no. 5 (1964): 917–42.

Enkiri, Jean Pierre. "Coup d'etat au Dahomey." *L'INA écalire l'actu*, December 22,1965. https://www.ina.fr/ina-eclaire-actu/video/caf96065107/coup-d-etat-au-dahomey.

Establet, Jean. *Mathieu Kerekou: L'inamovible président du Bénin*. Paris: Editions L'Harmattan, 1997.

Foccart, Jacques. *Foccart parle, entretiens avec Philippe Gaillard*, vol. 2. Paris: Fayard—Jeune Afrique, 1997. https://www.biblio.com/book/foccart-parle-entretiens-avec-philippe-gaillard/d/1010851214.

"The Foccart Syndrome: French policy in Africa, from 1959 to the Present Day." Paris: Folio, 2012.

"French 'Circles' Cited for Raid Against Benin." *New York Times*, April 7, 1977. Sec. Archives. https://www.nytimes.com/1977/04/07/archives/french-circles-cited-for-raid-against-benin.html.

French, Howard. "The Mercenary Position." *Transition* (Kampala, Uganda), no. 73 (1997): 110–21.

Gabon. "Letter Dated 22 May 1979 from the Permanent Representative of Gabon to the United Nations Addressed to the Secretary-General." New York: United Nations, May 23, 1979. https://digitallibrary.un.org/record/2907.

Gauthier-Villars, David. "Colonial-Era Ties to Africa Face a Reckoning in France." *Wall Street Journal*, May 17, 2007. Sec. Articles. https://www.wsj.com/articles/SB117926269972503926.

Genné, Marcelle. "La tentation du socialisme au Bénin (The Temptation of Socialism in Bénin)." *Études internationals* 9, no. 3 (1978): 383–404.

Ginette Co., "L'escalade de l'aggression." *Afrique-Asie*, no. 128, February 7–20, 1977, 15–17.

Global Security. "Benin Army (l'Armee de Terre)." Accessed November 18, 2021. https://www.globalsecurity.org/military/world/africa/bn-army.htm.

Grool, Marjolijn Aalders. *A Journey to Gods and Comrades: Recording Voodoo Stories in Benin (1975–1977, 2014, 2015).* Series: Topics in Interdisciplinary African Studies, vol. 45. Köln, Germany: Rüdiger Köppe Verlag· Köln, 2017.

Henri, Hugues. "La décolonisation de l'Afrique et les mercenaires," n.d. https://www.academia.edu/37523937/La_décolonisation_de_lAfrique_et_les_mercenaires.

Hessoun, Charly. "Bénin: Il y a 38 ans, l'historique agression du 16 janvier 1977 (vidéo)." *La Nouvelle Tribune* (blog), January 16, 2015. https://lanouvelletribune.info/2015/01/benin-il-y-a-38-ans-l-historique-agression-du-16-janvier-1977-video/.

———. "Bénin: Le voile se lève sur le coup d'état du 26 octobre 1972." *La Nouvelle Tribune* (blog), December 15, 2015. https://lanouvelletribune.info/2015/12/benin-le-voile-se-leve-sur-le-coup-d-etat-du-26-octobre-1972/.

———. "Janvier Assogba: 'Le coup d'etat du 26 octobre 1972, personne n'était demandeur.'" *La Nouvelle Tribune* (blog), December 11, 2015. https://lanouvelletribune.info/2015/12/janvier-assogba-le-coup-d-etat-du-26-octobre-1972-personne-n-etait-demandeur/.

Hoare, Mike. *Congo Mercenary.* London: Robert Hall, 1967.

Houndjahoué, Michel. "Notes sur les relations internationales du Bénin socialiste: 1972–1986." *Études internationales* 18, no. 2 (1987): 371. https://doi.org/10.7202/702168ar.

Houngnikpo, Mathurin C., and Samuel Decalo. *Historical Dictionary of Benin.* Lanham, MD: Scarecrow Press, 2012.

Hugounenc, Philippe. *Bob Denard, l'histoire d'un homme.* Paris: Philippe Hugounenc Editeur, 2020.

"Interview du general Soglo apres son coup d'état de 1965." YouTube video, posted by Jomalick1 on August 19, 2010. https://www.youtube.com/watch?v=JKFgQxNup08.

Jeune Afrique, April 1977.

———. May 1977.

Jeune Afrique avec AFP. "Bénin: L'ancien président Mathieu Kérékou en cinq mots." *JeuneAfrique.com*, October 15, 2015. Accessed November 23, 2021. https://www.jeuneafrique.com/271982/politique/benin-lancien-president-mathieu-kerekou-5-mots/.

Johnson, R. W. "Sekou Touré and the Guinean Revolution." *African Affairs* 69, no. 277 (1970): 350–65.

Kairouz, Matthieu. "Ce jour-là: Le 16 janvier 1977, Bob Denard lance 'l'Opération crevette' contre Kérékou au Bénin." *Jeune Afrique*, January 16, 2017. https://www.jeuneafrique.com/360952/politique/jour-16-janvier-1977-bob-denard-lance-l-operation-crevette-contre-kerekou-benin/.

Kérékou, Mathieu, Jacques Abouchar, and Pascal Michel. "Situation au Dahomey après le coup d'Etat: Interview du Président Kerekou." *L'INA éclaire l'actu*, October 29, 1972. https://www.ina.fr/ina-eclaire-actu/video/caf92015518/situation-au-dahomey-apres-le-coup-d-etat-interview-du-president-kerekou.

Kouyami, François. *Affaires d'état au Bénin: Le général François Kouyami parle: Livre-interview. Les grandes interviews.* L'Hay-les-Roses, France: Les Editions IBIDUN, 2011.

Kpatindé, Francis. "Benin: Pardon pour les 'Impenitents.'" *Jeune Afrique*, no. 1500, October 2, 1989.

Kroes, Claude. "Bob Denard et les 'services' au banc des accusés." *L'Humanite*, March 12, 1993. http://www.humanite.fr/node/51832.

"La frère Peter Onu envoyé spécial de l'OUA est arrivé à Cotonou." *Ehuzu*, February 18, 1977.

"L'ancien Président Zinsou dénonce la repression." *Le Monde*, November 6, 1975.

Laurent, Olivier. "Gabonese President Omar Bongo (1935–2009)." World Socialist Web Site, September 5, 2009. https://www.wsws.org/en/articles/2009/09/bong-s05.html.

"Le Bénin poursuit ses efforts pour faire annuler le 'sommet' de l'O.U.A." *Le Monde*, June 24, 1977. https ://www.lemonde.fr/archives/article/1977/06/24/le-benin-poursuit-ses-efforts-pour-faire-annuler-le-sommet-de-l-o-u-a_2866869_1819218.html.

"Le Colonel." *Orbs Patria Nostra.* Accessed November 19, 2021. https://www.orbspatrianostra.com/colonel.html.

"Le Dahomey autorise la croix-rouge à acheminer des secours à partir de son territoire." *Le Monde*, January 30, 1969. https://www.lemonde.fr/archives/article/1969/01/30/le-dahomey-autorise-la-croix-rouge-a-acheminer-des-secours-a-partir-de-son-territoire_2423063_1819218.html.

"L'élection présidentielle est annulée." *Le Monde*, May 15, 1968. https://www.lemonde.fr/archives/article/1968/05/15/l-election-presidentielle-est-annulee_2503546_1819218.html.

Le Figaro. April 1999.

Leluc, Alain. "Bob Denard, 20 Years as a Mercenary." *Historia*, n.d.

"Le Maroc justifie son retrait par une 'violation flagrante' de la Charte." *Le Monde*, March 1, 1977. https://www.lemonde.fr/archives/article/1977/03/01/le-maroc-justifie-son-retrait-par-une-violation-flagrante-de-la-charte_2862891_1819218.html.

"Le massacre a été évité de justesse à l'armée Béninoise le 16 janvier 1977." *Agence Benin Presse.* Accessed November 18, 2021. http://www.agencebeninpresse.info/web/message/%22Le%20massacre%20a%20%C3%A9t%C3%A9%20%C3%A9vit%C3%A9%20de%20justesse%20%C3%A0%20l%E2%80%99arm%C3%A9e%20b%C3%A9ninoise%20le%2016%20janvier%201977%22.

Le Monde, Decembre 1978.

———, January 1, 1993.

———, January 5, 1978.

———, January 10, 1978.

"Le president de la Republique du Gabon: 'Tout est faux.'" *Jeune Afrique*, April 29, 1977.

"Le président du Dahomey a été renversé par un putsch militaire." *Le Monde*, December 11, 1969. https://www.lemonde.fr/archives/article/1969/12/11/le

-president-du-dahomey-a-ete-renverse-par-un-putsch-militaire_2406371_1819218
.html.

"Le president Kérékou rejette l'idée du multipartisme." *Fraternité Matin* (Abidjan),
September 4, 1989.

"Le réponse de Togo." *Jeune Afrique*, no. 854, May 20, 1977.

"Les agresseurs avaient des complices africanisé—Interview du Président Mathieu
Kérékou,

le Dossier de l'aggression mercenaire." Ginette Co, *Afrique-Asie*, no. 138, June 27–
July 27, 1977, 29–64.

"Les suites judiciaires d'une tentative de coup d'etat au Bénin en 1977 l'embarrassant
procès de Bob Denard." *Le Monde*, September 20, 1991. https://www.lemonde.fr
/archives/article/1991/09/20/les-suites-judiciaires-d-une-tentative-de-coup-d-etat
-au-benin-en-1977-l-embarrassant-proces-de-bob-denard_4034196_1819218.html.

Loko, Marius. *La politique étrangère du Benin: D'hier à Aujourd'hui.*
Paris: L'Harmattan, 2022.

Lösch, Dieter. "Socialism in Africa." *Intereconomics* 25, no. 6 (1990): 300–306,
https://doi.org/10.1007/BF02928799.

Lunel, Pierre. *Bob Denard: Le roi de fortune.* Edition⁰ 1, 1991.

"M. Pierre Décamps ambassadeur au Bénin." *Le Monde*, October 23, 1978. https:
//www.lemonde.fr/archives/article/1978/10/23/m-pierre-decamps-ambassadeur-au
-benin_2978177_1819218.html.

Magazine, Editors of *Soldier of Fortune*. "The Lord of the Mercs, Part II." *Soldier Of
Fortune*, June 1, 2008.

"Mathieu Kerekou: 'Tous les Beninois peuvent renter.'" *Jeune Afrique*, December
4, 1989.

"Maurice Peyrot, au tribunal correctionnel de Paris Bob Denard, mercenaire ou corsaire?" *Le Monde*, March 12, 1993. https://www.lemonde.fr/archives/article/1993
/03/12/au-tribunal-correctionnel-de-paris-bob-denard-mercenaire-ou-corsaire
_3918299_1819218.html.

McNulty, Mel William Edward. "Military Intervention in Theory and Practice: French
Policy in Sub-Saharan Africa Since 1960." PhD dissertation, University of
Portsmouth, 1999. https://pure.port.ac.uk/ws/portalfiles/portal/12992283/McNulty
_M.W.E._PhD.

Merriam-Webster. "Cannon Fodder." Accessed November 28, 2021. https://www
.merriam-webster.com/dictionary/cannon+fodder.

Mockler, Anthony. *The New Mercenaries. The History of the Hired Soldiers from the
Congo to the Seychelles.* New York: Paragon House, 1987.

Mongbibeaux, Jean Francosi, and Bernard Sidler. "Bob Denard nous dit tout." *Le
Figaro Magasin*, April 1999.

Moreau Defarges, Philippe. "Samy Cohen et Marie-Claude Smouts (dir.): La politique extérieure de Valéry Giscard d'Estaing." *Politique étrangère* 51, no. 1
(1986): 310–12.

"Morocco Quits O.A.U. in a Rift." *New York Times*, February 26, 1977. Sec. Archives.
https://www.nytimes.com/1977/02/26/archives/morocco-quits-oau-in-a-rift.html.

Nicholson, Sophie. "Bob Denard." *The Guardian*, October 15, 2007. Sec. World News. https://www.theguardian.com/news/2007/oct/16/guardianobituaries.france.

Nohlen, Dieter, Bernard Thibaut, and Michael Krennerich, *Elections in Africa: A Data Handbook*. Oxford: Oxford University Press, 1999.

"Nom: Robert Denard, pseudonyme: Gilbert Bourgeaud." *Agence France Presse*, October 15, 2007.

"OAU Convention for the Elimination of Mercenarism in Africa." Organization of African Unity, 1977. https://doi.org/10.1163/9789004479708_016.

"Onze personnes sont condamnées à mort pour avoir participé au complot d'octobre 1975." *Le Monde*, February 5, 1976. https://www.lemonde.fr/archives/article/1976/02/05/onze-personnes-sont-condamnees-a-mort-pour-avoir-participe-au-complot-d-octobre-1975_2960450_1819218.html.

"OPS Bénin." *Orbs Patria Nostra*. Accessed November 18, 2021. https://www.orbspatrianostra.com/ops/ops-benin/temoignage-alain-marc.html.

Ordonnace no. 70-34 / CP du 7 mai 1970 portant Chartre du Conseil Présidentiel: https://sgg.gouv.bj/doc/ordonnance-1970-34/.O

ORTB. "Rappel historique des trois glorieuses." YouTube video, posted December 1, 2014. https://www.youtube.com/watch?v=sq8CZVYEpao.

———. "On October 26, 1972, in Benin, Mathieu Kérékou Took Power by Coup d'état." YouTube video, posted October 26, 2015. https://www.youtube.com/watch?v=jq2UNZCXy_M.

Osumane, Amadou. *Notre ami Kerekou*. Cotonou, Benin: Éditions Assuli, 2016.

Ouitona, Serge. "7 décembre 1989–7 décembre 2019: Il y a 30 ans, Mathieu Kérékou virait sa cuti." *Afrik.com*, December 7, 2019. https://www.afrik.com/7-decembre-1989-7-decembre-2019-il-y-a-30-ans-mathieu-kerekou-ravalait-ses-vomissures.

———. "Bénin: Il était une fois . . . le 26 octobre 1972." *Afrik.com*, October 26, 2020. https://www.afrik.com/benin-il-etait-une-fois-le-26-octobre-1972.

Panara, Marlène. "Indépendance du Bénin: Vous avez dit démocratie?" *Le Point Afrique*, August 1, 2020. https://www.lepoint.fr/afrique/independance-du-benin-vous-avez-dit-democratie-01-08-2020-2386323_3826.php#11.

Paris—Rabat—Libreville. "Les trois pôles de l'aggression, Mariam Sysle, *Afrique-Asie*, no. 131, March 2–April 3, 1977, 20–22.

Péan, Pierre. *Affaires africaines*. Paris: Fayard, 1983.

PBS. "Hopes on the Horizon—Benin Transcript." Accessed November 16, 2021. http://www.pbs.org/hopes/benin/transcript.html.

"Qui etes vous Docteur Zinsou?" *Jeune Afrique*, no. 396, August 11, 1968.

"Un rapport qui ne dissipe pas les equivoques." *Jeune Afrique*, March 25, 1977.

"Report of the Security Council: 16 June 1980–15 June 1981." Report of the Security Council. General Assembly. New York: United Nations, 1981. https://undocs.org/pdf?symbol=en/A/36/2(SUPP).

Reuters. "Upheaval in the East; Benin, Too, Gives Up Marxism for Reforms." *New York Times*, December 9, 1989. Sec. World. https://www.nytimes.com/1989/12/09/world/upheaval-in-the-east-benin-too-gives-up-marxism-for-reforms.html.

Riding, Alan. "A French Soldier of Fortune Tries on the Mantle of Patriot and Finds It Fits." *New York Times*, April 25, 1993. Sec. World. https://www.nytimes.com

/1993/04/25/world/a-french-soldier-of-fortune-tries-on-the-mantle-of-patriot-and-finds-it-fits.html.

Robert, Maurice. *Maurice Robert, "minister" de l'Afrique: Entretiens avec André Renault*. Paris: Seuil, 2004.

Roberts, Sam. "Mathieu Kérékou, Dictator Who Ushered in Democracy in Benin, Dies at 82." *New York Times*, October 16, 2015. Sec. World. https://www.nytimes.com/2015/10/16/world/africa/mathieu-kerekou-dictator-who-ushered-in-democracy-in-benin-dies-at-82.html.

Ronen, Dov. "The Colonial Elite in Dahomey." *African Studies Review* 17, no. 1 (April 1974): 55–76. https://doi.org/10.2307/523577.

———. *Dahomey: Between Tradition and Modernity*. Ithaca, NY: Cornell University Press, 1975.

"Roy Nesbit, Dudley Cowderoy, Sanctions Busters." *Flight International Magazine*, February 2, 1985.

Sabas, Andre. "Coup d'etat au Dahomey." *L'INA éclaire l'actu*, December 10, 1969. https://www.ina.fr/ina-eclaire-actu/video/caf96065113/coup-d-etat-au-dahomey.

Schmid, Peter. "Tshombe's Four Hundred." *The Reporter*, December 17, 1964.

"Security Council Official Records, 32nd Year: 2000th Meeting, 6 April 1977, New York." New York: United Nations, 1977. https://digitallibrary.un.org/record/224232.

"Security Council Official Records, 32nd Year: 2001st Meeting, 7 April 1977, New York." New York: United Nations, 1977. https://digitallibrary.un.org/record/224233.

"Security Council Official Records, 32nd Year: 2002nd Meeting, 12 April 1977, New York." New York: United Nations, 1977. https://digitallibrary.un.org/record/224234.

"Security Council Official Records, 32nd Year: 2003rd Meeting, 13 April 1977, New York." New York: United Nations, 1977. https://digitallibrary.un.org/record/224235.

"Security Council Official Records, 32nd Year: 2047th Meeting, 22 November 1977, New York." New York: United Nations, 1977. https://digitallibrary.un.org/record/224279.

Sedegan, Ebénézer Korê, and Olivier Djidénou Allocheme. *Histoire des coups d'état au Dahomey (1963–1972)*. Paris: L'Harmattan, 2021.

Shaxson, Nicholas. *Poisoned Wells: The Dirty Politics of African Oil*. First edition. New York: St. Martin's Press, 2007.

Siebert, Jean-Philippe. "Militaires, merrcenaires, contractors, volontaires. . . . à ne pas confondre." *Les Surligneur*, March 21, 2023. https://www.lessurligneurs.eu/militaires-mercenaires-contractors-volontaires-a-ne-pas-confondre/.

Skurnik, W. A. E. "Can the Military Modernize?" *Africa Today* 15, no. 2 (1968): 5–6.

"Smashing of a Plot Reported by Dahomey." *New York Times*, October 20, 1975. Sec. Archives. https://www.nytimes.com/1975/10/20/archives/smashing-of-a-plot-reported-by-dahomey.html.

"Sous le coup de deux mandats d'arrêt Le mercenaire Bob Denard souhaiterait rentrer en France." *Le Monde*, January 28, 1993. https://www.lemonde.fr/archives/article /1993/01/28/sous-le-coup-de-deux-mandats-d-arret-le-mercenaire-bob-denard -souhaiterait-rentrer-en-france_3926711_1819218.html.

"Sous le coup d'un mandat d'arrêt international: L'ancien mercenaire Bob Denard est rentré en France." *Le Monde*, February 2, 1993. https://www.lemonde.fr/archives /article/1993/02/02/sous-le-coup-d-un-mandat-d-arret-international-l-ancien -mercenaire-bob-denard-est-rentre-en-france_3920693_1819218.html.

Sovissi, Jules. "Bénin / coup d'etat du 26 Octobre 1972: Le Témoignage du Colonel Janvier Assogba." *Journal Adjinakou Benin* (blog), June 18, 2017. https://www .journal-adjinakou-benin.net/benin-coup-detat-du-26-octobre-1972-le-temoignage -du-colonel-janvier-assogba/.

Taylor, Mildred Europa. "How a Benin Royal Sold the Mighty Dahomey Kingdom to the French for a Title in 1894." *Face2Face Africa*, January 17, 2019. https://face2faceafrica.com/article/how-a-benin-royal-sold-the-mighty -dahomey-kingdom-to-the-french-for-a-title-in-1894.

"Togolese Reply to Benin Charges." Wikileaks Public Library of US Diplomacy. Togo Lomé, February 5, 1976. https://wikileaks.org/plusd/cables/1976LOME00264_b .html.

Tremblais, Jean-Louis. "Mercenaire de la République." *Le Figaro*, July 4, 2009. https: //www.lefigaro.fr/lefigaromagazine/2009/07/04/01006-20090704ARTFIG00098- -mercenaire-de-la-republique-.php.

"Un délegation du Conseil des ministres de l'OUA en mission d'enquête à Cotonu." *Ehuzu*, February 24, 1977.

UN Secretary-General and Gabon. President. "Letter Dated 77/04/04 from the Secretary-General Addressed to the President of the Security Council." New York: United Nations, April 4, 1977. https://digitallibrary.un.org/record/564428.

UN. Security Council (32nd year: 1977). "Resolution 405 (1977) / Adopted by the Security Council at Its 2005th Meeting, on 14 April 1977." New York: United Nations, April 14, 1977. https://digitallibrary.un.org/record/66646.

———. "Resolution 419 (1977) / Adopted by the Security Council at Its 2049th Meeting, on 24 November 1977." New York: United Nations, November 24, 1977. https://digitallibrary.un.org/record/66647.

UN. Special Mission of the Security Council Established under Resolution 404 (1977). "Report of the Security Council Special Mission to the People's Republic of Benin Established under Resolution 404 (1977)." New York: United Nations, 1977. https://digitallibrary.un.org/record/564622.

———. "Report of the Security Council Special Mission to the People's Republic of Benin Established under Resolution 404 (1977)." New York: United Nations, March 8, 1977. https://digitallibrary.un.org/record/564389?ln=en.

———. "Report of the Security Council Special Mission to the People's Republic of Benin Established under Resolution 404 (1977): Addendum." New York: United Nations, March 8, 1977. https://digitallibrary.un.org/record/564391.

University of Central Arkansas. "29. Dahomey/Benin (1960–Present)." Accessed November 16, 2021. https://uca.edu/politicalscience/dadm-project/sub-saharan -africa-region/dahomeybenin-1960-present/.

"Une Vie de Mercenaire." *La Liberte*, October 21, 2006.

Vignes, Jacques. "Benin: Une mystérieuse agression." *Jeune Afrique*, January 28, 1977.

Vinen, R. C. "Foccart parle, vol. 2, entretiens avec Philippe Gaillard." *English Historical Review* 114, no. 455 (1999).

Vucher-Bondet, Veronique. "Bénin, le cuisant échec d'un raid audacieux." *Historia*, no. 406, 1980.

Weinberg, Samantha. "France Blesses Its 'Dog of War': In His First Interview since Leaving Jail, Bob Denard Tells Samantha Weinberg in Paris of His Many French Connections." *The Independent*, April 7, 1993. https://www.independent.co .uk/news/world/europe/france-blesses-its-dog-of-war-in-his-first-interview-since -leaving-jail-bob-denard-tells-samantha-weinberg-in-paris-of-his-many-french -connections-1453994.html.

———. *Last of The Pirates: The Search for Bob Denard*. New York: Pantheon, 1995.

Whiteman, Kaye. "Hubert Maga." *The Guardian*, July 24, 2000. Sec. News. https:// www.theguardian.com/news/2000/jul/24/guardianobituaries2.

———. "The Man Who Ran Franafrique." *The National Interest*. The Center for the National Interest, September 1, 1997. https://nationalinterest.org/article/the-man -who-ran-franafrique-1005.

"'The Whole Truth about the Armed Aggression of 16 January.' Report of the Special Joint Session of the Central Committee of the PRPB, the Revolution Nation Council (CNR) and the MRG." *Ehuzu*, March 15, 1977.

Wiking, Staffan. *Military Coups in Sub-Saharan Africa: How to Justify Illegal Assumptions of Power*. Uppsala, Sweden: Scandinavian Institute of African Studies, 1986.

Yates, Douglas A. *The Rentier State in Africa. Oil Rent Dependency and Neocolonialism in the Republic of Gabon*. Trenton, NJ: Africa World Press, 1996.

Zinsou, Émile Derlin. *En ces temps là . . .* Paris: Riveneuve, 2013.

"Zinsou: Le Dahomey a Bouge 'Vers l'unite.'" *Jeune Afrique*, no. 396, August 1969.

Index

Abdallah, Ahmed, 57, 169, 174–77
Ahomadégbé, Justin, 6–7, 10–13,
  16–17, 21–22, 26–27, 29, 58, 187
Apithy, Migan, 4, 6–7, 9–14, 17, 25,
  27, 58

Ben Guerir Air Base, 66, 73–79, 111,
  150, 161
Bohiki affair, 10
Bongo, Omar, 47–48, 50, 65, 77–78,
  81–82, 116, 121, 131, 140, 147–48,
  150, 156–58, 162, 164, 179

Camp Guézo, 10–11, 37, 59, 61, 92, 98,
  101–2, 105–6, 110, 112–6, 119–120,
  122, 126, 137, 145
Cellule Africaine, 44
China, 24, 29, 36, 58
Chirac, Jacques, 158, 191
CIA, 87
civil war: Angola, 141; Biafra-Nigeria,
  78, 88; Congo, 88; mercenary
  recruitment, 67
Clan Gabonais, 78
Communism, xiv–v, 24, 33–34, 36–37,
  44, 56–57, 66, 87, 106, 183, 187;
  Communist China, 29
Congacou, Tahïrou, 11–12, 14

Congo (DRC), x–xi, xiv–v, xvii, 44, 56,
  60, 66–67, 73, 78, 82, 88–89, 97,
  112, 120–21, 159, 177
Cuba, 24, 34, 36, 56, 153

"the Dreadful," *les affreux*, xi, xiii,
  xiv, 67

Equatorial Guinea, 46, 56
d'Estaing, Giscard, 29, 49, 158–59,
  173, 175
European Union, 89
Eyadéma, Gnassingbé, 47–48, 50, 69,
  77, 162

Foccart, Jacques, 25, 29, 43–44, 48–51,
  150, 158–59, 162, 173, 179
FLERD, 38, 43–44, 46, 61, 65–66, 68,
  77, 79, 91, 95, 97, 99, 122, 163
Franco-Dahomean War, 3
French Sudan, 3, 141, 169

Germany, 5, 67–68, 90, 126, 141, 187
Ghana, 89, 183
*Gouvernement Militaire
  Révolutionnaire*, 27, 36
Green Berets, Legionaries from First
  Foreign Parachute Regiment
  (*Premier REP*), 69

Guinea, 3, 35–36, 59, 68, 147, 153–55, 163, 169, 171–73

Hassan II, 45, 47, 49–50, 65, 66, 79, 150, 161–62, 191
Hoare, Mike, xi, xiv
Hoxhaist, 34

Indochina, ix, x, 66, 73, 79, 82, 177
Ivory Coast, 3, 13, 43–44, 50–51, 68, 75, 96, 154–56, 158, 162, 190

Khadafi, Colonel Muammar, 135
Kouandété, Maurice Iropa, 12–13, 15–17, 21–22, 24, 27
Kovacs affair, 27, 30–31, 37, 40
Kovacs, Louis, 27, 37

Luanda Trials, 141, 169

Madagascar, ix, 153
Marxism, 9, 29, 33, 36–39, 45–47, 50, 55–56, 58–59, 68, 96, 185, 187–88, 191; Marxism-Beninism, 34, 188; Marxism-Leninism, 29, 33–34, 36, 55, 58, 105, 186
Maga, Hubery, 6–7, 9–14, 16–17, 21–22, 24–27, 58, 114, 187
mercenary training, 74
Mobutu, General, then President, xi, xiv, 78, 159, 179
Morocco, ix, x, 43, 47–50, 65–66, 73–74, 79–80, 87, 99, 111, 121, 149–50, 155–56, 158, 160–65, 177, 191

Nigeria, xi, 1, 16, 34, 78, 88, 109, 122, 129, 154–55, 163, 171–72
North Korea, 24, 29, 36, 61, 102–6, 120, 127–28, 136, 138–40

Organization of African Unity (OAU), 14, 43, 81, 117, 130, 140, 153, 155, 163, 170
Organisation Armée Secrète (OAS), xiii

Pognon, Gratien, 14, 43–46, 61, 65, 68, 79–80, 91, 96, 99, 121–22, 141, 149, 188–90
POLISARIO (*Frente Popular de Liberaciónde Saguía el Hamra y Río de Oro*), 49, 161–62, 178
presidential triumvirate, 17, 25, 27

Revolutionary Military Committee (*Comité Militaire Révolutionnaire* or CMR), 24
Rhodesia, xiii, 87–88, 165
Robert, Maurice, 23, 43–44, 49, 51, 78, 97, 158, 160, 162, 178

Sao Tome and Principe, 46, 56, 165
Sarkozy, Nicolas, 25
SDECE, xi, 23, 43–46, 49, 51–52, 60, 68, 95–97, 103, 158, 160, 178
Senegal, 3, 14, 23, 44, 50–51, 58, 68, 76, 153–55, 162
socialism, xv, 33, 36, 56, 102, 184
Soglo, Christophe, 7, 9–13
South Africa, xi, 88, 174, 176–77
Soviet Union, 29, 36, 58, 33, 49, 187; Communism, xiv
Steiner, Rolf, 141, 169

Tanzania, 36
Togo, 1, 11, 13, 38, 43–44, 47–48, 50–52, 55, 57, 60, 69, 77, 84, 92, 102, 114, 125, 153, 155, 158, 161
Touré, Sékou, 35, 50, 59, 68, 154

United Nations, 46–47, 56, 76, 87–88, 102, 119, 128, 130, 136, 147, 153–63, 170, 189

Western Sahara, 48–49, 161, 165
World War II, ix–x, 3, 56, 82, 87

Zaire, 89, 112, 129, 179
Zedong, Mao, 24

About the Authors

Les Sosnowski and **Monique Sosnowski** have spent years documenting mercenary activities across Africa. Les began his career doing so as a doctoral student studying international public law at Jagiellonian University (PhD 1974, Habilitation 1982) where he later taught political science for fifteen years. His research has spanned the legal position of mercenaries in modern international law (resulting in several academic articles as well as a published book); though various postcolonial independence movements across African nations, such as Namibia and Djibouti; and the unification of the African Union (both topics being examined in further academic articles and books). Monique similarly has studied security issues across Africa, focusing more so on issues of criminal justice and crime prevention. A PhD from the John Jay College of Criminal Justice in New York, her research has focused on examining illicit trades within source countries in Africa. This has led to a wide range of academic article and book chapter publications primarily on the illegal wildlife and drug trades. Her work has resulted in her being named a UNODC Education for Justice Young Scholar, UN Youth Representative, and a Department of State grant recipient. She currently also works with a field-based organization in southern Africa developing security protocols. Both Les and Monique have spent notable time in southern Africa scouring libraries for primary source material to support their work on mercenaries.

Milton Keynes UK
Ingram Content Group UK Ltd.
UKHW021651210224
438176UK00037B/43

9 781666 911237